Official Cookbook

70 RECIPES INSPIRED BY THE
SANDERSON SISTERS,
MAX, DANI AND BEYOND

BY ELENA CRAIG & S. T. BENDE

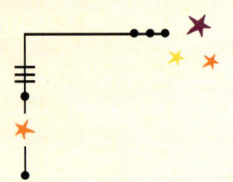

Table of Contents

Introduction 9

Starters and Sides 11
  Graveyard Cheeseboard 13
  Billy Butcherson Zombie Fingers 14
  All Hallows' Eve Feast Grazing Board 17
  Miss Olin Nutty Brown Bread 21
  Massachusetts Baked Beans 22
  Ten Chocolate Bars, No Liquorice, Candy Toll 23
  Pretty Black Meatball Spiders 24
  Circle of Salt Soft Pretzels 26
  Pan Hag 27
  "Amok, Amok, Amok" Guacamole and Homemade Chips 29
  "No Witches Here" Pumpkin Butter 30
  The Master's Fried Peppers 31
  Dead Man's Toes 33
  "Oh, Cheese and Crust" Homemade Crackers 34
  Popping Cranberries 35
  Roach Muffins 37
  Pastry Boots 38

Main Dishes 41
  Mrs Dennison's Roasted Pumpkin Tacos 43
  Shishkebaby 45
  "Another Glorious Morning" Breakfast Sandwiches for Dinner 46
  Winifred's Guts for Garters Squash 49
  Knockout Skillet French Toast 50
  Full Moon Blue Cheese Onion Tart 53
  Mummy's Scorpion Pie 57
  "Who's Going for the Jacuzzi" Lobster 59
  Spicy Cauliflower Ears 60
  Roasted Red Spice Chicken 61
  Maggot-Stuffed Pork Chop 62
  Green Mummy Roll-Ups 65
  Rat Loaf 69
  Spicy Nightshade Stir-Fry 70
  Pumpkin Risotto 72
  Waterwheel Pot Pie 75
  Sanderson Sisters Barbecue Fillet 77
  Cheese Puff Chicken Tenders 79
  Graveyard Gnocchi Grubs 80
  Hollywood Barbecue Chicken Pizza 83
  Tie-Dye California Smoothie Bowl 84

Desserts 87

Blood Orange Jack-O'-Lantern Tarts 88
Halloween Candy Ice Cream with Gummy Worm Ganache 91
Thackery Binx Treats 92
"Hey, Cupcake" Cupcakes 95
Winnie's Spellbook Cake 99
Classic Caramel Apple Dip 103
Broomstick, and Other Transport, Treats 105
Winnie's Magical Popping Candy 108
Black River Brownie Bars 109
Gravestone Sugar Cookies 111
Witch Cookie Lollies 113
Dad-cula Fang Strawberries 117
Twisted Winifred Spirals 118
Puffed Rice Potion Bottles 121
Tart Face Tart 122
Cat Tongue Cookies 125
"Bonjour!" Crème Brûlée 126
Fly Ice Cream 127
Frogspawn Boba Matcha Cheesecake 129
Dust Bombs 131

Drinks 133

Most Refreshing Drink 135
"I Put a Spell on You" Brew 136
Life Potion Witches' Drink 139
Renaissance Party Cider 140
Pumpkin Spiced Golden Milk 142
Burning Rain of Death Drink 143
Winnie's Popping Potion 145
Sarah's Sassy Sipper 146
Mary's Magic Elixir 149
Sunrise Punch 150
"Ice" Cream Float 152
Pink Smoke Drink 153

Conclusion 155
Dietary Considerations 156
Fry Station Safety 157
Glossary 158

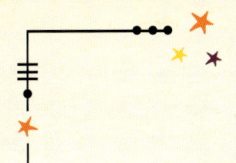
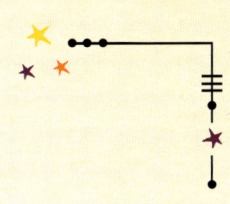

Introduction

The magical world of *Hocus Pocus* has put a spell on us from the moment we first met its charmingly cursed sisters. With their penchant for plotting, fondness for mischief and unrelenting spirit of determination, Winifred, Mary and Sarah Sanderson have inspired the curious, the daring and, of course, the adventurous souls ever since they first arrived in Salem. And while some of the sisters' schemes *may* have been slightly unscrupulous, one need not view their plotting through fearful eyes. After all, as they say, the legend of the Sanderson sisters is just a bunch of *hocus pocus*, right?

But even legends have their dangers, dancing – as they so often do – along the razor-thin veil that separates truth and fantasy. After a three-hundred-year absence, the Sandersons are more than ready to squeeze every drop of life from whatever time they might have in our mortal realm. There's no finer way to embrace earthly offerings than by sampling their finest cuisine, so we've put together a mesmerising menu that's sure to impress even the most wanton of witches. From Circle of Salt Soft Pretzels (page 26) to "I Put a Spell on You" Brew (page 136), these enticing treats carry all the magic that their namesake curses – and clever spell-casters – hold so dear. Billy Butcherson Zombie Fingers (page 14) are equal parts garish and irresistible, while Massachusetts Baked Beans (page 22) are the quintessential Salemite side dish.

For those who prefer their culinary experiences to mirror the macabre, The Master's Fried Peppers (page 31) and Dead Man's Toes (page 33) will offer up a proper scare. Graveyard Gnocchi Grubs (page 80) and Maggot-Stuffed Pork Chop (page 62) offer an exotic, earthy twist on beloved classic dishes. And our dearest Winifred would no doubt delight in serving up her Spellbook Cake (page 99) – so long as no one tries to steal it from her, of course! Throughout these pages, recipes may be marked with a few interesting runes: GF, GF*, V, V*, V+, or V+*. These runes indicate the following dietary considerations:

GF: Gluten-free

GF*: Easily adapted to be gluten-free

V: Vegetarian

V*: Easily adapted to be vegetarian

V+: Vegan

V+*: Easily adapted to be vegan

It's a *thrill* to share these otherworldly recipes for the very first time. We hope you've brought a hunger for dastardly dishes, devilish desserts and a cupcake worthy of the black flame candle itself. So, gather your coven, summon your favourite broomstick – or vacuum – and prepare to embark upon an epicurean adventure of ghoulish proportions. After all, we only have until morning. So, come … we fly!

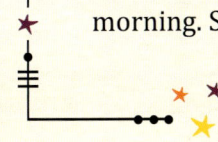
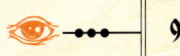

Starters and Sides

Winifred, Mary and Sarah have been gone three hundred years – *right down to the day*! But now the witches are back. And their appetites are sure to be positively ghoulish. Whether you're planning a calming circle for three wayward witches or a dinner party for several hungry humans, no menu would be complete without these starters and sides, inspired by Salem's favourite witchy trio. From "Amok, Amok, Amok" Guacamole and Homemade Chips (page 29) to Dead Man's Toes (page 33), each of these recipes will whet the appetite of even the most ravenous of witches. Provided, of course, they don't put a spell on you first!

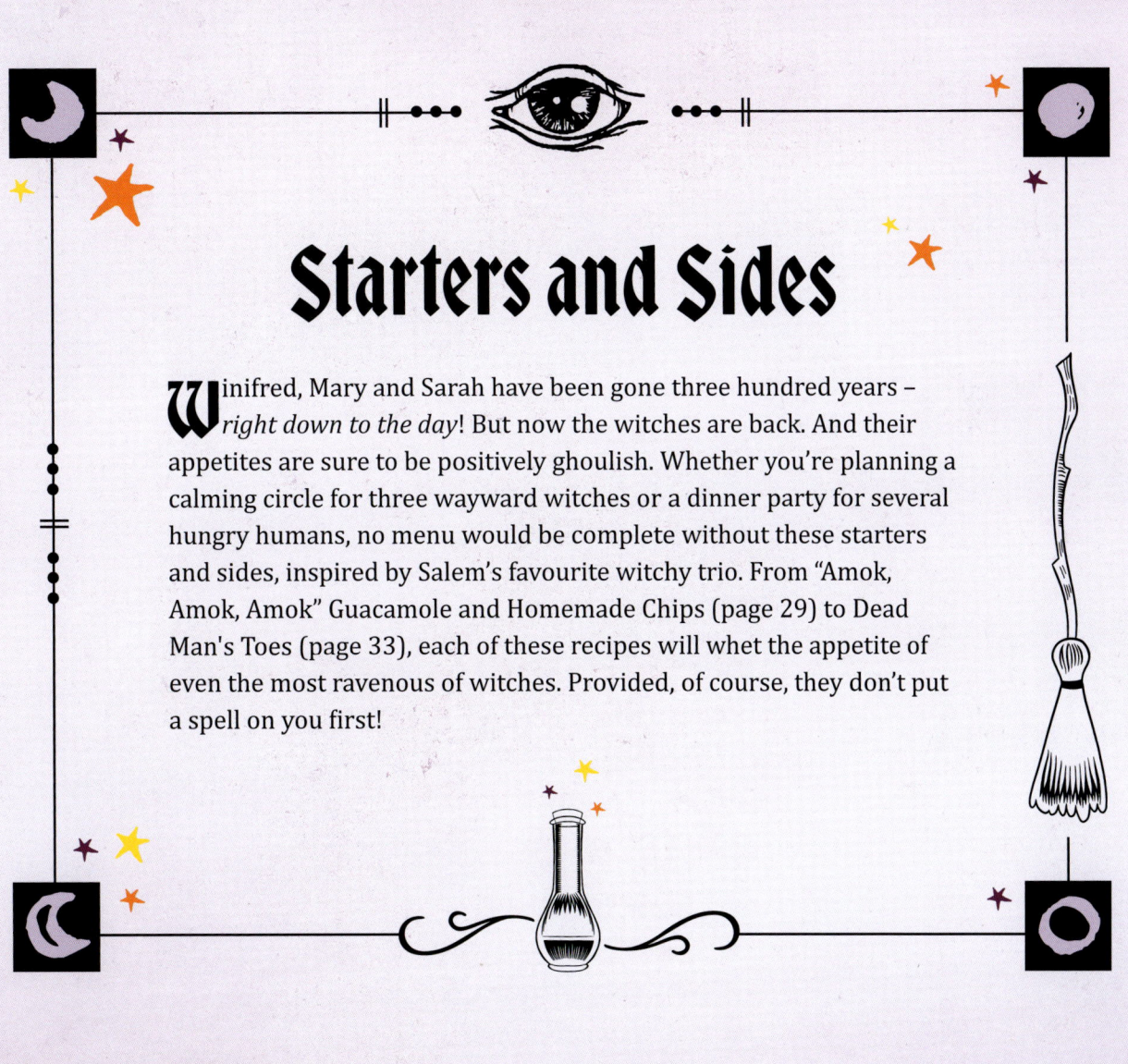

Graveyard Cheeseboard

To create a board divine,
Itch-it-a-cop-it-a, Mel-a-ka-mys-ti-ca.
Gather fromages most fine.
Itch-it-a-cop-it-a, Mel-a-ka-mys-ti-ca.
Set them in a tidy row,
Itch-it-a-cop-it-a, Mel-a-ka-mys-ti-ca.
Placed beside a wedge of dough.
Itch-it-a-cop-it-a, Mel-a-ka-mys-ti-ca.
Serve to guests, who will be floored,
Itch-it-a-cop-it-a, Mel-a-ka-mys-ti-ca.
By this cheesy graveyard board.
Itch-it-a-cop-it-a, Mel-a-ka-mys-ti-ca.

Yield: *8 to 12 servings* | GF*, V

- 4 to 5 blocks (rectangle or square in shape) firm cheeses, such as Cheddar, Cheshire or Red Leicester
- 1 to 2 tablespoons poppy seeds
- 1 to 2 tablespoons balsamic vinegar
- 1 to 2 interesting-shaped cheeses, such as logs, trapezoids or wedges (these can be softer cheeses)
- 2 to 3 types dark-coloured crackers (gluten-free, if desired)
- Sliced baguette and/or squares of pumpernickel bread for serving
- 1 bunch black seedless grapes
- Pea crisps, pistachios and/or blue corn chips for "graveyard dirt" (optional)
- Pickled onions, dark olives and fig or balsamic jam (optional)

Have a large chopping or serving board standing by.

Cut the firm blocks of cheese into various headstone shapes, making sure to leave the base wide and flat enough that it will stand up. Cut a coffin shape if desired. Save any trimmings to create smaller "broken" headstones or graveyard rubble. Use a toothpick or skewer to carve names, dates and/or symbols into the headstones and coffin.

To darken your carvings, cover with the poppy seeds and gently press them into the carving. Over a small plate, brush off excess poppy seeds, leaving them only in the carved areas. To darken with the balsamic, use a small pastry brush to paint inside the carved area. This will cause an eerie dripping effect when the headstone is standing.

Arrange each of these cheese headstones on the serving board, spacing them out to create the feeling of a wandering path in between. Add the additional cheeses as monuments. Fill in your graveyard with the crackers, baguette, grapes and pea crisps (if using). Add small dishes of pickled onions, olives and jam (if using).

Set out cheese knives and serve.

Note

This recipe is easily made gluten-free by using gluten-free crackers and/or bread.

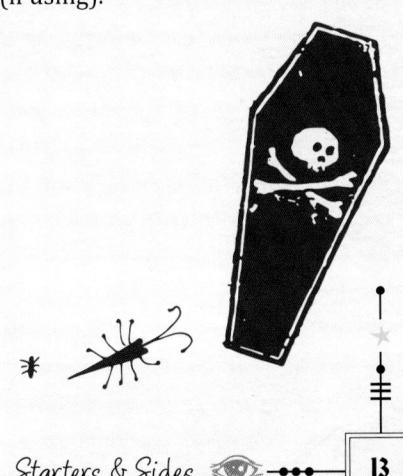

Starters & Sides 13

Billy Butcherson Zombie Fingers

When Winifred's beau was caught sporting with her sister Sarah, he found himself in quite the pickle. Winifred's jealous streak would be Billy Butcherson's downfall … but it was an unfortunate incident with a manhole cover that ultimately inspired this tangy dish. Brine, garlic and a smattering of dill create this most unusual – and decidedly delicious! – finger food.

Yield: 12 pickles | GF, V, V+

6 baby cucumbers
12 cloves garlic, peeled
4 to 6 sprigs fresh dill
180 ml cold water
120 ml red wine vinegar
60 ml spicy apple cider vinegar
1 tablespoon rock salt
¾ teaspoon sugar
½ tablespoon black peppercorns
½ teaspoon fennel seeds
½ teaspoon celery seeds
2 bay leaves

Specialist Tools
2 sealable jars, wide enough to hold 6 pickles, such as 680 gram mason jars

Break each cucumber in half and score the non-broken end with an X about ½ cm deep. Gently press a clove of garlic into each scored end. Place six pieces of cucumber, standing on end with the garlic facing up, into each of two 680 gram mason jars. They should fit snugly. Place 2 or 3 sprigs of dill in each jar. Set aside.

In a 480 ml measuring jug, combine the water, red wine vinegar, apple cider vinegar, salt and sugar, stirring to combine. Set aside.

Warm a medium saucepan over a medium heat and add the peppercorns, fennel, celery seeds and bay leaves. Toast, moving constantly, for 2 minutes. Add the vinegar mixture and bring to a simmer. Carefully pour the hot brine into each jar, making sure that the cucumbers are covered. Make sure to get a bay leaf and about half of the spices into each jar. Add more water if needed to cover.

Seal the jars and allow them to cool to room temperature, then refrigerate. Pickles are ready to eat the next day; however, the longer they sit, the more flavourful they become. Pickles can be stored in the refrigerator for up to two months. Note that the garlic cloves may come loose from the pickles, but they can be pressed back in for serving if desired.

Starters & Sides

All Hallows' Eve Feast Grazing Board

According to Allison, Halloween is based on an ancient feast called All Hallows' Eve – the one night of the year when spirits can come back to roam the earth. And there's no better way to welcome ghostly guests than with this grazing board. This savoury plate serves up candied clementines, kale chips, baked Brie with pesto and the ever-appetising "mouldy" grapes. It's an ideal offering of sinister snacks for any soul feeling the slightest bit peckish – be they living … or deceased! Most of the components can be made in advance, but the Brie should be baked just before serving.

Yield: 6 to 8 servings | GF*, V*, V+*

For the Kale Chip Bat Wings

1 bunch curly kale, washed and dried very well

60 ml olive oil

1 tablespoon balsamic vinegar

½ teaspoon rock salt

¼ teaspoon harissa powder

For the Candied Orange Dark Moons

4 clementines or mandarin oranges

400 grams sugar

60 grams dark chocolate or chocolate chips

For the Mouldy Grapes

1 bunch purple grapes

50 grams roasted salted pistachios, crushed

110 grams goat's cheese, slightly softened

For the Baked Swampy Brie with Pesto

220 gram wheel of Brie

2 tablespoons homemade pesto (see page 65) or shop-bought pesto

1 teaspoon balsamic vinegar

1 tablespoon grated Parmesan cheese

For Assembly

The Master's Fried Peppers (page 31)

Assorted cheeses (see note)

Assorted charcuterie (see note)

Assorted olives and antipasto

Jams or dips of choice

Crackers and/or baguette slices

Notes

For the cheese, plan on 30 grams of each cheese per person. So, if you are serving three cheeses to six people, you need 180 grams of each cheese. For charcuterie, plan on 60 to 90 grams per person, making sure you have that amount of each item. Since leftovers store well, feel free to make your grazing board look bountiful.

For dietary restrictions, select the items that fit your needs. The kale chips are gluten-free, vegetarian and vegan; the moons are gluten-free and vegetarian; the grapes are gluten-free and vegetarian; and the pesto is gluten-free and vegetarian. The entire board can be made gluten-free by using gluten-free crackers and bread.

continued on page 18

Starters & Sides

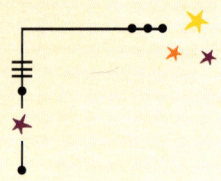

continued from page 17

To make the kale chips: Have 2 rimmed baking sheets standing by. Preheat the oven to 150°C.

To stem the kale, take each piece, fold the leaves away from the stem and gently pull them off the stem. This will leave you with two long pieces of kale. Repeat until all the kale is stemmed and set it aside.

In a small bowl, whisk together the olive oil, vinegar, salt and harissa. Using a pastry brush, paint a thin layer of the mixture over the surface of each baking sheet. Lay out the kale leaves in a single layer without overlapping on the baking sheets. Brush the top of each kale leaf with a light coating of the oil mixture.

Bake for 8 to 12 minutes, or until the kale is crisp but not brown. At the 8-minute mark, check carefully and take out any kale chips that are already done and rotate the sheets. It is okay if the kale chips are still a bit soft in the middle; they will continue to crisp as they cool. Allow to cool completely on a baking sheet and then store in an airtight container until serving.

To make the candied oranges: Slice each orange into ½-cm-thick slices, discarding the ends. Gently remove any seeds from each slice and discard. Set the slices aside.

In a large saucepan over a medium-high heat, bring 480 ml water to the boil and add the sugar. Stir until sugar is completely dissolved. Add the orange slices and press a piece of parchment paper down to rest on top of the oranges. Turn the heat down to low and maintain a simmer for 1 hour.

Place a wire rack set on a rimmed baking sheet. Using tongs or a slotted spoon, remove each orange slice and place it on the rack. Reserve the orange syrup for an alternate use. Allow to dry for 5 to 7 hours, or until firm and slightly tacky.

Line a baking sheet with parchment paper. In a medium microwave-safe bowl, melt the chocolate in 30-second bursts and stir until completely smooth. Do not overheat.

Dip each orange slice halfway into the chocolate, then place on the baking sheet. Refrigerate for 7 to 10 minutes, or until chocolate is set. Store in an airtight container between layers of parchment for up to three days.

To make the grapes: Remove the grapes from the stem. Place the pistachios on a shallow plate. Spread a small amount of goat's cheese on to the stem end of the grape. Being a bit messy here is just fine. Roll the goat's cheese in the crushed nuts. Continue until all the grapes are covered. Serve immediately or gently store in an airtight container in the refrigerator for up to one day.

To make the Brie: Have an ovenproof dish, large enough to hold the Brie with some room to spare, standing by. Preheat the oven to 180°C.

Using a sharp knife, score the Brie with deep cuts, about every 2 cm all the way across, rotate the Brie, then make the same cuts across the other direction, making a crosshatch. Be careful not to cut all the way through (placing a chopstick on either side of the Brie to stop your knife can help with this). Gently open up the crosshatches a bit by bending back the wheel of Brie and then place it in the ovenproof dish. Spread the pesto over the top of the Brie, drizzle with the balsamic vinegar and sprinkle with the Parmesan cheese. Bake for 15 to 20 minutes, or until the cheese is bubbly and gooey. Serve immediately.

To assemble: Arrange two or three chopping or serving boards on your table. Arrange all the items using small bowls or plates to hold items such as olives, the candied oranges, the Master's Fried Peppers, jams and dips. Kale chips, some crackers and/or breadsticks can be served standing up in glasses or wide-mouth jars to create height. Set the cheeses with appropriate cheese knives scattered around the boards. Arrange the various charcuterie, grouped by type, directly on the board or on small plates. Tuck crackers, mouldy grapes, other fruit and baguette slices in the empty spaces. Have a heatproof spot, such as a trivet or chopping board, to place the Brie once it is out of the oven, surrounded by bread or crackers and with a serving knife tucked in. Have small side plates available for serving.

Miss Olin Nutty Brown Bread

A stickler for accuracy, Max and Allison's teacher Miss Olin holds her students to *particularly* high standards. This lover of lore appreciates attention to detail – whether she's retelling the legend of the Sanderson sisters or baking a loaf of delightful brown bread. This Miss Olin–inspired confection combines hints of hazelnut with golden raisins in a blend that is both sweet and tangy – just like the teacher herself.

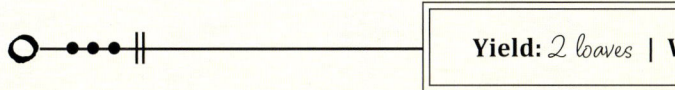

Yield: 2 loaves | V

Butter or coconut oil for greasing

390 grams wholewheat flour

120 grams plain flour

110 grams dark brown sugar

1 tablespoon baking soda

1 teaspoon salt

300 ml buttermilk

280 grams pomegranate syrup

200 grams golden raisins

150 grams chopped hazelnuts

Warm softened butter or "No Witches Here" Pumpkin Butter (page 30) for serving

Preheat the oven to 180°C.

Use the butter to grease two 20-by-12-cm loaf tins and line each with a wide central strip of parchment paper that goes along the bottom and overhangs slightly from each end.

In a large bowl, mix together the wholewheat flour, plain flour, brown sugar, baking soda and salt.

In a medium bowl, whisk together the buttermilk and pomegranate syrup until well combined. Stir the buttermilk mixture into the flour mixture and continue to stir until all the dry ingredients are moistened. Fold in the raisins and hazelnuts.

Split the batter between the two tins and bake for 35 to 40 minutes, or until a skewer comes out clean. Allow to cool in the tin for 15 minutes, then use the parchment to lift the loaves and transfer them to a wire rack to cool. Serve warm with softened butter.

Leftover bread can be stored in an airtight container for up to four days. It can be served at room temperature, toasted or rewarmed in the oven.

Starters & Sides — 21

Massachusetts Baked Beans

Ask any Salemite for a quintessential hometown recipe, and they're sure to mention baked beans. These sweetly seasoned legumes are a statewide staple – served at barbecues, family feasts and festive autumn gatherings alike. Just as Sarah Sanderson knows that boys will love her for her beauty, purveyors of baked beans can be confident that guests will *adore* this sure-to-be classic recipe.

Yield: 8 servings | GF

450 grams dried haricot beans, soaked (see note)

2 sprigs fresh thyme

1 sprig fresh rosemary

1 tablespoon rock salt

1 bay leaf

1 dried red chilli

3 cloves garlic, smashed

140 grams pomegranate syrup

2 tablespoons Dijon mustard

1 tablespoon Worcestershire sauce

225 grams bacon, chopped into 2.5 cm pieces

1 onion, diced

Note

Dried beans should be rinsed and picked through to remove any debris. They should then be soaked overnight, a minimum of 6 hours. This method is best as the beans will retain the best texture. If you are short on time, you can quick-soak the beans by putting them in a large pan, covering with water and bringing to a rapid boil. Boil for 2 minutes, remove from the heat and let soak for 1 hour. Drain and rinse the beans.

Add the soaked beans, thyme, rosemary, 2 teaspoons of the salt, the bay leaf, chilli, and smashed garlic to a large pot. Add enough water to cover the beans by about 5 cm (about 2 litres). Bring to the boil over a medium-high heat, turn the heat to medium-low and simmer until the beans are just tender, about 30 minutes. Check the pot periodically and add more water as necessary to keep the beans covered.

Once the beans are tender, drain the beans, reserving the cooking liquid. Remove any of the woody stems of herbs, leaving behind any herb leaves, the bay leaf, garlic cloves and dried chilli. Put the pomegranate syrup in a 1 litre measuring jug. Add the mustard, Worcestershire sauce and the remaining 1 teaspoon of salt. Add enough reserved cooking liquid to the measuring jug to create 480 ml of liquid. Stir until the pomegranate syrup is completely dissolved.

Preheat the oven to 180°C

In a large casserole dish over a medium-high heat, cook the bacon for about 5 minutes, rendering off most of the fat. Add the onion and continue to cook until the bacon is crisp and the onion is brown. Add the pomegranate syrup mixture and the beans and stir to combine. If the beans are not completely submerged, add additional cooking liquid until the beans are just under the surface.

Place in the oven and bake for 2½ to 3 hours. After 1 hour, stir the beans and shake the pot to level it, then add more of the reserved cooking liquid so the beans stay barely submerged. The goal is to keep the beans under a thin layer of liquid so the top ones don't dry out but not so much liquid as to prevent browning. Continue to check on the liquid level about once an hour.

The beans are ready when they are completely tender and have developed a deep brown sauce. Serve immediately. Leftovers can be stored in the refrigerator in an airtight container for up to three days. They can be rewarmed on the stove top, with a little added water or stock to loosen if needed.

Starters & Sides

 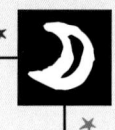

Ten Chocolate Bars, No Liquorice, Candy Toll

Salem's resident bullies *always* demand a Halloween candy toll – ten chocolate bars, *no liquorice*. But should a trick-or-treater wish to hold on to their haul, this sweet, crunchy recipe might just distract a would-be candy thief. Crispy cereal and salty pretzels pair perfectly with a smattering of bite-size Halloween treats. Guaranteed to distract any mouth breather ... provided you don't gobble up this treat yourself!

Yield: *About 10 servings* | **GF*, V**

Ingredients

- 120 grams toasted oats cereal (like Cheerios)
- 120 grams square cereal (like Golden Grahams)
- 120 grams mini shredded wheat cereal
- 120 grams mini pretzels
- 60 grams unsalted butter
- 1½ tablespoons treacle
- 70 grams light brown sugar
- ½ teaspoon ground cinnamon
- 1 teaspoon rock salt
- ¼ teaspoon baking soda
- 500 grams assorted mini or bite-size Halloween candies of choice
- 50 grams raisins

Method

Preheat the oven to 190°C and line two rimmed baking sheets with parchment paper or silicone baking mats.

In a large bowl, stir together the toasted oats cereal, square cereal, mini shredded wheat cereal and pretzels. Set aside.

In a medium saucepan, combine the butter, treacle and brown sugar. Cook over a medium-high heat, stirring continually, until the mixture comes to a rolling boil, 3 to 5 minutes. Remove from the heat and stir in the cinnamon, ½ teaspoon of the salt and the baking soda. Immediately pour this mixture over the cereal mixture and stir thoroughly to coat.

Turn out the mixture on to the two baking sheets and spread into even layers. Bake for 15 minutes, stirring every 5 minutes, or until golden brown and fragrant. Sprinkle with the remaining ½ teaspoon of salt. Allow to cool almost completely before adding candy and raisins.

Once completely cool, store in an airtight container until serving.

> **Note**
>
> For a gluten-free option, choose only gluten-free cereals, omit the pretzels (or use gluten-free pretzels) and use your favourite gluten-free candies.

Starters & Sides

Pretty Black Meatball Spiders

Sarah Sanderson loves to snack on a good spider – especially the pretty ones! But when *actual* spiders aren't available, these meatball spiders make for the next best thing. Fried chow mein noodles combined with a dash of tangy mustard are sure to enchant *any* arachnid aficionado. Just watch out for those spindly legs – they've been known to tickle!

Yield: About 25 spiders

For the Spiders

120 grams tahini (see note)

3 to 5 drops black food colouring

1 tablespoon Worcestershire sauce

1 teaspoon paprika

400 grams ready cooked chow mein noodles

450 grams sausage meat

2 tablespoons chopped shallot

For the Dipping Sauce

4 tablespoons Dijon mustard

1 tablespoon apple cider vinegar

1 tablespoon honey

½ tablespoon chilli paste or hot sauce

> **Note**
>
> Have black tahini on hand? Use that and omit the food colouring!

To make the spiders: Preheat the oven to 120°C. Line two rimmed baking sheets with parchment paper.

In a small bowl, whisk together the tahini, food colouring, Worcestershire sauce and paprika until well blended. Mix 2 tablespoons of the sauce mixture with 2 tablespoons of water until well combined.

In a medium bowl, toss the thinned sauce with 200 grams of the noodles. Spread the noodles out in an even layer on one of the prepared baking sheets. Bake for 10 minutes, then set aside and allow to cool completely. Keep the oven on but raise the temperature to 190°C.

In a food processor, pulverise the remaining 200 grams of noodles into fine crumbs. Mix the remaining sauce mixture with the sausage, noodle crumbs and shallot.

Form the spiders by scooping up about 2 tablespoons of the sausage mixture at a time, rolling into a ball and inserting eight noodle "legs", four on each side. Set on the prepared baking sheets. Bake for 15 minutes, or until an instant-read thermometer inserted into the centre of the spiders registers 75°C.

These can be made ahead and chilled for up to 4 hours before baking.

To make the dipping sauce: While the meatballs are baking, whisk together the mustard, vinegar, honey and chilli paste in a small bowl. Set aside until ready to serve.

Serve the meatballs warm with the dipping sauce.

Starters & Sides

Circle of Salt Soft Pretzels

After three hundred years, the Sanderson sisters are ready to run *amok, amok, amok*! And as everyone knows, only a circle of salt can protect the innocent from such formidable witches. While some might sprinkle the crystals around their bodies (or even around a grave!), others may opt for a less conventional means of protection. The cleverest of white witches can conjure their safeguard into a delightful snack – one specifically designed to twist even the most wicked spell into knots. Light, doughy and sure to pack a protective punch, these pretzels are a favourite of any Salemite worth her salts.

Yield: About 24 pretzels | V

240 ml warm water (about 45°C)

70 grams pomegranate syrup

1 packet (7 grams) rapid-rise active dry yeast

300 grams plain flour

130 grams dark rye flour

1 tablespoon rock salt

90 grams unsalted butter

240 ml sparkling apple juice

115 grams baking soda

About 75 grams pretzel salt or other coarse salt

In a medium bowl, mix together the water, pomegranate syrup and yeast. Let stand for 5 to 10 minutes, until foamy.

In the bowl of a food mixer fitted with the hook attachment, mix together the plain flour, dark rye flour and rock salt. Cut the butter into small pieces, then work it into the flour with a pastry cutter or your hands until it is crumbly. Add the yeast mixture and mix on low speed, stopping and scraping the bowl as necessary, until all the flour has been incorporated.

With the mixer still on a low speed (or the manufacturer's recommended setting for dough), mix the dough until it is smooth and elastic, 4 to 6 minutes. Remove the dough from the bowl, form it into a ball and wrap it in cling film. Refrigerate for 8 hours or overnight.

Preheat the oven to 200°C. Line two baking sheets with parchment paper. On a lightly floured work surface, roll out the dough to a roughly 30-by-35-cm rectangle. Cut the dough into long strips, about 2.5 cm wide. Working with one strip at a time, roll it into a long rope about 45 cm long, then halve it. Form each half into a circle, pressing the ends together, then place them on the baking sheets. Repeat with the remaining dough. Cover the pretzels with a clean tea towel.

In a large, deep pan set over a medium-high heat, bring 2 litres of water, the vinegar and the baking soda to a simmer. Gently lower one or two pretzels into the water bath and simmer for about 30 seconds. Use a large sieve or slotted spoon to remove the pretzels, then place them back on the prepared baking sheets. Sprinkle each pretzel with the pretzel salt. Repeat with the remaining pretzels, then bake for 10 to 12 minutes, or until they are dark brown.

Starters & Sides

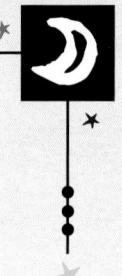

Pan Hag

Winifred Sanderson is *not* impressed when Thackery Binx calls her a hag ... and declares that there are not enough children in the world to make her young and beautiful! Naturally, she's quick to anger – and even quicker to dole out vicious vengeance. But even a witch as wrathful as Winnie would be blown away by Pan Hag. Cheesy potatoes with just a hint of rocket are cooked to a crisp in a cast-iron skillet, creating a crunchy, savoury side that's destined to become a beloved part of any All Hallows' Eve celebration.

Yield: 6 servings | GF, V

- 60 grams salted butter
- 1 onion, diced
- 200 grams baby rocket leaves, washed and dried well
- 900 grams golden potatoes, peeled and sliced thin
- 1 teaspoon salt
- 225 grams white sharp Cheddar cheese, grated
- Freshly ground black pepper

In a 25-cm cast-iron skillet or ovenproof pan over a medium-high heat, melt 30 grams of the butter until it foams. Add the onion and sauté until translucent but not brown, 2 to 3 minutes. Add the rocket and continue to sauté until just wilted, 2 to 3 minutes more. Transfer the mixture to a bowl and set aside.

Preheat the oven to 220°C.

Add 15 grams of the butter to the pan, still over a medium-high heat, and let it melt. Remove the pan from the heat and place a single layer of potatoes, slightly overlapping each other, on the bottom of the pan. Sprinkle on ⅓ teaspoon of the salt and season with black pepper to taste. Add a third of the onion mixture and a third of the cheese. Cover with another layer of potatoes, season with ⅓ teaspoon of the salt and black pepper to taste. Repeat with another third of the onion mixture and cheese, then repeat the layering once more with the remaining third of the onion mixture and cheese. Top with the remaining potatoes and remaining ⅓ teaspoon of salt. Season with black pepper to taste.

Place the pan over a medium heat and cook until the bottom layer of potatoes is brown, 7 to 10 minutes.

Dot the top with the remaining 15 grams of butter and bake for 40 to 45 minutes, or until the potatoes are fork-tender and the top is golden brown.

Allow to cool for 10 minutes before slicing and serving.

Starters & Sides

"Amok, Amok, Amok" Guacamole and Homemade Chips

Winifred is horrified to discover that after three hundred years, All Hallows' Eve has become a night of frolic. But Sarah dances delightedly at the news. Nothing could be better than children dressing up in costumes and running *amok, amok, amok*! Since such shenanigans require sustenance, this recipe for guacamole and homemade chips provides the perfect salty snack. While hobgoblins abound and trusty brooms may disappear, this go-to starter offers a bounty of tantalising tastes to anyone bold enough to cross paths with a witch ... or three!

Yield: 6 servings | GF*, V*, V+*

For the Homemade Chips
- 6 sheets spring roll wrappers
- About 1 litre sunflower oil for frying

For the Guacamole
- 3 ripe avocados, halved and pitted
- Juice of ½ lime
- 1 teaspoon shichimi togarashi seasoning (see note)
- 3 cloves black garlic, peeled

Note
Shichimi togarashi seasoning has bonito fish flakes, so this dish is not vegetarian or vegan. For a vegetarian option, simply omit the seasoning from the recipe, and add a pinch of red pepper flakes. To make the dish gluten-free, use regular corn chips instead of the homemade ones.

To make the chips: Cut each spring roll wrapper into strips about 2.5 cm wide. Pour the oil into a large, heavy-bottomed pan until it reaches 7 ½ cm deep, then place over a medium-high heat until it reaches 180°C. Have a plate lined with paper towels standing by.

Fry the strips in batches using a spider or slotted spoon to turn the strips gently while they cook (see Fry Station Safety on page 157). Strips are ready when they are golden brown, about 1 minute. Remove the strips with the spider and place them on the prepared plate to drain. As soon as they are cool to the touch, they are ready to serve, or they can be stored in an airtight container for up to two days.

To make the guacamole: Scoop the flesh of the avocados into a medium serving bowl. Pour the lime juice over the avocado, sprinkle with the seasoning and blend briefly with a fork.

On the surface of a small chopping board, with the blade of a knife facing away from you, use the flat side of the knife to smash the garlic cloves into a jam-like consistency. Scrape the garlic into the avocado mixture and use the fork to blend and incorporate it.

Serve with homemade chips.

Starters & Sides

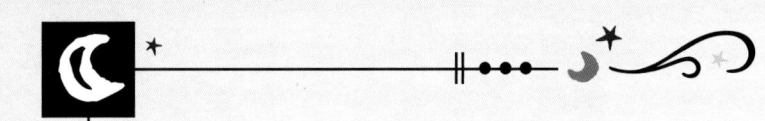

"No Witches Here" Pumpkin Butter

When the people of Salem set out to find Thackery Binx, they pound angrily on the Sandersons' door. The villagers are on a witch hunt ... and they're determined to reveal the true identities of the women responsible for Thackery's disappearance. But Winifred pleads ignorance, claiming "there be no witches here" – only kindly old spinster women with their cauldrons of rich, bubbling brew. Either way, the Sandersons are well-known for their sinister recipes – witchy or otherwise. And the troublesome trio wouldn't be able to resist this rich, creamy concoction. With plenty of pumpkin cooked down with sugar and spices, this pumpkin butter is the perfect complement to a loaf of Miss Olin Nutty Brown Bread (page 21) ... and, of course, a quiet evening at home.

Yield: *About 900 grams* | **GF, V, V+**

1.35 kilograms pumpkin or butternut squash

240 ml apple juice

2 tablespoons bourbon or vanilla extract

220 grams dark brown sugar

1 teaspoon ground cinnamon

¼ teaspoon ground clove

Specialist Tools
Eight 110 gram or four 225 gram jars

Have ready eight 110 gram or four 225 gram jars with tight-fitting lids, well washed or sterilised. Preheat the oven to 180°C.

Halve the pumpkin or squash and scoop out the seeds and stringy pulp. Cut the stem end off and discard it.

Pour 120 ml of the apple juice with 120 ml water into a roasting tray. Place the pumpkin pieces, cut-side down, in the tray and roast for 45 to 50 minutes, or until very tender when poked with a fork.

Allow the pumpkin to cool for 10 minutes, then use a fork and spoon to scrape the flesh from the skin. Place all the flesh and the cooking liquid in a large, heavy-bottomed saucepan. Discard the skin.

Add the remaining 120 ml of apple juice, the bourbon, brown sugar, cinnamon and clove. Place over a medium heat and cook, stirring, until the mixture begins to bubble, about 10 minutes. Turn the heat down to low, cover partially and simmer for 20 to 25 minutes, or until the mixture clings to a spoon for several seconds before falling back in the pan.

Remove from the heat and use an immersion blender to puree into a smooth texture. Immediately fill the clean jars and seal with tight-fitting lids. Allow to cool to room temperature and then refrigerate. The pumpkin butter will store in the refrigerator for up to three weeks.

The Master's Fried Peppers

The Sanderson sisters revere their master – that pitchfork-wielding, red-horned fellow whose dastardly tendencies often land him in hot water. But Master's spicy proclivities extend beyond mere mischief-making. With tastes that run hotter than the temperature of his abode, Master would surely find these fried peppers to be a devilish delight. No doubt, they'll keep *anyone* dancing well into the night.

Yield: 4 to 6 servings | GF, V, V+

2 tablespoons avocado oil

110 grams padron peppers

About 2 teaspoons black and/or red lava salt

In a medium stainless-steel or cast-iron skillet, heat the oil over a high heat until it shimmers. Add the peppers and stir or shake the pan to coat the peppers in oil.

Cook, stirring or shaking the pan occasionally, for 4 to 5 minutes, until the peppers blister on all sides. Remove the pan from the heat and transfer the peppers to a serving plate.

Serve with the black and red salt in a small dish and sprinkle a few grains of salt on to each pepper just before eating.

Starters & Sides — 31

Dead Man's Toes

Tis time. Yes, tis time for a potion, forsooth!
One meant to restore sisters' glorious youth.
Flip open the book, add ingredients vile –
Toss oil and hair and red herb to the pile.
Most precious of all is the rare dead man's toe.

It needs to be fresh – so perhaps one should know
Just how to prepare it: sausage you shall need.
Add dough, an almond, and some herbs – oh indeed
You'll find that this toe is a flavourful treat.
One certain to sweep you right off your feet.

Yield: About 24 toes

450 grams Italian sausage meat
150 grams panko breadcrumbs
1 large egg, separated
One 500 gram packet puff pastry, thawed
24 Marcona almonds
1 tablespoon dried rosemary

Line a rimmed baking sheet with a silicone baking mat or parchment paper.

In a large bowl, combine the sausage, breadcrumbs, and egg yolk. Set the egg white aside.

On a lightly floured work surface, cut each sheet of puff pastry into three 7 ½-cm-wide strips. Roll each strip out a bit until it reaches about 30 cm in length. Cut each strip into four 7 ½ cm squares.

Whisk the egg white with 1 teaspoon water to create an egg wash.

Brush the edges of one pastry square with the egg wash. Form about 1½ tablespoons of the sausage mixture into a rough log. Place the sausage log in the centre of the pastry square, leaving a bit of sausage overhanging one end. Fold the sides of the pastry square over the sausage, overlapping in the middle, and place it, seam-side down, on the prepared baking sheet. Pinch and tuck the pastry end until it is completely closed and slightly rounded.

Egg wash the entire sausage "toe" and press one almond into the pastry end of the roll. Use a sharp knife or pastry wheel to score a knuckle towards the nail end of the toe. Sprinkle the knuckle with a few rosemary "hairs".

Repeat this process until you've used all the pastry and sausage mixture. Chill the toes in the refrigerator for at least 20 minutes or up to 1 hour.

Bake at 200°C for 20 to 25 minutes, or until golden brown and an instant-read thermometer inserted into the centre of the sausage registers 75°C.

Starters & Sides

"Oh, Cheese and Crust" Homemade Crackers

In a magic-filled world, it can be difficult to keep one's head – a truth Winnie learns when an errant tree branch sends Billy Butcherson's head flying. The frustrated witch shouts, "Oh cheese and crust!" which inspires Billy to get moving. Conveniently enough, it *also* inspires this guaranteed crowd-pleaser. With hints of white Cheddar and a smattering of chives, these crackers are sure to make even the surliest Sanderson take her broom to the skies in delight.

Yield: *About 72 crackers* | **V**

- 120 grams unsalted butter
- 170 grams sharp white Cheddar, cut into chunks
- 25 grams grated Parmesan cheese
- 180 grams plain flour
- 2 tablespoons double cream
- 1 teaspoon dried chives
- ¼ teaspoon salt

In the bowl of a food processor, combine the butter, Cheddar cheese and Parmesan cheese and pulse a few times to combine. Add the flour, double cream, chives and salt and pulse until the dough just comes together. It will still be a bit crumbly.

On a chopping board, split the dough into thirds and shape each third into a log about 20 cm long. Wrap each log in parchment paper and refrigerate for at least 1 hour.

Preheat the oven to 180°C. Line a baking sheet with parchment paper or a silicone baking mat.

Slice each log into 3-mm-thick slices and place on the prepared baking sheet. Bake for 10 to 12 minutes, or until lightly browned and crisp. Transfer the crackers to a wire rack to cool and serve warm or at room temperature.

Dough can be kept in the refrigerator for up to three days or frozen for up to one month. If frozen, set aside for 1 hour, or until it's easy to slice.

Starters & Sides

Popping Cranberries

The Sanderson sisters spend a *lot* of time crafting potions. And these popping cranberries would make an ideal ingredient for any one of the witchy sisters' bubbling brews. After a simmering syrup bath and receiving a generous sprinkle of sugar, these sweetly tart cranberries will practically pop with flavour. How *glorious*!

Yield: 480 ml | GF, V, V+

200 grams fresh cranberries
400 grams granulated sugar
1 tablespoon fresh lemon juice
150 grams caster sugar
¼ teaspoon ground cinnamon

In a colander, rinse and sort the berries, removing any debris or bruised fruit. Set aside to drain.

In a large saucepan over a medium-high heat, bring 480 ml of water to the boil, then turn the heat to low and add the granulated sugar, stirring until completely dissolved. Remove from the heat and add the lemon juice and cranberries. Stir to combine. Pour the mixture into a heatproof bowl and transfer to the refrigerator (covering is fine but not required). Allow to chill and infuse for 8 hours or overnight.

In a small bowl, combine the caster sugar and cinnamon and spread it out over a large rimmed baking sheet. Strain the cranberries and reserve the liquid for future use, such as Mary's Magic Elixir (page 149). Scatter the cranberries over the baking sheet and shake the sheet back and forth to coat the berries. Allow to dry for 1 hour, or until dry.

These make a great addition to the All Hallows' Eve Feast Grazing Board (page 17), as a drink garnish and dessert topping – or simply serve them as a snack on their own. Store in an airtight container in a cool, dark place for up to one week. To gift, place in parchment-paper-lined containers and seal.

Starters & Sides

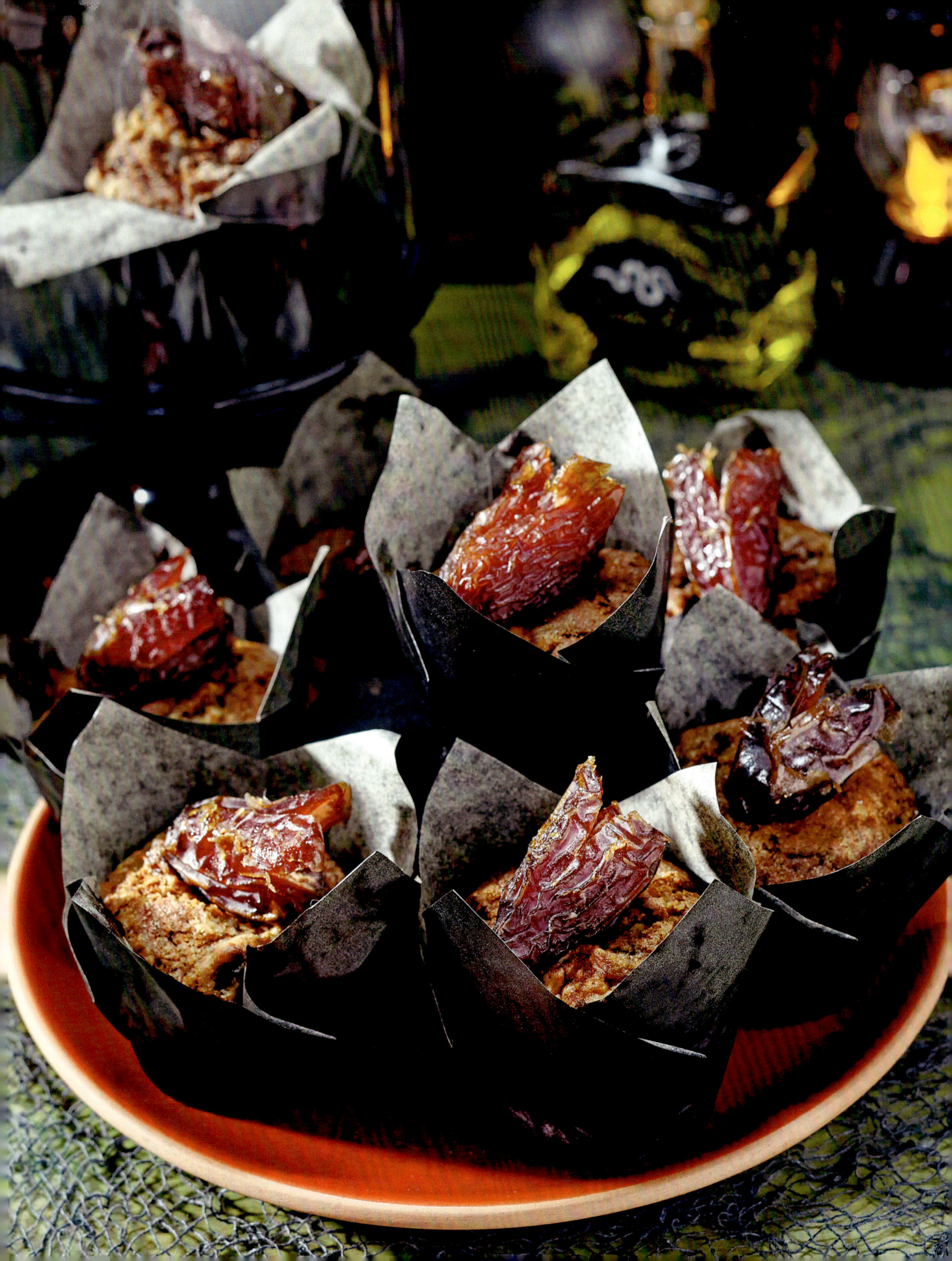

Roach Muffins

Witches have rather peculiar tastes. They think nothing of serving up a side of hag ... or a spot of Dead Man's Toes (page 33). And while the mention of cockroaches might cause the occasional fainting spell, this roach-free recipe will have even mortal guests scurrying about with delight. Apples, dates and cinnamon combine to make these muffins a perennial favourite – of witches, warlocks and humans alike!

Yield: 12 muffins | V

210 grams plain flour

1 teaspoon baking soda

1 teaspoon baking powder

2 teaspoons ground cinnamon

½ teaspoon salt

1 large apple

1 tablespoon fresh lemon juice

50 grams sugar, plus 2 teaspoons

340 grams whole pitted dates (see note)

60 ml boiling water

120 grams unsalted butter, softened

110 grams dark brown sugar

2 large eggs, at room temperature

1 tablespoon vanilla extract

Preheat the oven to 220°C. Line a 12-hole muffin tray with cupcake cases.

Whisk 180 grams of the flour, the baking soda, baking powder, 1 teaspoon of the cinnamon and the salt together in a large bowl. Set aside.

Peel, core and dice the apple. Place in a small bowl with the lemon juice and mix. Set aside. In a small bowl, mix 2 teaspoons of the sugar and the remaining 1 teaspoon of cinnamon together and set aside.

Reserve 12 whole dates for the garnish and finely chop the rest. In a heatproof bowl or measuring jug, cover the chopped dates with the boiling water, stir to combine and set aside.

In a large mixing bowl using a hand mixer or in the bowl of a food mixer fitted with the paddle attachment, beat together the butter, brown sugar and the remaining 50 grams of sugar on a high speed until smooth and creamy, about 2 minutes. Add the eggs and vanilla. Beat on a medium speed for 1 minute, then turn to a high speed and beat until the mixture is combined and mostly creamy. (It's OK if it appears somewhat curdled.) With the mixer running on a low speed, add the flour mixture and continue to mix until it is incorporated. Fold in the dates with their liquid.

Toss the apples with the remaining 30 grams of flour and fold the apple mixture into the batter. Fill each muffin case two-thirds of the way full and top with about ¼ teaspoon of the cinnamon sugar for each muffin.

Bake for 5 minutes at 220°C, then, keeping the muffins in the oven, reduce the oven temperature to 180°C. Bake for 12 to 15 minutes more, or until a skewer inserted in the centre comes out clean.

While the muffins are baking, prepare the cockroach garnish. Take each reserved whole date and make a cut down the top centre, starting at the hole. Leave 1 cm uncut at the other end. Next, cut the same line, about 1 cm to the left and right of the centre cut, creating two wings. Gently lift the wings away from the body and pose as desired. As soon as the muffins come out of the oven, place one date roach on each muffin.

> **Note**
> Not a fan of insect decor? Decrease the amount of dates to 110 grams and just add them to the batter.

Starters & Sides

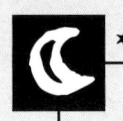

Pastry Boots

Winnie, Mary and Sarah eagerly embrace their witchy wardrobe. With flowing gowns, bristly brooms and, of course, their trademark jet-black boots, the Sandersons make for picture-perfect witches. These black puff pastry boots evoke the essence of the sisters – while offering up a savoury twist. Stuffed with spinach, feta and a hint of sweet pepper, these pastries are sure to kick any menu up a notch.

Yield: *About 24 boots* | V

1 tablespoon olive oil

2 tablespoons salted butter

2 cloves garlic, crushed

1 yellow pepper, diced

One 450 gram bag frozen spinach, thawed and drained

960 grams frozen puff pastry sheets

170 grams feta cheese, crumbled

2 egg whites

2 to 3 drops black food colouring

Specialist Tools

Boot-shaped cookie cutter

> **Note**
>
> Want to make these ahead? Assemble the boots as above and instead of chilling in the refrigerator, freeze on the baking sheets until solid, about 1 hour. Then transfer to an airtight container and continue to freeze until needed, for up to one month. Bake as directed above, but note that the pastry may need a few extra minutes to cook.

In a large skillet over a medium heat, add the olive oil and butter. When the butter begins to foam, add the garlic, stir for 1 minute until fragrant, then add the pepper. Stir to coat and cook for 2 to 3 minutes more, until just barely tender. Pull out 24 pieces of pepper and reserve in a small bowl. Stir in the spinach and cook for 1 to 2 more minutes. Remove from the heat, transfer to a bowl and allow to cool.

While the spinach mixture is cooling, defrost the puff pastry according to directions on the pack. Once the spinach mixture is cool to the touch, stir in the feta and set aside.

Line two baking sheets with parchment paper or silicone baking mats. In a small bowl, whisk the egg whites with 2 tablespoons of water until frothy, add the food colouring and stir to combine.

On a lightly floured surface and working with one piece of puff pastry at a time, roll out the pastry to about ½-cm thickness. Use a boot-shaped cookie cutter to cut out pairs of boots. Place half of the boots on one prepared baking sheet and spread a heaped tablespoon of filling on to each boot, leaving a blank border around the edge. Place another boot on top of the filling, stretching gently if needed, and use a fork to crimp the edges closed. Using a pastry brush, brush the whole boot with the egg wash, prick the boot (at the bottom of the shaft) with the prongs of the fork and cover the holes with a reserved piece of pepper to create the buckle. Once the baking sheet is full, transfer it to the refrigerator and chill for at least 20 minutes.

Preheat the oven to 220°C.

Continue to make more boots by rolling out the other pieces of puff pastry one at a time and repeating the above steps.

Bake the pastries, rotating the sheets halfway through baking, for 15 to 20 minutes, or until golden brown and crisp. Allow to cool for 5 minutes before serving. Serve warm or at room temperature. Pastries can be stored in an airtight container in the refrigerator for up to three days and reheated in a 180°C oven for 10 minutes.

Starters & Sides

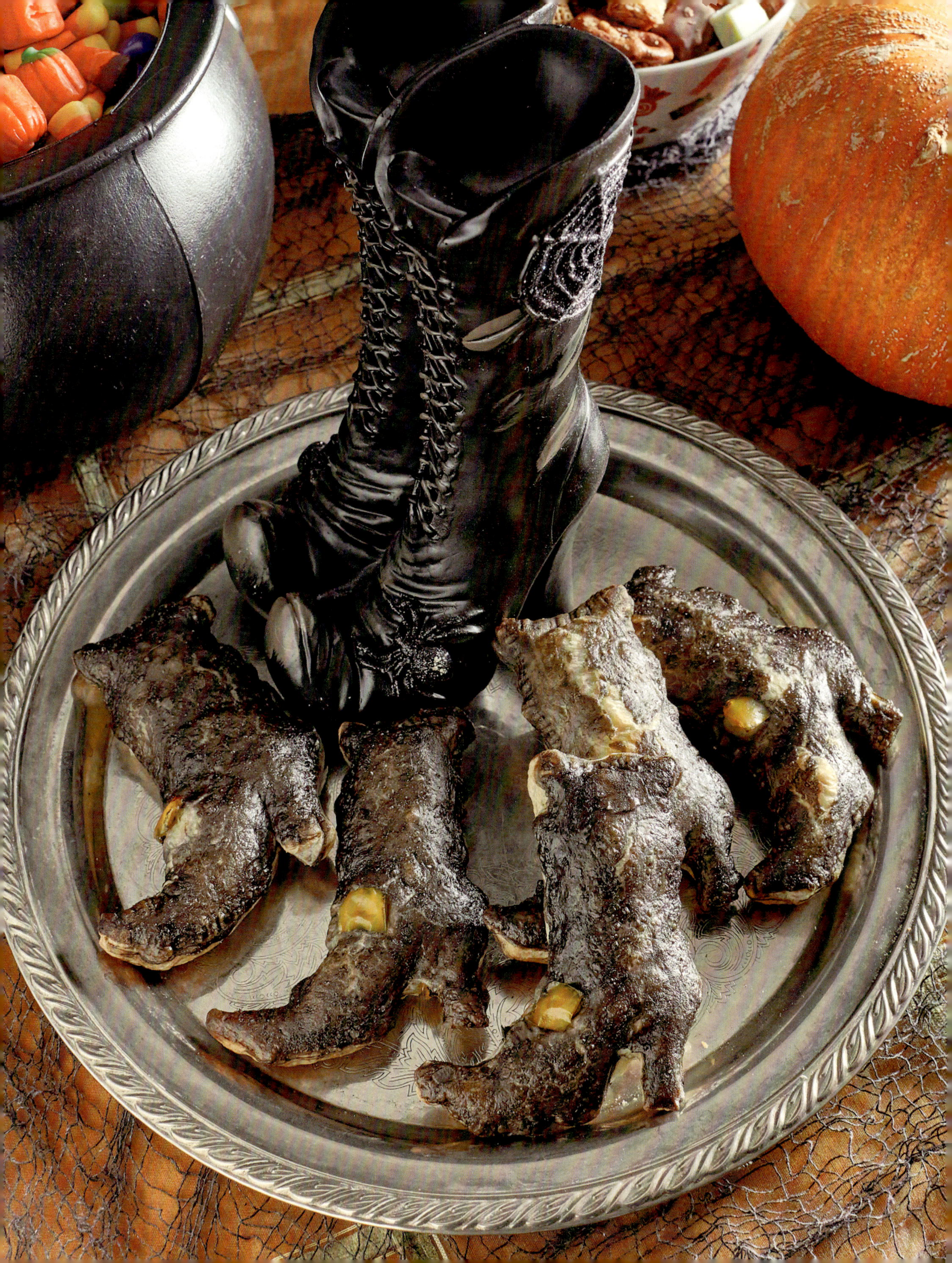

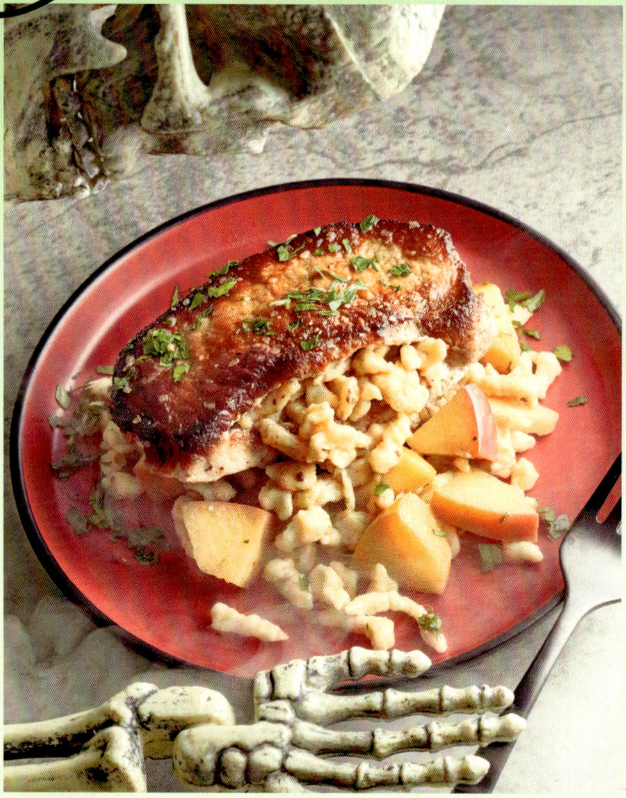
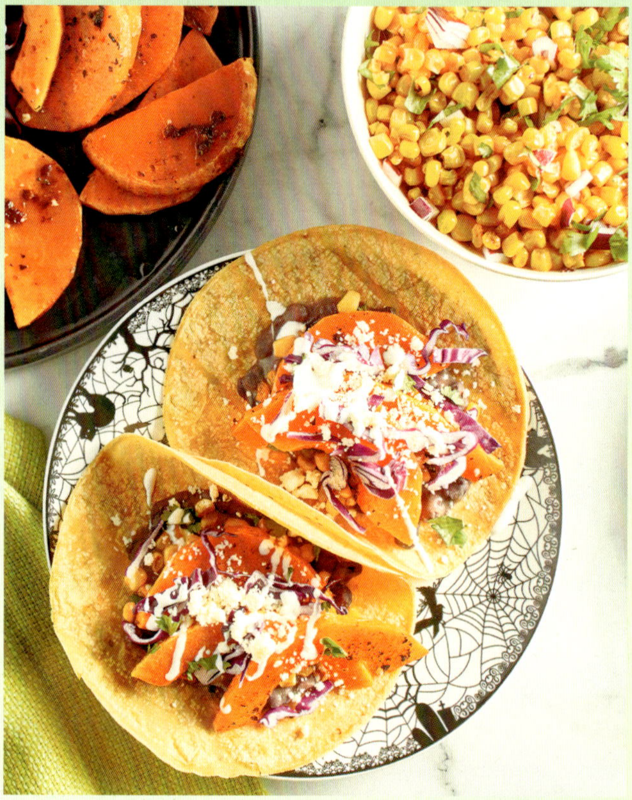
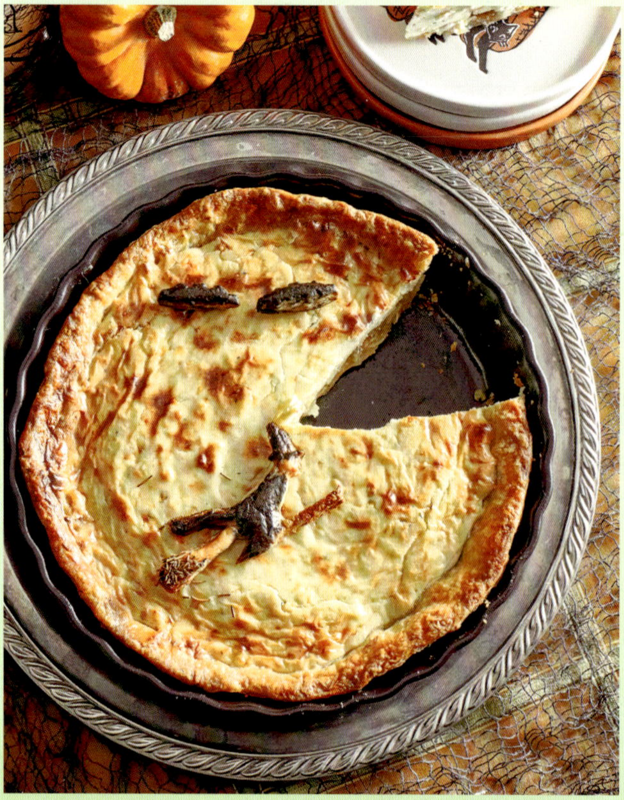
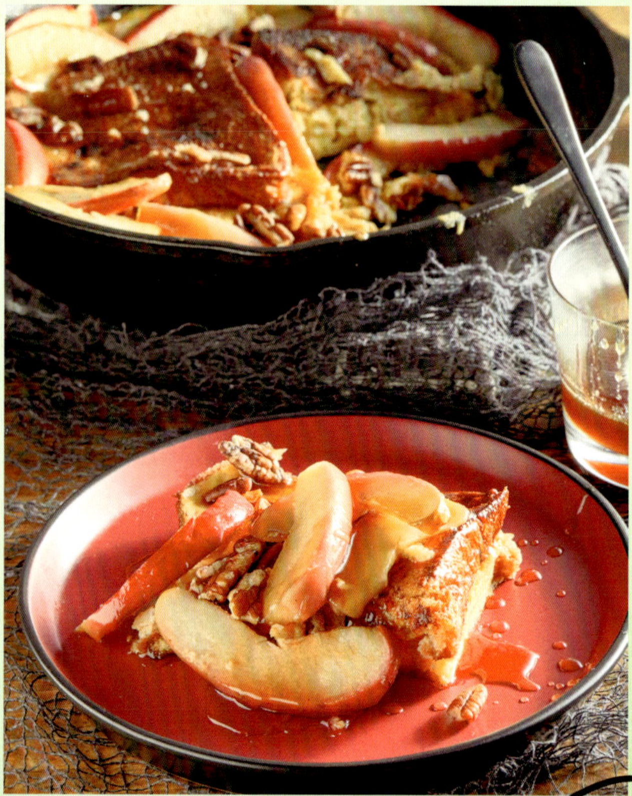

Main Dishes

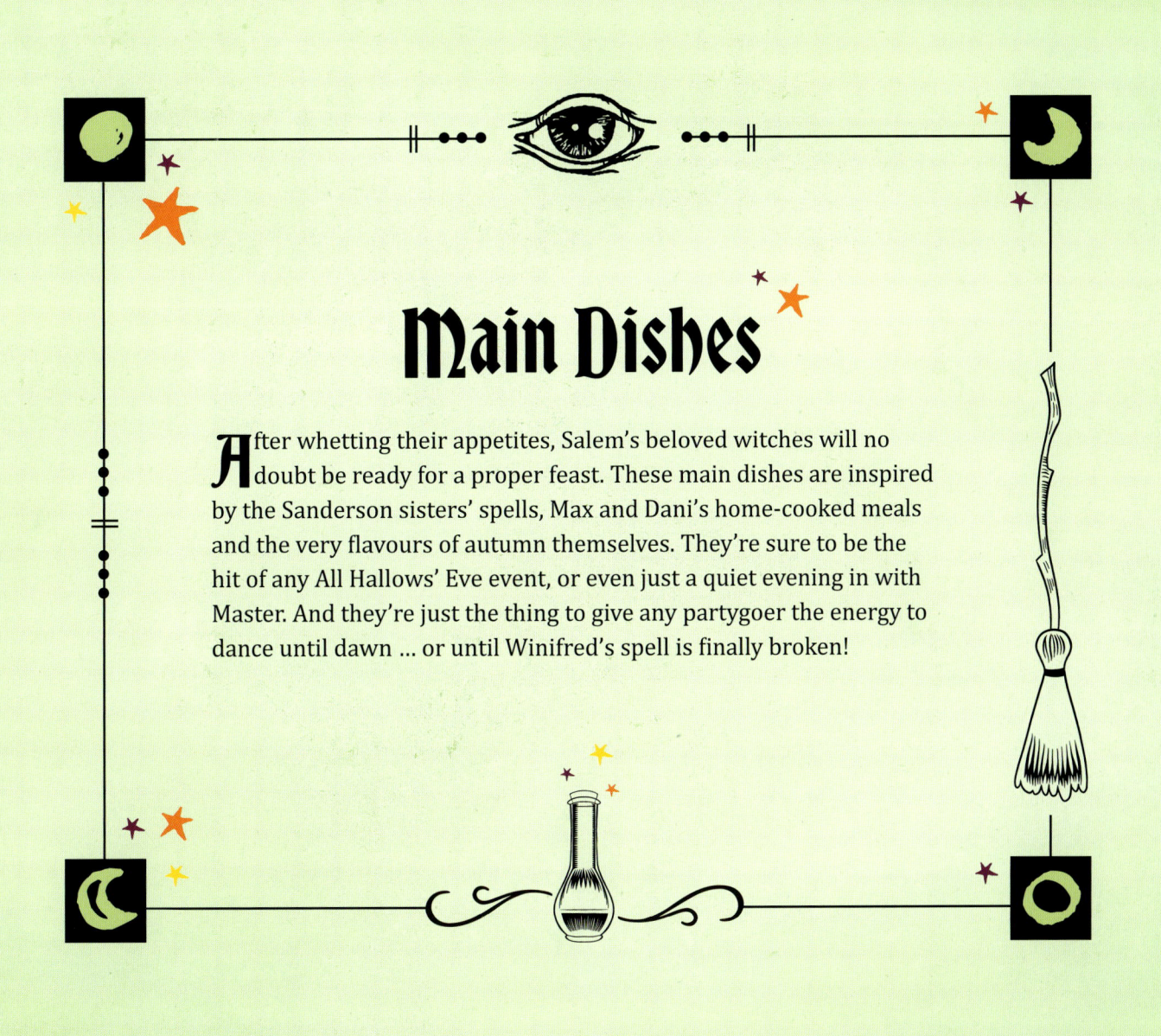

After whetting their appetites, Salem's beloved witches will no doubt be ready for a proper feast. These main dishes are inspired by the Sanderson sisters' spells, Max and Dani's home-cooked meals and the very flavours of autumn themselves. They're sure to be the hit of any All Hallows' Eve event, or even just a quiet evening in with Master. And they're just the thing to give any partygoer the energy to dance until dawn … or until Winifred's spell is finally broken!

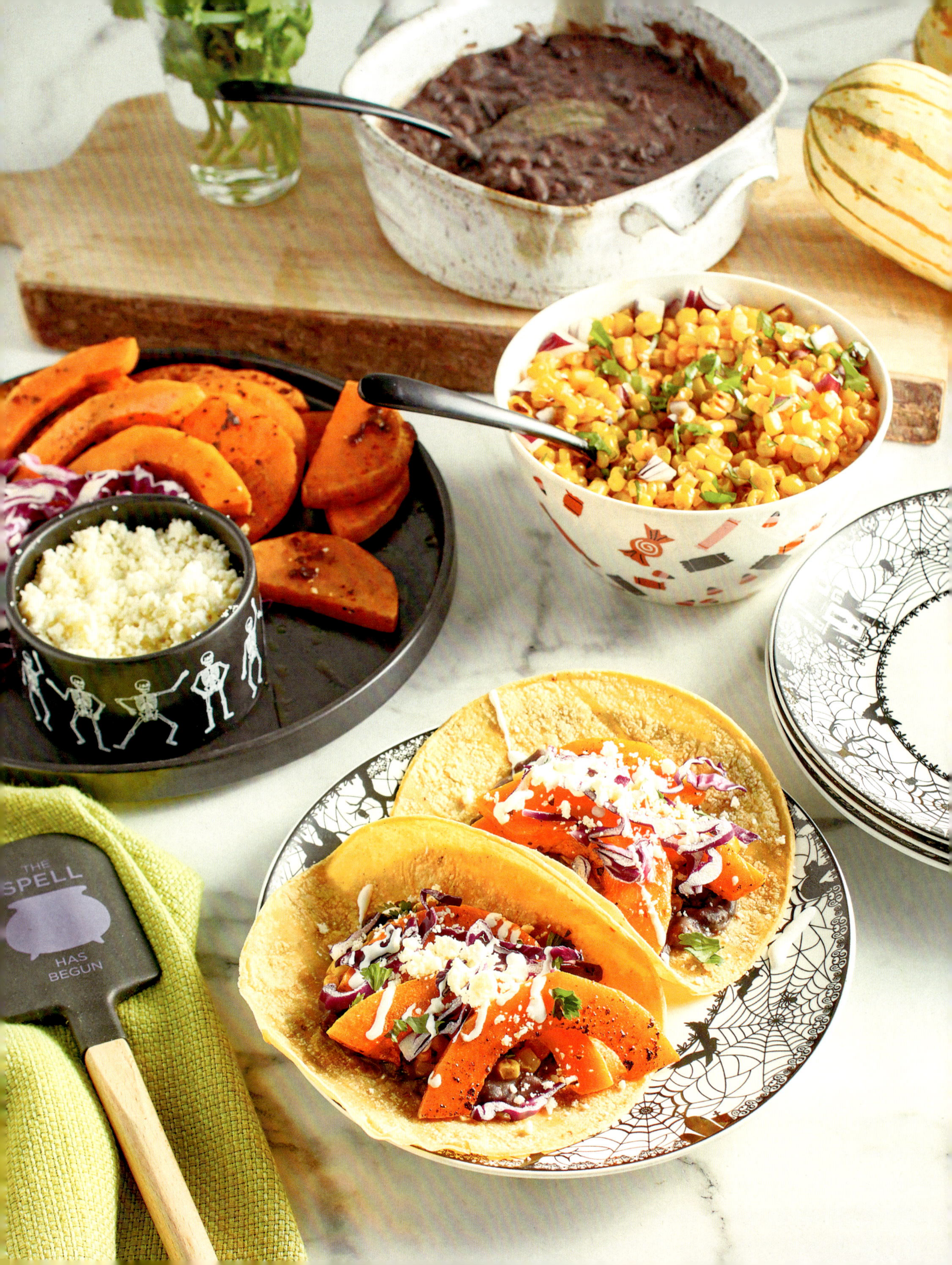
THE
SPELL
HAS
BEGUN

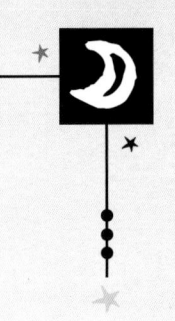

Mrs Dennison's Roasted Pumpkin Tacos

In California, where the Dennisons are from, tacos are a staple. And this pumpkin-based meal provides a Halloween twist on a Hollywood classic, something Mrs Dennison would surely make for Max and Dani during their transition to Salem. Roasted vegetables, savoury spices and the most quintessential of autumn foods come together to make this meal an instant favourite. With sun-hued tones that evoke an air of serenity, this dish is perfect to serve at your next family dinner. You see, they're very health-conscious in Los Angeles ... and Mrs Dennison's tacos are the perfect way to bring a slice of California – and one of Salem too! – into your own home.

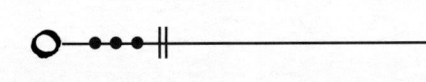

Yield: 4 servings | GF*, V, V+*

For the Pumpkin Tacos
- 1 tablespoon olive oil
- 1 teaspoon adobo sauce (from canned chipotles in adobo)
- Juice of ½ lime
- ½ teaspoon salt
- ½ teaspoon dried oregano
- ¼ teaspoon ground cinnamon
- 900 grams pumpkin or butternut squash, peeled, seeded and sliced into 5-cm strips

For the Corn Salad
- 1 tablespoon vegetable oil
- 1 chipotle pepper in adobo sauce, drained and diced
- 600 grams fresh or thawed frozen corn kernels
- ½ teaspoon salt
- 15 grams picked fresh coriander leaves
- ½ red onion, diced
- Juice of ½ lime

For the Refried Black Beans
- 30 grams salted butter
- Two 425-gram cans black beans, liquid reserved from 1 can
- 1 bay leaf
- ½ teaspoon salt
- ¼ teaspoon garlic powder
- ¼ teaspoon ground coriander

For Assembly
- 8 corn tortillas
- Shredded cabbage (optional)
- Cotija cheese, or feta (optional)
- Crema (optional)

continued on page 44

Note

This recipe can be easily made gluten-free and vegan by swapping the butter for coconut oil, swapping the Cotija cheese for a vegan cheese, omitting the crema and using gluten-free tortillas.

Main Dishes

continued from page 43

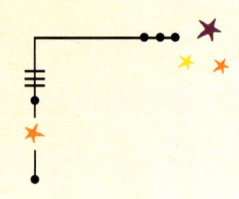

To make the pumpkin tacos: Preheat the oven to 200°C.

In a large bowl, combine the olive oil, adobo sauce, lime juice, salt, oregano and cinnamon. Whisk to combine. Add the pumpkin slices and toss to coat thoroughly. Arrange the pumpkin slices in a single layer on a rimmed baking sheet and roast for 15 to 20 minutes, or until tender and starting to caramelise.

While the pumpkin is roasting, make the corn salad and black beans.

To make the corn salad: In a large sauté pan over a medium heat, combine the oil and the chipotle. Sauté for 2 to 3 minutes, until fragrant and sticky. Add the corn and salt to the pan and stir to coat. Continue to sauté, stirring occasionally, until the corn is starting to brown in places, 7 to 10 minutes. Transfer the corn to a large bowl. Roughly chop the coriander leaves and add them to the corn along with the onion and lime juice. Stir to combine and set aside until serving.

To make the black beans: In the same sauté pan (now with browned chipotle bits) over a medium heat, melt the butter until it foams. Add the beans and the reserved liquid of one can. Fill the can halfway with water and add it to the beans. Add the bay leaf, salt, garlic powder and coriander, stirring to combine.

Bring the beans to a low boil, then turn down the heat to low and simmer for 10 to 15 minutes, until most of the liquid has been reduced. Remove from the heat and use the back of a wooden spoon to smash most of the beans. Stir to combine. Keep warm until serving.

To assemble: In a lightly greased pan over a medium-high heat, warm each tortilla for 1 to 2 minutes per side. Smear each tortilla with black beans, then add corn salad and three to four slices of pumpkin. Top with cabbage, cheese and/or crema (if using). Alternatively, heat all the tortillas and keep them warm in a tortilla warmer. Set up all the components as a taco bar and allow guests to assemble their own.

Shishkebaby

When Dani finds herself facing her soon-to-be nemeses, she puts on her bravest face and pretends to be a witch herself. Dani clings to her false alias, even when Mary pokes at her and declares her to be a well-fed "shishkebaby". In this play on Dani's unwanted nickname, speared cauliflower, peppers and onions are seasoned with balsamic vinegar, olive oil and salt, creating a burst of roasted flavour that's delightfully bold – just like Dani herself.

Yield: 8 servings as a main course or up to 16 as a starter | GF, V, V+

For the Marinade

Juice and zest of 1 orange

60 ml balsamic vinegar

120 ml olive oil

1 teaspoon rock salt

1 teaspoon freshly ground black pepper

For the Skewers

1 bunch (about 450 grams) rainbow carrots

450 grams baby potatoes

900 grams mini sweet peppers

1 head Romanesco cauliflower, broken into bite-size florets

One 400 gram bag baby onions

Specialist Tools

Thirty-two 25-cm bamboo skewers

To make the marinade: In a medium bowl, whisk together the orange juice and zest, balsamic vinegar, olive oil, salt and black pepper. Set aside.

To make the skewers: Preheat the oven to 190°C and have two rimmed baking sheets standing by.

Halve the carrots lengthwise. Cut each half, at an angle, into 1-cm slices. Alternating vegetables, load up each skewer with at least one piece each of carrot, potato, sweet pepper, cauliflower and onion, doubling up on smaller ones, such as onion and carrot. Continue until all the skewers are complete. Any extra vegetables can be roasted separately or saved for another use.

Line up the skewers in a single layer on each baking sheet, drizzle with the marinade and shake to coat. You may not need all the marinade. Let stand for 10 minutes, then roast for 20 to 25 minutes, or until the potatoes are fork-tender and vegetables are well browned.

As a main dish, serve over rice or noodles drizzled with any remaining marinade. As a starter, serve warm or at room temperature drizzled with any remaining marinade.

"Another Glorious Morning" Breakfast Sandwiches for Dinner

Winifred Sanderson has never been a morning person. She disliked the dawn long before her three-hundred-year rest, and she positively loathes it now. But while glorious mornings make Winifred sick, this sandwich is sure to make any dinner a truly extraordinary experience. With eggs, cheese and ham, these sandwiches will leave diners – and talking black cats! – clamouring for more.

Yield: 4 sandwiches

For the Béchamel

- 30 grams unsalted butter
- 2 tablespoons plain flour
- 240 ml whole milk
- 2 teaspoons Dijon mustard
- ½ teaspoon salt
- ¼ teaspoon ground nutmeg

For the Sandwiches

- 8 slices sourdough bread
- 60 grams unsalted butter, softened
- 200 grams finely grated Gruyère cheese
- 340 grams ham, sliced (2 to 3 slices per sandwich)
- 50 grams grated Parmesan cheese
- 4 large eggs

To make the béchamel: In a medium saucepan over a medium heat, melt the butter until it foams. Add the flour and, stirring continuously, cook the mixture until the flour smells nutty and a smooth paste has formed, about 2 minutes.

Slowly whisk in the milk and continue whisking until smooth. Add the mustard, salt and nutmeg. Continue to whisk, making sure to scrape the bottom and around the edges of the pan, until the mixture thickens, 3 to 5 minutes. Remove from the heat, cover and set aside.

To make the sandwiches: Heat a cast-iron griddle or large skillet over a medium-high heat. While the pan is heating, pair up the slices of bread and spread the butter on one side of each slice. Grill the bread, butter-side down, until toasted and golden brown, about 2 minutes. Once all the slices have been toasted on one side, lay them in pairs on a chopping board, toasted-side up.

Over a medium-low heat, gently rewarm the béchamel and keep warm. Spread each piece of bread on the toasted side with about 1 tablespoon of béchamel. Top one piece of each bread pair with about 25 grams of the Gruyère, 2 to 3 slices of ham, and another 25 grams of the Gruyère. Place the second piece of bread (untoasted-side up) on top and continue until all four sandwiches are made.

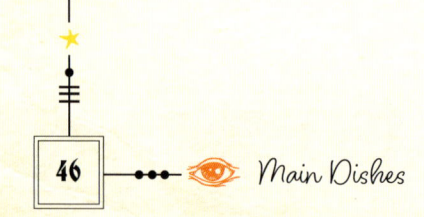

Working with one sandwich and one egg at a time, spread one side of the sandwich with more butter, then press 1 tablespoon of Parmesan cheese into the butter coating the bread. Place the sandwich into the skillet, or on the griddle, over a medium-high heat, cheese-side down, and cook for 2 to 3 minutes. While the sandwich is cooking, spread more butter on to the side facing up and press another 1 tablespoon of Parmesan cheese on to it. The sandwich is ready to flip when it can move easily with a spatula and is deep golden brown on the bottom. While the sandwich is cooking, crack one of the eggs on to the other side of the griddle and cook sunny-side up or over easy to desired firmness.

Halve each sandwich and place on a plate, slightly separated. Spoon a bit of extra béchamel in between the two halves, top with an egg and serve immediately. This is a knife-and-fork sandwich!

Note

This sandwich is best served to order with the sandwich grilling and egg cooking at the same time. If you want all the sandwiches ready at once, preheat the oven to 120°C before you begin grilling the assembled sandwiches. Place a baking sheet fitted with a rack in the oven. As each sandwich is ready, place it in the oven to stay warm. Once all the sandwiches have been cooked, fry all the eggs, then plate as above.

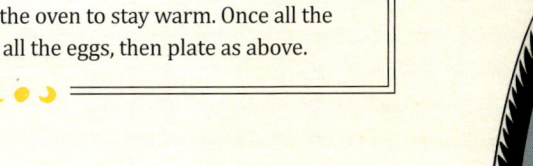

Main Dishes

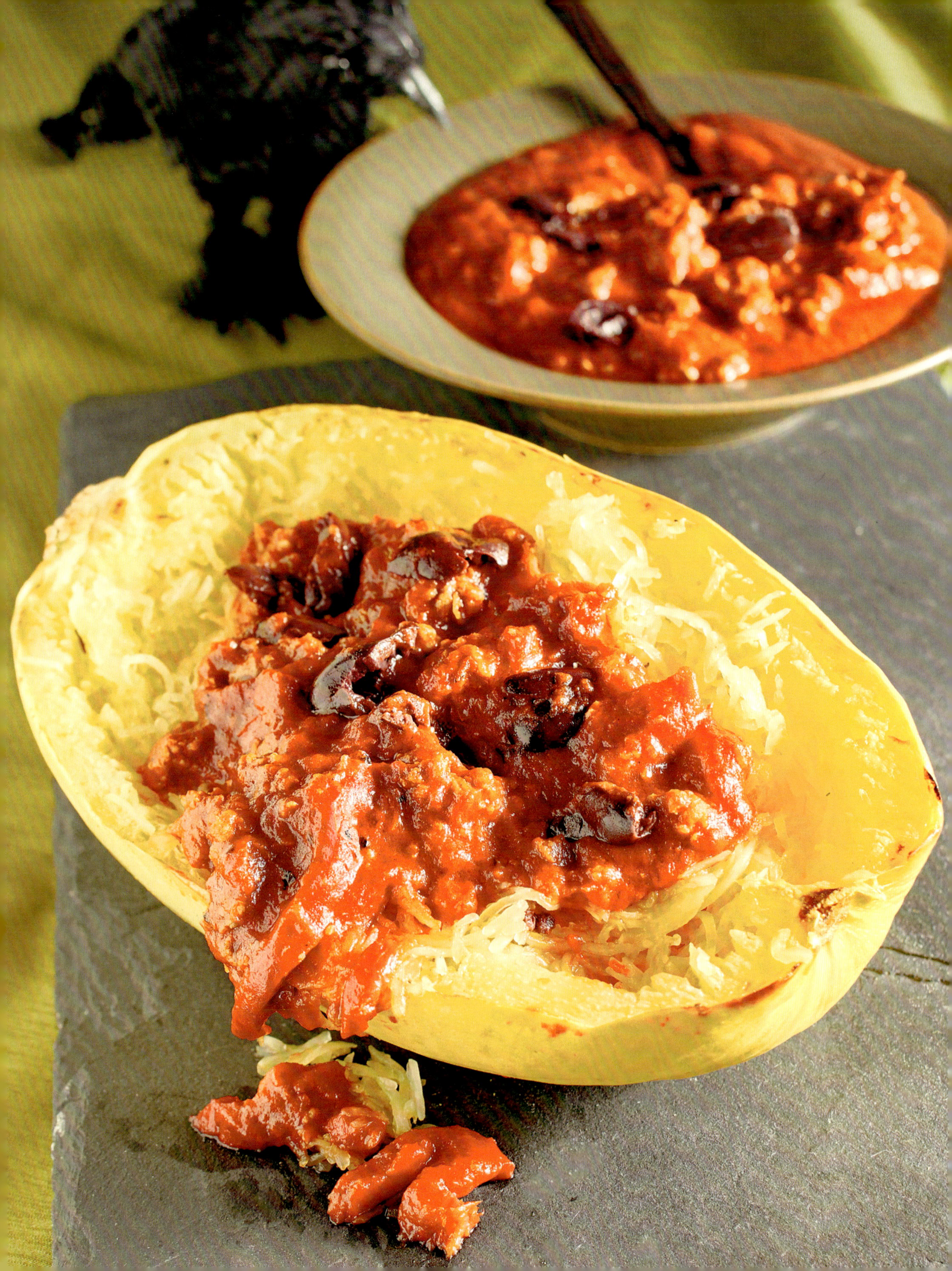

Winifred's Guts for Garters Squash

Double, double, toil and trouble,
Bring your cauldron to a bubble.
Blood-hued sauce with savoury meat
Make squash entrails a witchy treat.
The sisters three would gobble up

This sausage-laden, gourd-filled cup.
A spell, of course, is not required
To make this dish that's so inspired.
Lest the mood turn rather tragic,
Add olives. (They're filled with magic!)

Yield: 4 servings | GF

2 spaghetti squash (about 450 grams total)

2 tablespoons plus 1 teaspoon olive oil

1 teaspoon salt

450 grams Italian sausage meat

4 cloves garlic, crushed

One 450 gram jar roasted red pepper strips

¼ teaspoon red pepper flakes

Freshly ground black pepper

One 170 gram jar tomato paste

One 425 gram jar tomato sauce

2 tablespoons balsamic vinegar

About 12 pitted whole Kalamata olives (optional)

Preheat the oven to 200°C.

Halve each spaghetti squash lengthwise and scrape the seeds out with a spoon. Place the halves on two rimmed baking sheets and brush 1 teaspoon of the olive oil on the inside of all four halves. Sprinkle a bit of salt on all four halves (about ½ teaspoon total), then turn them over so the cut sides are face down. Roast for 25 to 30 minutes, or until fork-tender.

In a large, high-walled sauté pan over a medium-high heat, heat the remaining 2 tablespoons of olive oil until it shimmers. Add the sausage and cook, stirring continuously to break it up, until there is no more pink, 5 to 7 minutes. Add the garlic, stir to coat, and sauté until it is fragrant, 2 to 3 minutes more.

Add the roasted red pepper, the remaining ½ teaspoon of salt and the red pepper flakes. Season with black pepper to taste, stir to coat and continue to cook for 3 to 5 minutes more, stirring occasionally.

Add the tomato paste and tomato sauce. Fill the tomato paste jar with water and stir, scraping up any leftover tomato paste. Add the tomato paste water to the tomato sauce jar, then add the balsamic vinegar. Stir together and add this mixture to the sauce in the pan. Bring to a low boil, stirring occasionally, then turn the heat to low and simmer for 10 to 15 minutes, or until the sauce has thickened.

Smash each olive (if using) with the flat side of a knife and set aside.

To serve, scrape each half of the squash from the outside edges towards the centre, pulling up all the strands. Be careful not to pierce the shells. Spoon the sauce into each shell and scatter the olives between the halves. Place each squash half on a plate or into a shallow pasta bowl.

Main Dishes

Knockout Skillet French Toast

*A*llison doesn't pull any punches when it comes to protecting Dani. When she sees what the witches have in store, the brave young Salemite grabs a frying pan and wallops Mary, knocking the witch out just long enough for Dani to run away. Just like its namesake, this dish is sure to knock the socks off even the pickiest eaters. Custard-coated bread picks up hints of brown sugar, cinnamon and apples as it crisps in a buttery skillet. It's the perfect way to kick off time spent catching up with – or digging up! – old friends.

Yield: 4 servings | GF*, V

110 grams golden brown sugar

Juice of 1 lemon

½ teaspoon ground cinnamon

2 apples

75 grams salted butter

Six 1-cm slices brioche or buttermilk bread

120 ml whole milk

120 ml double cream

3 large eggs

75 grams chopped walnuts or pecans (optional)

Note
This recipe can be easily made gluten-free by using your favourite gluten-free bread.

In a medium bowl, mix together the sugar, lemon juice and cinnamon. Core and slice each apple, adding the slices to the bowl and stirring to coat. Let the apples macerate in the mixture for 5 to 10 minutes.

In a 25-cm cast-iron or ovenproof skillet over a medium-high heat, melt 30 grams of the butter until it foams. Add the apples and all their juices. Simmer the apples until just tender, about 5 minutes. Remove from the heat and use a slotted spoon to remove the apples from the juices and set aside.

Return the skillet to a medium-high heat and simmer the juices until they reduce enough to coat the back of a spoon, 3 to 5 minutes. Transfer to a heatproof container and set aside.

In a large bowl big enough to dunk the slices of bread, whisk together the milk, cream and eggs, then set aside.

Heat 15 grams of the butter in the skillet until it foams. Place two pieces of bread in the skillet and brown for about 1 minute on each side. Repeat with the remaining 30 grams of butter and slices of bread until all six slices have been browned on both sides. Remove the pan from the heat.

Preheat the oven to 180°C.

Dunk each piece of bread into the egg custard and place it in the skillet. Tuck apple slices in between each piece of bread. Stagger the top layer, tucking apples into the nooks. Pour the remaining custard into the pan. Let the bread absorb the custard while the oven preheats. Bake for 25 to 30 minutes, until a knife inserted into the centre comes out clean. Sprinkle the top with the walnuts (if using) in the last 10 minutes of baking.

Serve with the reserved apple syrup.

Main Dishes

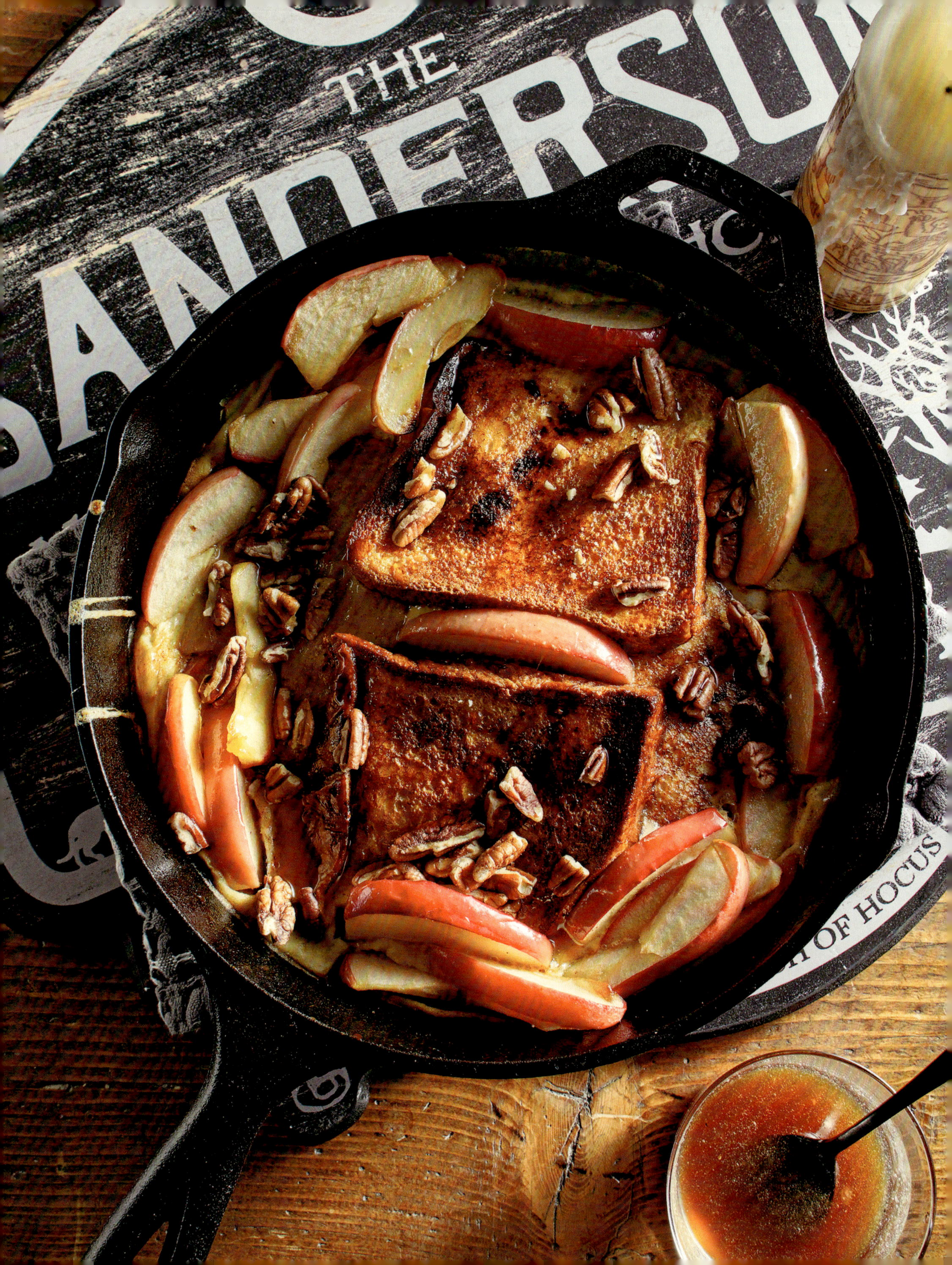
THE
OF HOCUS

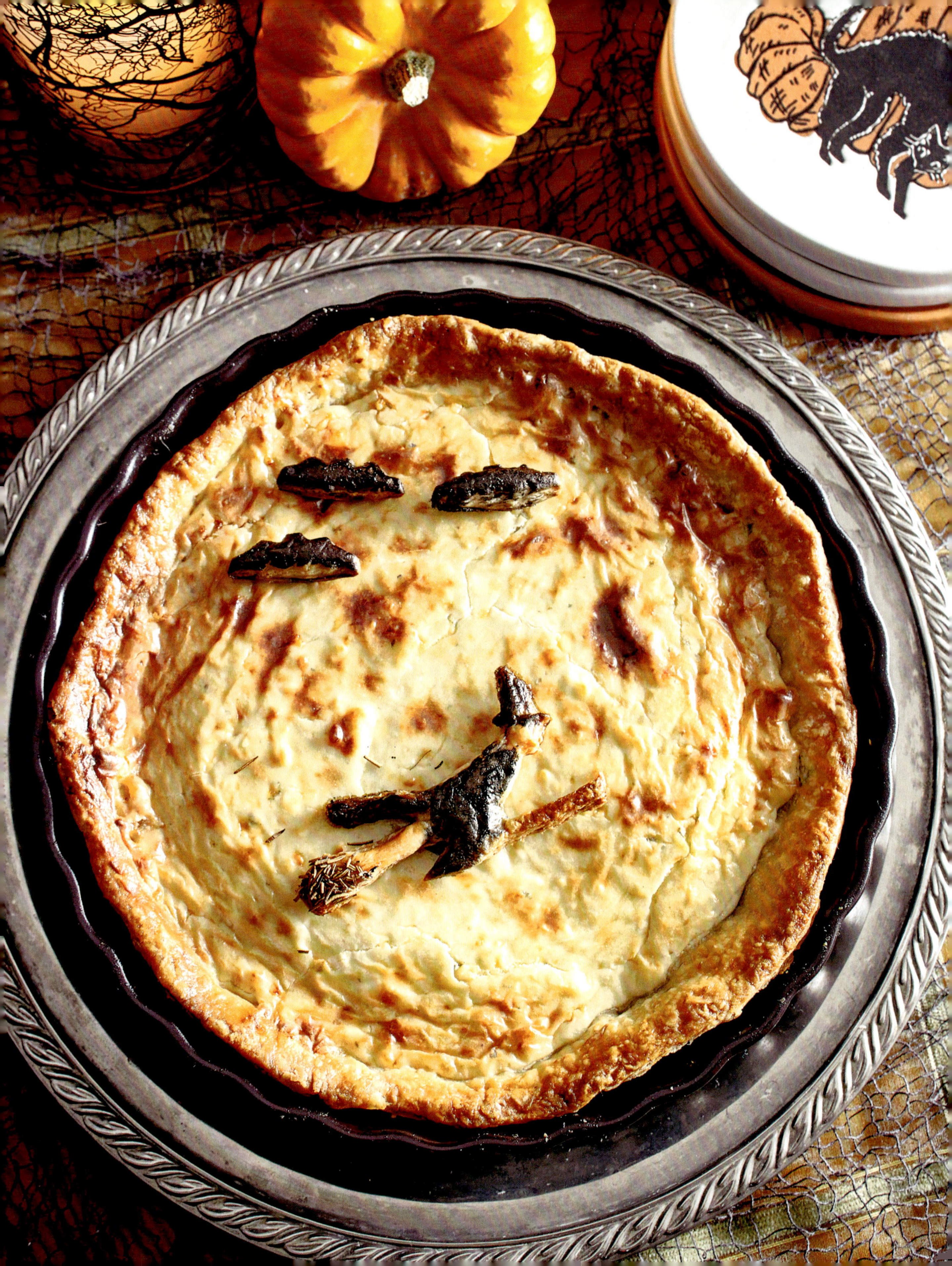

Full Moon Blue Cheese Onion Tart

Magic is at its most powerful at the full moon. It's these nights when witches fly broomsticks – or vacuums – across starlit skies, and the veil between two worlds grows precariously thin. It's *also* the perfect time to bake this tart. This dish pairs blue cheese with caramelised onions, creating a cheesy, savoury delicacy that's revered in this realm … and beyond.

Yield: *6 servings as a main course or up to 10 as a starter* | V

For the Crust

- 150 grams plain flour
- ½ teaspoon salt
- 60 grams unsalted butter, very cold
- 30 grams vegetable fat, very cold
- 4 tablespoons ice water
- 1 egg white
- Dried herbs, such as rosemary, for decorations (optional)
- Black food colouring (optional)

For the Filling

- 1½ tablespoons olive oil
- 15 grams salted butter
- 2 onions, thinly sliced
- ½ teaspoon rock salt
- 3 sprigs fresh thyme
- ½ teaspoon freshly ground black pepper
- 225 grams cream cheese, softened
- 110 grams blue cheese, crumbled
- 60 ml sour cream
- 1 large egg
- 2 tablespoons plain flour

Specialist Tools

- 22-cm tart tin
- Broom- and bat-shaped cookie cutters (optional)
- Pie weights or dried beans

To make the crust: Have a 22-cm tart tin standing by. In a large bowl, combine the flour and salt. Using a pastry cutter or two forks, cut the butter and fat into the flour until the mixture is sandy without any pieces larger than a pea. Slowly add the ice water and continue to gently work the mixture just until the dough comes together. You may need a bit more water.

On a lightly floured surface, roll out the dough into a 30-cm circle. Fit the dough into the tart tin by gently pressing it to the bottom and into the sides. Use a knife to remove the excess dough. Chill the tart tin in the refrigerator for at least 30 minutes. While the dough is chilling, preheat the oven to 200°C.

If creating the decorations, reroll the excess dough to ½-cm thickness and use the cookie cutters to cut out brooms and bats. Place them on a baking sheet and refrigerate until needed.

Remove the tart tin from the refrigerator. Prepare the dough for blind baking by lining it with two pieces of overlapping aluminum foil so that the entire crust is covered. Fill the centre of the tart shell with pie weights. Bake for 10 minutes.

While the crust is baking, prepare an egg wash by combining the egg white with 1 tablespoon water and whisking until frothy.

At the 10-minute mark, remove the tart shell from the oven, carefully lift out the foil and weights, and set aside. Brush the whole tart shell with the egg wash and return to the oven for 5 to 7 minutes more, or until just golden brown. Remove from the oven and set aside.

continued on page 54

Main Dishes

continued from page 53

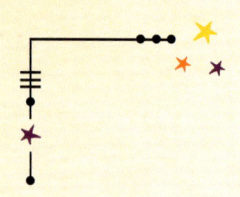

To finish the decorations, brush the broom shapes with egg wash and add some dried herbs (if using) to create the end of the broom. Add a few drops of black food colouring (if using) to the remaining egg wash and brush the bat shapes. Bake for 5 to 7 minutes, or until crisp. Allow to cool completely and store in an airtight container until needed.

To make the filling: Heat the oil and butter in a medium pan over a medium-high heat until the butter foams. Add the onions and toss to coat with oil and butter. Sprinkle the salt evenly across the onions, turn the heat to a medium-low, add the thyme sprigs and cook, stirring frequently, until the onions are soft and fully caramelised, about 20 minutes. Remove the thyme sprigs and discard. Season with the black pepper, then set aside.

Preheat the oven to 180°C.

In a medium bowl using a hand mixer on a medium speed, beat the cream cheese until smooth. Add the blue cheese, sour cream, egg and flour. Beat again on a medium speed until the mixture is thoroughly combined and mostly smooth with some chunks of blue cheese. Set aside.

To assemble, spread the onions in an even layer on the bottom of the crust. With a large spoon, drop large dollops of filling across the onions and smooth out in an even layer. Bake for 20 to 25 minutes, or until the top is golden brown.

Cool for 10 minutes, decorate with the pastry brooms and bats and serve.

Notes

The tart shell and decorations can be made up to a day ahead and stored in an airtight container until needed.

This dish pairs well with a green salad or sliced thin as part of the All Hallows' Eve Feast Grazing Board (page 117).

Main Dishes

Main Dishes
55

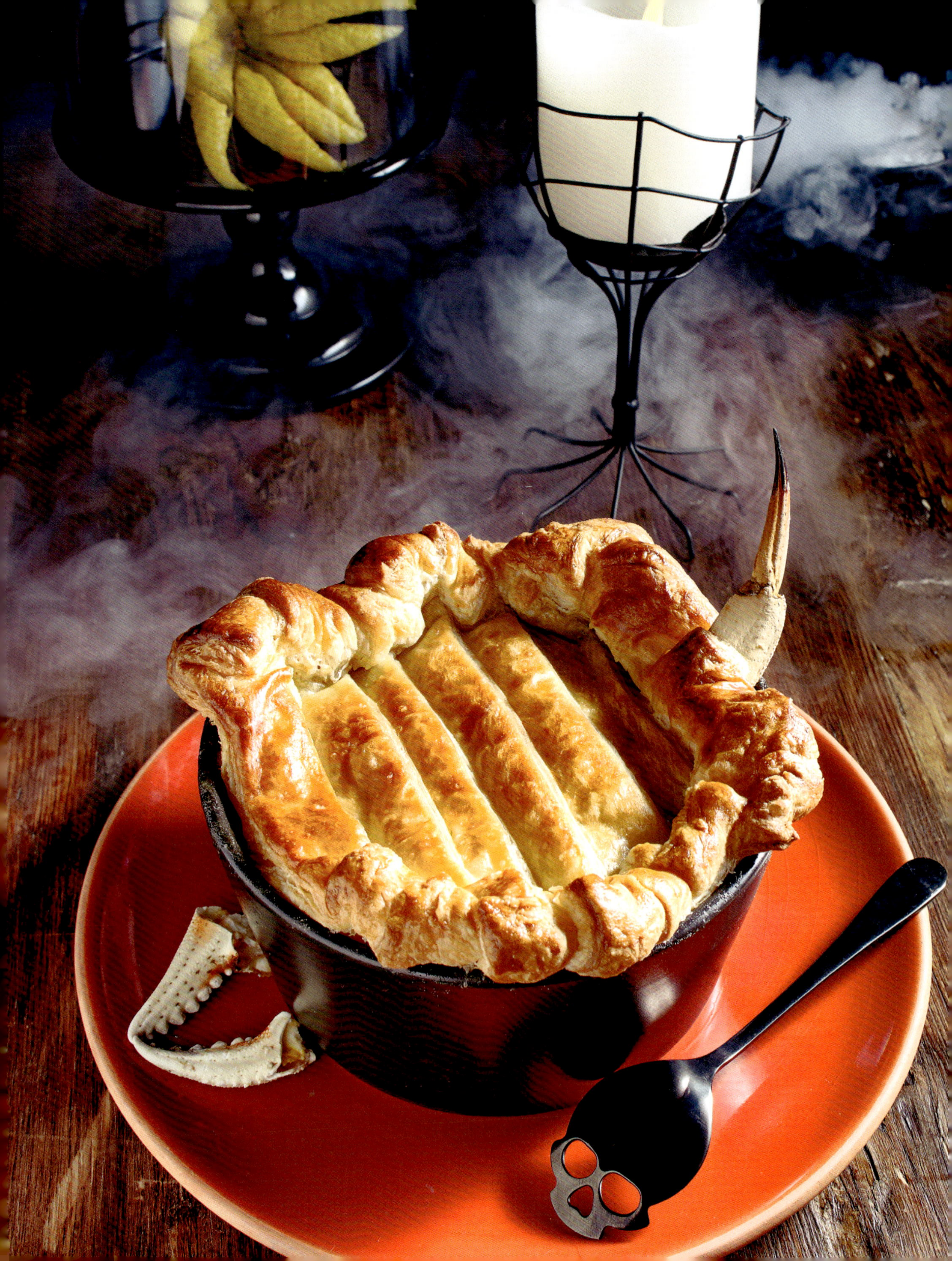

Mummy's Scorpion Pie

Winifred, Mary and Sarah have fond memories of the woman who brought them into the world. Mummy taught them everything she knew – and instilled in them a fondness for her beloved Scorpion Pie. With butter, crabmeat and corn, this dish is best served with a side of nostalgia. It's perfect for sharing at a family gathering, a séance and, of course, your next calming circle.

Yield: *4 servings*

675 grams whole crab (see note)

1 tablespoon olive oil

150 grams thawed frozen sweetcorn

30 grams unsalted butter

1 small onion, diced

3 or 4 stalks celery, preferably from the heart with leaves

2 tablespoons plain flour

1 teaspoon rock salt

450 grams new potatoes, quartered

480 ml vegetable stock

Zest and juice of 1 lemon, separated

2 tablespoons chopped fresh parsley

1 tablespoon chopped fresh dill

1 large egg

400 grams frozen puff pastry, thawed and standing by in the refrigerator

Specialist Tools
Four 450 gram ovenproof bowls

If using whole crab, remove all the crabmeat from its shell, making sure to get the claw meat. Reserve some of the larger shell pieces to add to the stock and save four of the walking (side) legs for garnish. These will be your "scorpion stingers". Refrigerate until needed.

In a large pot or casserole dish over a medium-high heat, place ½ tablespoon of the olive oil and the corn in a single layer. Leave undisturbed for 1 to 2 minutes, then stir and continue to cook, stirring only occasionally, until the corn begins to brown, about 5 minutes.

Transfer the corn to a plate – it's fine to leave a few kernels behind – and set aside. Add the remaining ½ tablespoon of olive oil and the butter and heat until the butter foams. Add the onion, stir to coat and sauté for 1 to 2 minutes. Add the celery and sauté 3 to 5 minutes more, or until the onion and celery soften.

Add the flour and salt, stir again, and cook for 1 to 2 minutes or until the flour smells nutty. Add the potatoes and stir to coat. Add the stock and reserved pieces of crab shell, if using. Bring to a simmer, then turn the heat to low and add the lemon zest. Simmer for 10 minutes, or until the potatoes are just tender. Remove from the heat and remove and discard the crab shell. Stir in the corn, lemon juice, parsley, dill and crabmeat.

Preheat the oven to 220°C.

Meanwhile, in a small bowl, whisk together the egg with 1 tablespoon water to make an egg wash. Split the filling mixture between four 450 gram ovenproof bowls, filling them almost to the top.

continued on page 58

Main Dishes

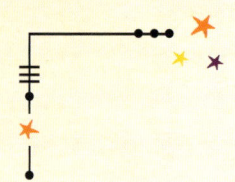

continued from page 57

Cut 2½-cm-wide strips of puff pastry. Using a pastry brush, brush the edges of the bowls with the egg wash, then begin layering the strips across each bowl. The strips should hang over the edge of the bowl by about ½ cm on either side. Trim as necessary. Brush each strip with egg wash before adding the additional strips. Continue until the surfaces of the bowls have been covered in pastry. Fold the edges towards the centre of the bowls and press down gently to stick to the edge. Create the "stinger" by tucking a reserved crab leg, if using, into the pastry at one end of the bowl.

Bake for 15 to 20 minutes, or until the pastry is puffed and golden brown. Allow to cool for 5 minutes before serving. Caution: The filling will be hot!

Note

Crab is normally sold live or cooked, with the latter being the most common at your local supermarket. The fish counter should be able to crack and clean the crab for you, but you may need to ask them to do it. This makes prep at home much easier. If whole crab is not available, purchase 280 grams of crabmeat.

"Who's Going for the Jacuzzi" Lobster

With the Sandersons chasing them down, Max, Allison and Dani hide in a back alley. As they cower beside a lobster tank – and watch in silence while a jovial cook asks an unfortunate crustacean, "Who's going for the Jacuzzi?" – the kids furiously plot to get the witches into hot water. Inspired by their Jacuzzi-bound friend, this meal pairs succulent seasonings with a generous dollop of butter. Rich, savoury and always appetising, this lobster is sure to please even the crabbiest of crowds.

Yield: 2 servings | GF*

90 grams salted butter
3 cloves garlic, peeled
30 grams parsley leaves
Zest of 1 lemon
50 grams grated Parmesan cheese
½ cup fine dried breadcrumbs
Four 100 gram raw lobster tails
120 ml white wine
1 bunch asparagus, snapped
1 tablespoon olive oil
½ teaspoon rock salt

Note
This recipe can be easily made gluten-free by using gluten-free breadcrumbs, gluten-free panko or even crushed almonds.

In a small microwave-safe bowl or small saucepan, melt 60 grams of the butter and set aside to cool.

In the bowl of a food processor, pulse together the garlic and parsley until finely chopped. Add the lemon zest and Parmesan cheese and pulse again until the mixture is sandy. Add the breadcrumbs and pulse just to combine. Transfer the mixture to a medium bowl and stir in the melted butter.

Preheat the oven to 220°C.

Using kitchen scissors, cut the shell on the underside of each lobster tail down the centre, leaving the tail fan intact. Remove any swimmerets as well. Holding each tail, cut facing up, and bend away from you, loosening the meat. Gently pull the tail meat out of the shell, being careful to leave it attached to the tail fan, and bring it back down to rest on the shell beneath. The meat should look like it is riding piggyback on its shell. Repeat with the remaining three tails.

Grease a baking dish with the remaining 30 grams of butter and pour in the white wine.

Place the tails in the baking dish and divide the crumb mixture evenly between them. Press the mixture on to the lobster meat, completely coating it.

Place the asparagus on a rimmed baking sheet, drizzle with the olive oil, and sprinkle the salt over the stalks. Shake the pan to coat.

Bake the lobster tails and the asparagus for 8 minutes. Remove the asparagus, turn the grill to high, and grill for 2 minutes, or until the breadcrumbs are brown.

Serve immediately with the lobster tails plated over a grid of the asparagus and drizzle with the juices from the bottom of the lobster pan.

Main Dishes

Spicy Cauliflower Ears

It's a little-known fact that a witch's curse cannot take hold if its victim never hears it. When the Sanderson sisters begin to sing, Thackery's dad warns the villagers, "Listen to them not!" And again three hundred years later when Winnie, Mary and Sarah burst into a more *robust* song, Dani screams for everyone to cover their ears. These cauliflower ears – covered in a tasty buffalo wing sauce – are a vegetarian twist on a tangy classic. But watch out – *they* might just put a spell on you!

Yield: 4 servings as a main course or up to 8 as a starter | GF*, V, V+

90 grams plain flour

½ teaspoon salt

1 teaspoon garlic powder

1 teaspoon smoked paprika

Freshly ground black pepper

240 ml oat or other plant-based milk

1 cauliflower head, broken into bite-size florets

225 grams panko breadcrumbs

Homemade barbecue sauce (page 83)

Line a rimmed baking sheet with parchment paper and preheat the oven to 190°C.

In a large bowl, combine the flour, salt, garlic powder and paprika. Season with black pepper to taste and stir to combine. Add the oat milk and stir until well combined, noting that some lumps are OK. Add the cauliflower and stir until the florets are well coated in the batter.

Working in batches, place about 75 grams of breadcrumbs in a small bowl and add the florets in small batches. Toss to coat and place the coated florets on the prepared baking sheet. Repeat with the remaining breadcrumbs and florets, keeping them in a single layer on the baking sheet.

Bake for 20 minutes, remove from the oven and drizzle with the barbecue sauce. Use a spatula to turn the florets and coat thoroughly with the sauce. Reserve the remaining sauce for serving. Return the cauliflower to the oven and bake for 15 to 20 minutes more, or until the florets are fork-tender and the glaze is set and starting to brown.

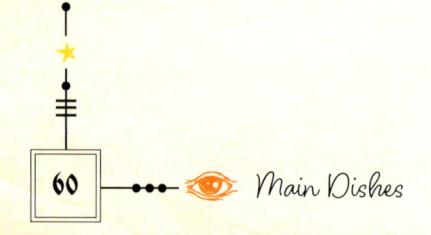

Notes

Serve with extra barbecue sauce and/or your favourite wing dip!

This recipe can be easily made gluten-free by using a gluten-free flour, such as rice or chickpea, and omitting or using gluten-free panko breadcrumbs.

Roasted Red Spice Chicken

Winifred Sanderson has been called many things – but bland is most definitely *not* one of them. This chicken dish conjures her spicy essence, with its combination of heat-inducing herbs and a fiery harissa rub. As the witch herself once said while trapped inside a prison for children, "Hot! Hot!"

Yield: 6 servings | GF

- 3 or 4 sprigs fresh oregano, gently crushed
- 6 cloves garlic, smashed
- 120 ml avocado or olive oil
- 120 ml apple cider vinegar
- 2 tablespoons pomegranate syrup
- 4 teaspoons harissa powder or paste
- 1½ teaspoons rock salt
- ½ teaspoon ground sumac
- 1.35 kilograms boneless skinless chicken thighs

In a container that seals well, combine the oregano, garlic, olive oil, vinegar, syrup, harissa, salt and sumac. Stir well to combine. Add the chicken pieces to the marinade and make sure they are coated well. Marinate in the refrigerator for at least 30 minutes or up to 2 hours.

To cook the chicken, heat a grill to about 190°C. Grill the chicken, turning at least once, for 7 to 10 minutes, or until an instant-read thermometer inserted into the thickest part of the meat registers 75°C.

Alternatively, bake the chicken. Preheat the oven and a rimmed baking sheet to 190°C. Place the chicken in a single layer on the preheated baking sheet and bake for 5 minutes. Flip the thighs and bake for 3 to 5 minutes more, or until an instant-read thermometer inserted into the thickest part of the meat registers 75°C.

Note

If you prefer bone-in, skin-on chicken, this marinade still works well, but allow about 30 more minutes for cooking.

Main Dishes

Maggot-Stuffed Pork Chop

Billy Butcherson may be a "maggoty-mouth peasant" – at least according to Winifred. After all, he *has* been buried for centuries ... and he almost definitely was caught sporting with the wrong Sanderson sister. But whatever else Billy may be, he would most certainly be a lover of this pork chop – or, he *would* have been ... before his mouth was sewn shut by that woefully wounded Winifred!

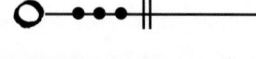

Yield: 4 servings

For the Spaetzle Maggots

- 120 grams plain flour
- 1 teaspoon salt, plus more for boiling
- ¼ teaspoon white pepper
- ½ teaspoon ground nutmeg
- 60 ml single cream
- 2 large eggs
- 60 grams unsalted butter, melted

For the Pork Chops

- 4 thick-cut boneless pork chops (about 900 grams)
- 2 teaspoons salt
- 2 teaspoons vegetable oil
- 60 grams unsalted butter

For the Apples and Assembly

- 60 ml apple cider vinegar
- 1 large apple, cored and chopped into 2½ cm pieces
- ½ teaspoon dried thyme
- 60 grams fresh parsley leaves, roughly chopped (optional)

Specialist Tools

Spaetzle maker or flat cheese grater

To make the maggots: In a medium bowl, mix together the flour, salt, white pepper and nutmeg. In a separate small bowl, whisk together the cream and eggs. Make a well in the flour mixture, add the egg mixture and stir to combine.

Allow the batter to rest while bringing a large pan of salted water to the boil and placing the melted butter in a large bowl.

When the water is boiling, turn the heat to medium and maintain a low boil. Use a spaetzle maker or flat cheese grater to press the batter through, a small portion at a time, into the boiling water. Cook for 2 to 3 minutes, or until all the dumplings are floating. Remove from the water with a spider or large sieve, transfer to the melted butter and stir to combine.

Continue this process until all the batter has been used. Make sure the spaetzle is well coated in butter and set aside.

To make the pork chops: Preheat the oven to 180°C.

Cut a deep slit about 7½ cm long into the thick side of each pork chop, being careful not to pierce through to the other side. Season the inside and outside with the salt. In a large ovenproof skillet over a medium-high heat, combine the vegetable oil and butter and heat until the butter foams. Add the pork chops and brown on each side without disturbing for 3 to 4 minutes. Transfer the browned pork chops to an ovenproof casserole dish. Cover with aluminum foil and cook for 10 to 15 minutes, or until an instant-read thermometer inserted into the thickest part of the meat registers 65°C. Allow to rest 3 to 5 minutes.

continued on page 64

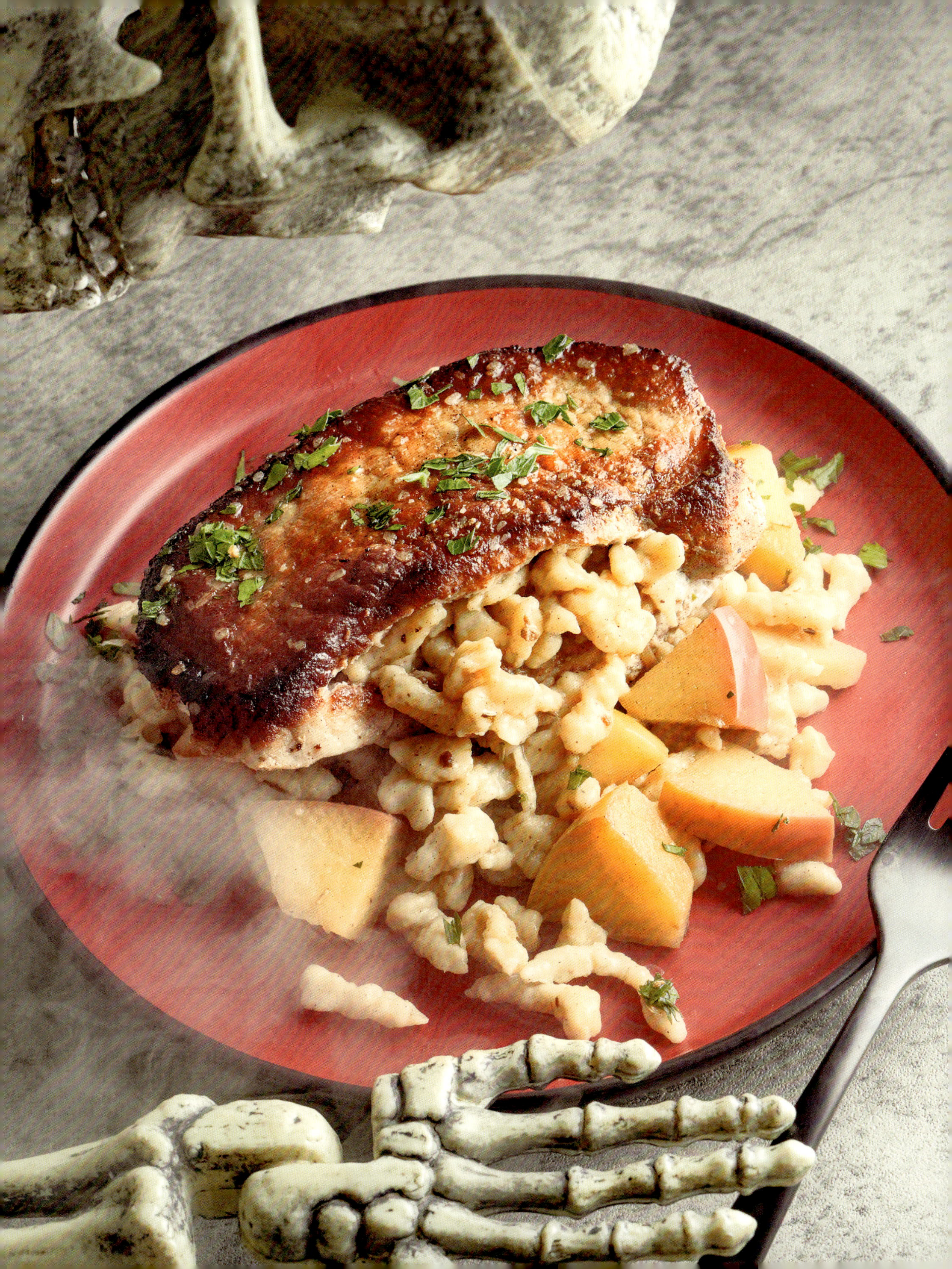

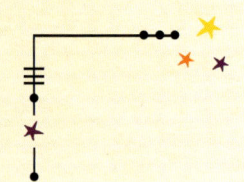

continued from page 62

To make the apples and assemble: While the pork finishes cooking in the oven, deglaze the skillet over a medium-high heat with the apple cider vinegar, stirring for 2 to 3 minutes. Add the apples and thyme and cook the apples until most of the liquid has been absorbed and the apples are tender, about 7 minutes.

Add the spaetzle, stir to make sure everything is well coated, and sauté for 3 to 5 minutes more, continuing to stir so the spaetzle does not stick.

Stuff each pork chop with the spaetzle mixture by using tongs to stand the pork chop on the intact edge. Plate each stuffed chop on top of more of the spaetzle mixture. Scatter the parsley (if using) over each plate.

Green Mummy Roll-Ups

Halloween conjures a bounty of images – jack-o'-lanterns, black flame candles and, of course, *mummies*. These courgette-based rolls might seem a bit greener than their white-wrapped bipedal brethren, but their mozzarella filling is packed with frightfully fabulous flavours. Bone-*appétit!*

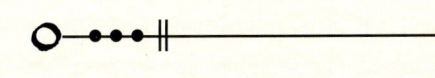

Yield: 4 to 6 servings | GF, V

For the Pesto

- 3 large cloves garlic, smashed
- 75 grams toasted walnuts (see note)
- 60 grams fresh basil leaves
- 60 grams fresh parsley leaves
- 50 grams grated Parmesan cheese
- 60 ml olive oil
- 60 ml double cream
- ½ teaspoon salt
- Freshly ground black pepper
- Juice of ½ lemon

For the Roll-Ups

- 450 grams low-moisture ricotta cheese
- ½ teaspoon salt
- Fresh ground black pepper
- 1 large egg
- 450 grams grated mozzarella cheese
- 50 grams grated Parmesan cheese
- 2 large courgettes
- 4 to 6 Kalamata olives, sliced (optional)

To make the pesto: In the bowl of a food processor, pulse the garlic a few times until roughly chopped. Add the walnuts, pulse again, then add the basil and parsley leaves. Run the food processor until everything is finely chopped, about 30 seconds.

Add the Parmesan cheese, then run the food processor again until everything comes together as a paste, about 30 seconds.

With the machine running, add the olive oil in a slow stream until it is completely incorporated. Stop the machine and scrape down the sides. With the machine running, add the double cream slowly until it is completely incorporated. Add the salt and season with black pepper to taste. Pulse again to combine. Add the lemon juice, run the food processor another 30 seconds and then set the pesto aside.

To make the roll-ups: Preheat the oven to 200°C. In a large bowl, mix together the ricotta cheese, salt, black pepper to taste, egg, 225 grams of the mozzarella cheese and the Parmesan cheese. Set aside.

Using a wide vegetable peeler, peel off most of the dark green skin of each courgette and discard. Continue to peel each courgette in wide ribbons until you begin to reach the seeds. Set all the ribbons aside. Quarter the core of each courgette and dice into ½-cm pieces.

In a 22 by 33 cm casserole dish, spread half of the pesto mixture on the bottom of the dish.

continued on page 67

Note

To toast the walnuts, heat a small stainless-steel or cast-iron pan on the stove over a medium-high heat for about 1 minute. Add the nuts, stir and then remove the pan from the heat. Continue to stir the nuts until fragrant, about 2 minutes.

Main Dishes

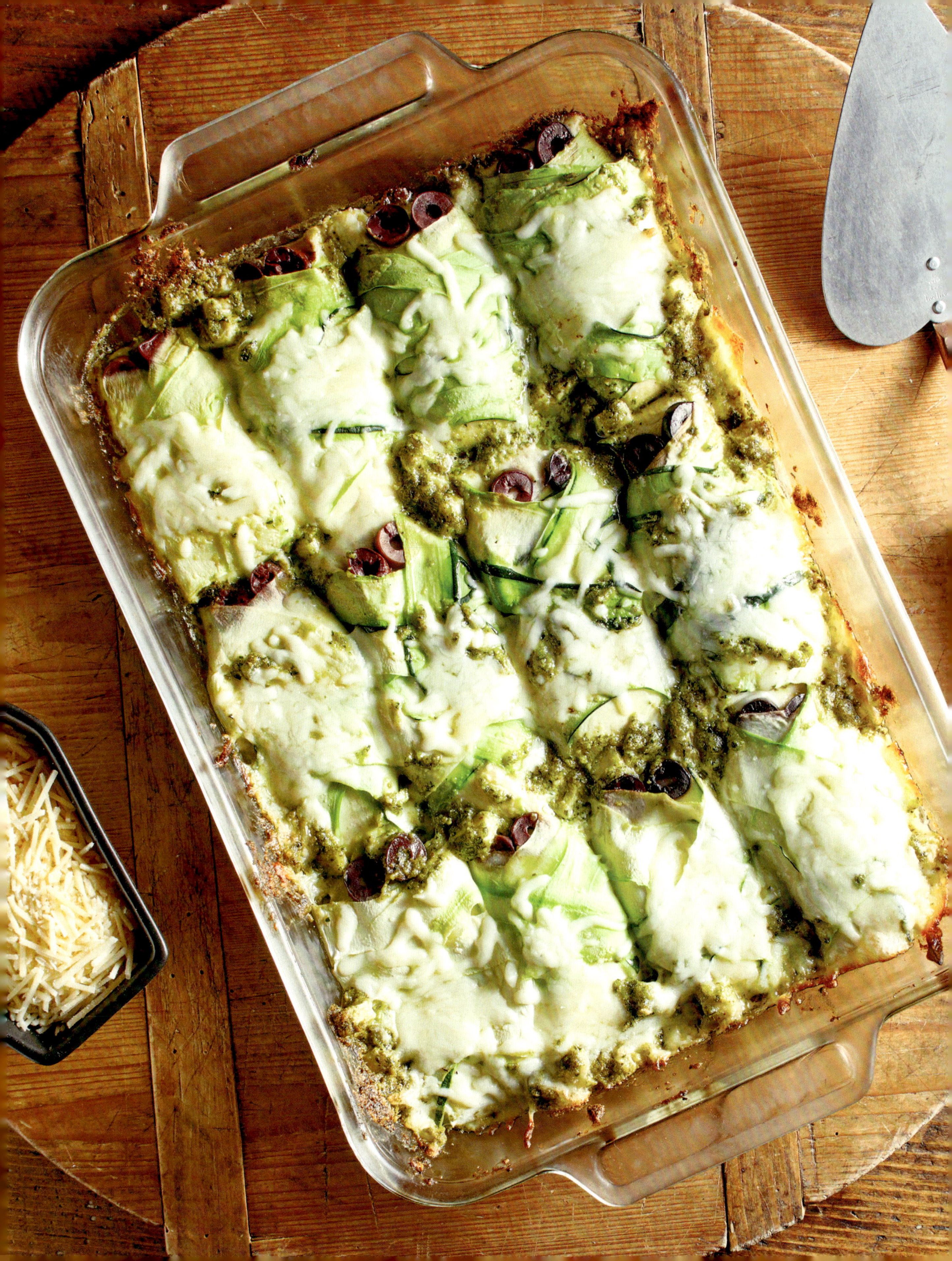

continued from page 65

On a work surface, layer four to six courgette ribbons, slightly overlapping, to create a "sheet" of courgette. Lay another two strips vertically down the centre of the sheet so their ends stick out past the top and bottom of the sheet. Place about 4 tablespoons of the ricotta mixture in the centre of the sheet and form it into a log shape down the centre.

Pull the top and bottom overhanging pieces towards the centre to help close the ends. Fold each side ribbon of courgette towards the centre, overlapping and alternating, to create a mummied effect. Once the filling is all wrapped up, make eyes by tucking two olive slices (if using) into the top of the mummy. Use a spatula to transfer the completed mummy to the casserole dish. Repeat with the remaining courgette ribbons until filling is all used. Leave about 2½ cm in between each mummy.

Mix the cubed courgette with the remaining pesto and scatter it in between and around each mummy. Bake for 15 to 20 minutes, until bubbling and beginning to brown.

Remove from the oven and sprinkle the remaining 225 grams of mozzarella cheese on each mummy. Return to the oven. Bake for 15 minutes more, or until the mozzarella is bubbly and brown.

Main Dishes

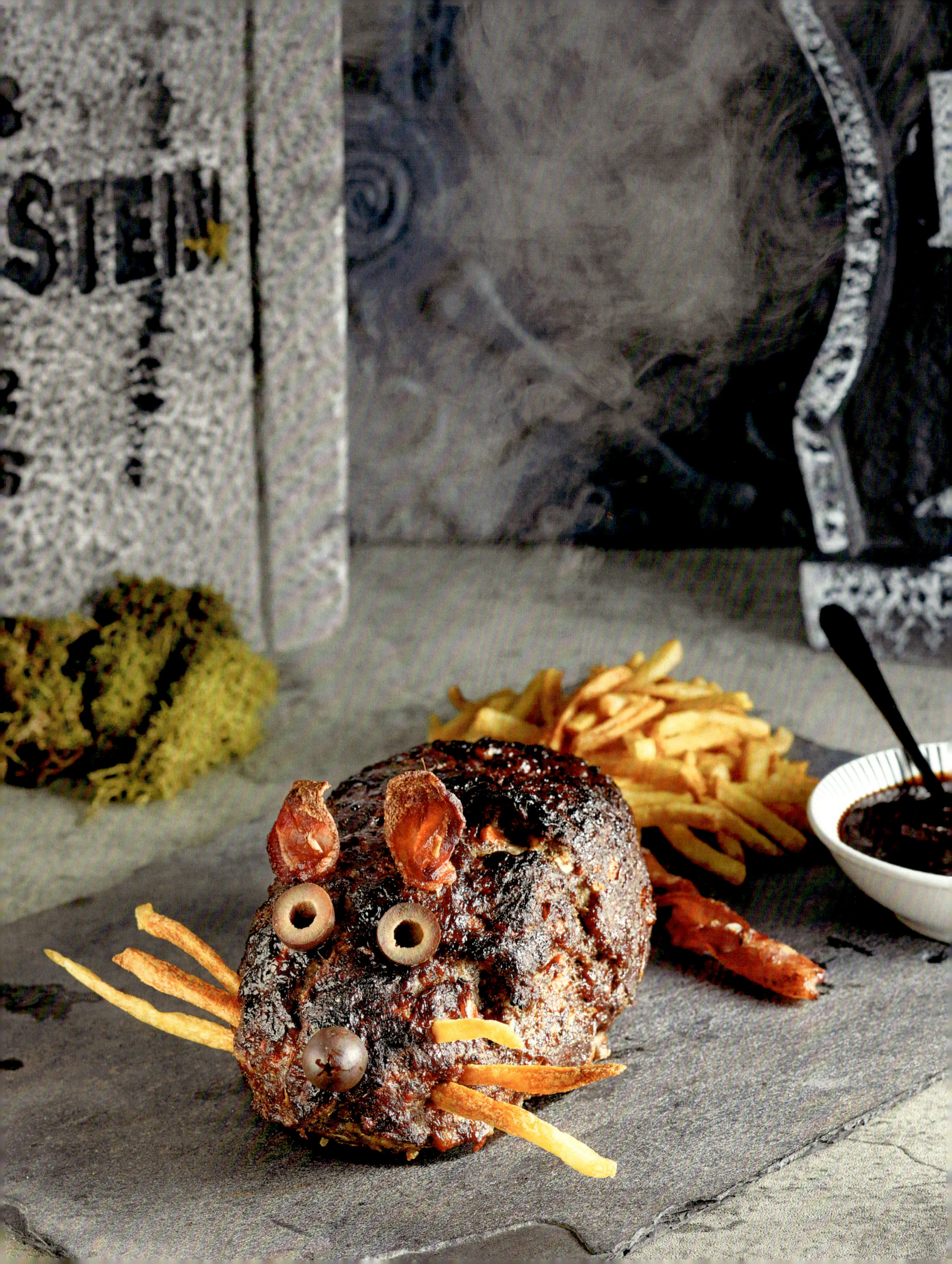
STEIN

Rat Loaf

Once the Sandersons make their triumphant return to Salem, Sarah immediately sets out to find one of her most treasured items. When she locates her lucky rat tail – *right where she left it!* – she clutches it gleefully in her hands. In honour of Sarah's happy reunion, this loaf offers up a *highly* palatable main course. Don't worry – it isn't made from the repugnant rodents that scurry through the Salem crypt. Instead, this dish gets its flavour from the more commonly used minced beef, with olives for eyes, clever fry-based whiskers and a bacon tail and ears. Salty, savoury and with just a hint of horror, this dish offers an unconventional twist on a classic family dinner.

Yield: 6 to 8 servings | **GF***

- 900 grams minced beef
- 75 grams diced carrots
- ½ cup diced onion
- 1 teaspoon salt
- ¼ teaspoon red pepper flakes
- Freshly ground black pepper
- 1 large egg
- 75 grams Italian breadcrumbs
- 120 grams ketchup
- 70 grams pomegranate syrup
- 2 tablespoons Worcestershire sauce
- 2 rashers bacon
- 6 shoestring fries, cooked
- 3 black olives

Notes

This recipe can be easily made gluten-free by using gluten-free breadcrumbs or panko.

This dish pairs well with shoestring fries and Massachusetts Baked Beans (page 22).

In a large bowl, combine the beef, carrots, onion, salt and red pepper flakes. Season with black pepper to taste. Mix gently to combine. Add the egg and breadcrumbs and continue to mix until combined.

In a small bowl, whisk together the ketchup, pomegranate syrup and Worcestershire sauce and set aside.

Preheat the oven to 190°C.

In a large baking dish, shape the beef mixture into a rat shape, giving it a long body, rounded bottom and pointy nose. Glaze the entire rat loaf with the ketchup mixture. Transfer any extra glaze to a small saucepan and set aside to heat for serving.

Bake the loaf for 30 minutes and remove from the oven. Add the bacon details by twisting one piece of bacon into a rope and placing it at the end of the rat for a tail. Cut two rounded pieces of bacon from the second strip and use toothpicks to attach them to the head for ears. Roughly chop any remaining bacon and add to the bottom of the pan. Bake for 15 to 25 minutes more, or until an instant-read thermometer inserted into the centre of the loaf registers 70°C.

Allow the loaf to rest for 5 minutes, then transfer to a serving platter or chopping board. Transfer the tail and reposition. Use a skewer to poke three holes on each side of the "face" and place the fries as whiskers. Add the black olive eyes and nose. Slice and serve.

Main Dishes

Spicy Nightshade Stir-Fry

All Hallows' Eve – that trick-filled night
When ghouls descend to give a fright.
And costumed children fill the streets
To reap their share of tricks – or treats!
Before the fun gets under way,

One must fill up – so one can play!
This nightshade stir-fry's sure to please,
With garlic, ginger and veggies.
So, fill those plates up good and high.
Eat up! Because tonight, we fly!

Yield: 4 servings | GF*, V, V+*

For the Sauce

1 tablespoon grated fresh ginger

4 cloves garlic, crushed

60 ml soy sauce

1 teaspoon sesame oil

1 teaspoon chilli-garlic sauce

1 teaspoon cornflour

For the Stir-Fry

3 tablespoons sunflower oil (or other high-smoke-point oil)

1 onion, thinly sliced

2 orange peppers, cut into thin strips

12 small cremini mushrooms, halved (see note)

1 Chinese aubergine, halved lengthwise, then sliced into half moons

¼ teaspoon rock salt

Cooked rice or noodles for serving

4 spring onions, white and light green parts only, sliced (optional)

75 grams roasted salted cashews, roughly chopped (optional)

To make the sauce: In a small bowl, combine the ginger, garlic, soy sauce, sesame oil and chilli-garlic sauce. Set aside. In another small bowl, make a slurry by whisking together the cornflour and 2 tablespoons water. Set aside.

To make the stir-fry: In a large wok or high-sided sauté pan over a medium-high heat, heat half of the sunflower oil until it shimmers. Add the onion and cook, stirring continuously, until it is translucent and begins to brown, 3 to 4 minutes. Add the peppers, stir to combine and cook 3 to 4 minutes more, until the peppers soften slightly and brown in some spots.

Using tongs, transfer the peppers and onions to a plate. Add the remaining half of the oil and heat until it shimmers. Add the mushrooms and aubergine, stirring to combine. Cook for 4 to 5 minutes, until browning and softened. Add the peppers and onions back to the pan, add the sauce and stir to combine. Cook for 1 to 2 minutes, then add the cornflour slurry. Stir to combine and cook for 1 to 2 minutes more, until the sauce thickens.

Serve over rice or noodles with the spring onions and cashews as a garnish (if using).

Notes

Want to turn your mushrooms into ghouls? Leave them whole and use a straw to poke out two holes for the eyes. Use a paring knife to carve a line to create the mouth. Sauté them whole with the aubergine.

This recipe can be made gluten-free and vegan by swapping out the soy sauce for a gluten-free vegan version and serving with rice.

Main Dishes

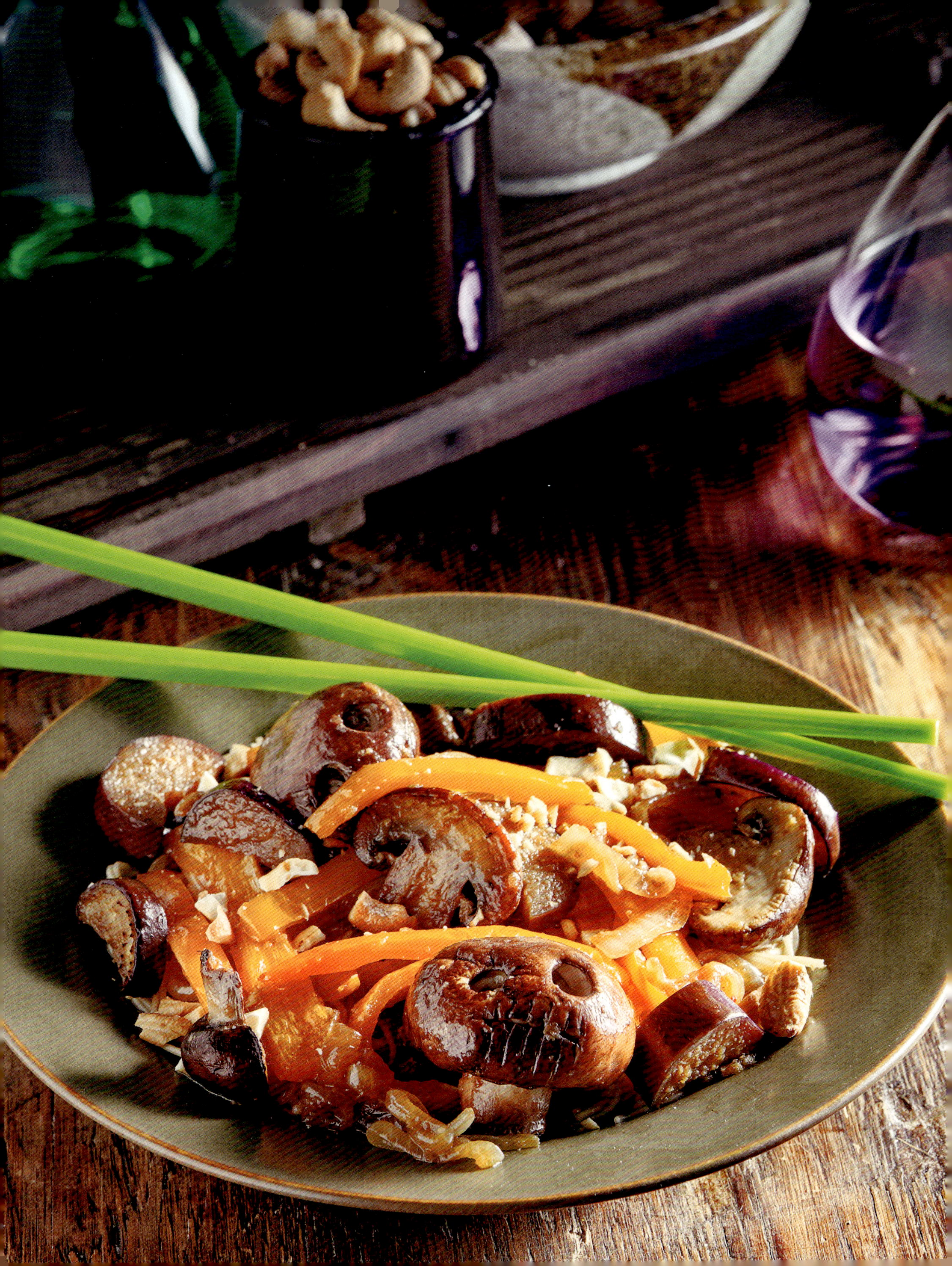

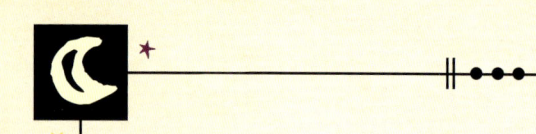

Pumpkin Risotto

Pumpkins are the seminal symbol of autumn. And they're packed with antioxidants, minerals and perhaps even a sprinkle of magic. Maybe that's why they're found in just about *every* kitchen in Salem – including Master's! Winnie, Mary and Sarah aren't at all surprised to find Master's countertop covered with gourdy goodness. Inspired by his *very* sensible tastes, this risotto serves up a vitamin-rich dish that's guaranteed to make any aspiring spell-caster feel right at home. After all, nothing says autumn more than pumpkin-flavoured *everything* – a fact that makes this the perfect dish to serve at All Hallows' Eve … or on any other night of frolic!

Yield: 6 servings | GF, V, V+*

For the Topping

60 grams raw pumpkin seeds or pepitas

1 teaspoon maple syrup

¼ teaspoon rock salt

¼ teaspoon smoked paprika

For the Risotto

900 grams pumpkin or butternut squash

2 tablespoons olive oil

1 teaspoon rock salt

2 litres vegetable stock

90 grams unsalted butter

¼ teaspoon smoked paprika

1 shallot, thinly sliced

600 grams arborio rice

120 ml dry white wine

50 grams grated Parmesan cheese, plus more for serving

To make the topping: Heat a medium skillet over a high heat. Once the pan is hot, add the pumpkin seeds and stir continuously for 1 minute. Lower the heat to medium and add the maple syrup, salt and paprika. Continue cooking and stirring until all the liquid is absorbed and the pumpkin seeds are coated. Remove from the heat and transfer to a bowl. Set aside.

To make the risotto: Preheat the oven to 200°C.

Peel the pumpkin or squash with a vegetable peeler, then halve, scrape out the seeds and cut into 5-cm chunks. Toss the pumpkin chunks with 1 tablespoon of the olive oil and ½ teaspoon of the salt. Roast for 20 to 25 minutes, or until fork-tender and starting to caramelise. Remove from the oven and set aside.

In a large saucepan, bring the vegetable stock to a simmer, then turn off the heat and cover to keep warm.

In a large, high-walled sauté pan, heat the remaining 1 tablespoon of olive oil and the butter. When the butter begins to foam, add the shallot. Stir until the shallot starts to become translucent, then add the rice. Continue to stir until the edges of the rice become translucent.

Add the wine and stir until the liquid is absorbed but the pan is not dry, about 2 minutes. Add a ladle (about 240 ml) of warm stock and the remaining ½ teaspoon of salt. Continue to stir until the stock is absorbed but the pan is not dry, about 4 minutes. Add three more ladles of stock in the same manner, using about half of the stock.

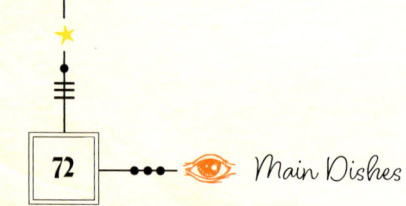

Main Dishes

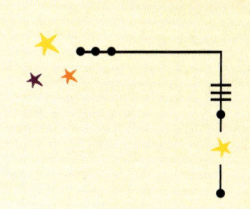

Smash half of the pumpkin pieces with the back of a fork and stir them into the risotto mixture. Add two ladles of stock, stirring and letting it absorb after each addition.

Taste the rice for desired texture. If the rice has reached the desired tenderness, add the cheese, remaining pumpkin and one more ladle of stock, stirring to combine.

If more tenderness is desired, add a ladle of stock, stirring and letting it absorb, and then proceed with cheese, pumpkin and a final ladle of stock.

Sprinkle the pumpkin seeds on each serving, then serve.

> **Note**
>
> This recipe can be easily made vegan by swapping the butter for coconut oil and omitting the cheese or using a plant-based substitute.

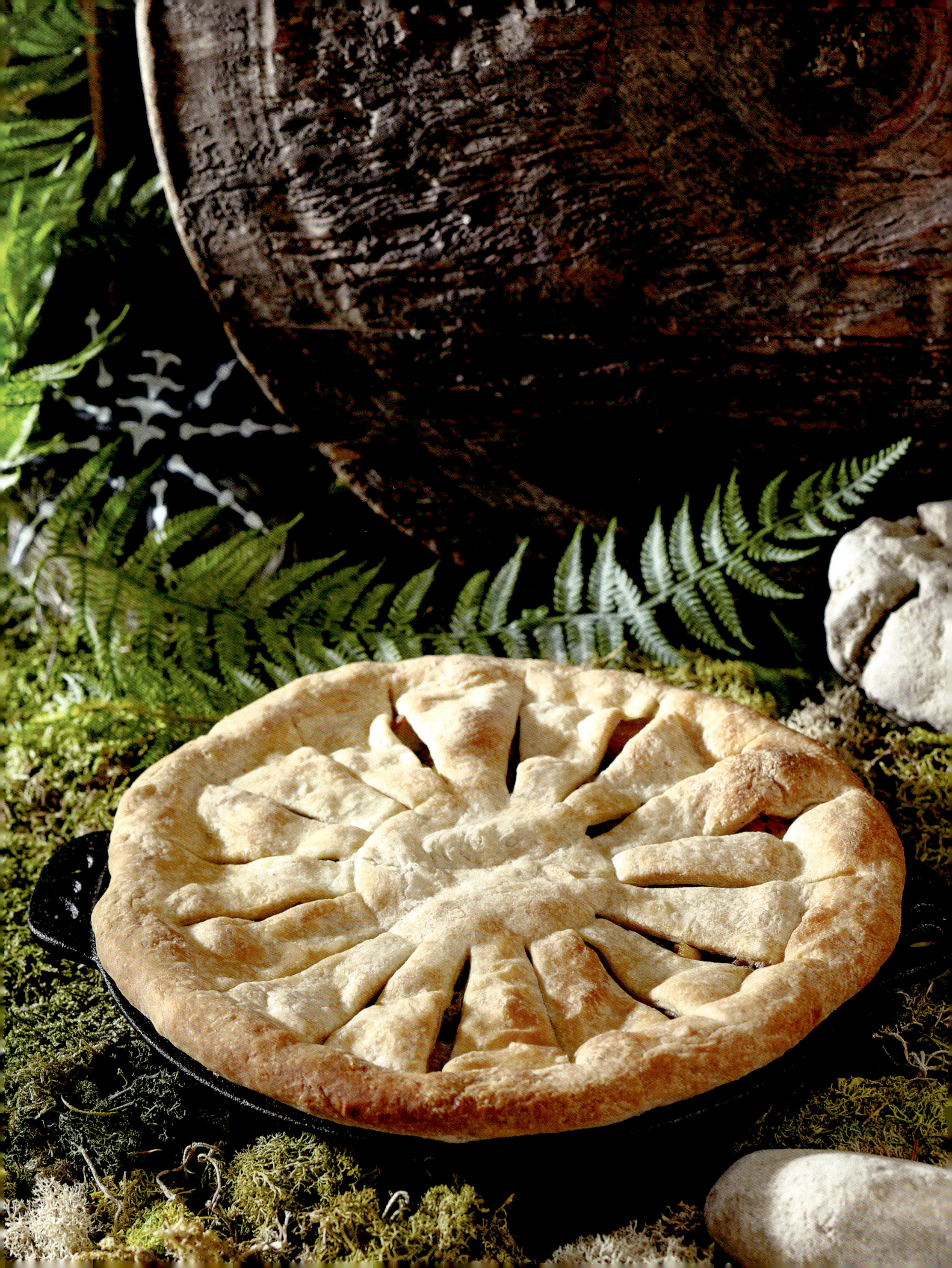

Waterwheel Pot Pie

The waterwheel at the Sanderson homestead served as a pillar of the original Salem community. And while it turned for many years, its gears eventually slowed … as did the caretakers who so lovingly maintained it. With this pot pie, Salem's relic need not be forgotten. Simply line a dish with pastry, fill it with vegetables and delight in this time-honoured piece of Salem's history.

Yield: 6 servings | V

For the Crust

- 300 grams plain flour
- 1 teaspoon salt
- 120 grams unsalted butter, very cold
- 50 grams vegetable fat, very cold
- 80 ml ice water

For the Filling

- 2 tablespoons vegetable oil
- 60 grams salted butter
- 2 leeks, well washed and trimmed, sliced
- 4 to 6 stalks celery, preferably from the heart with leaves, sliced
- 1 teaspoon salt
- ½ teaspoon ground sumac
- ½ teaspoon dried thyme
- ¼ teaspoon white pepper
- 2 tablespoons plain flour
- 480 ml vegetable stock
- 4 large carrots, sliced on an angle into ½-cm pieces
- 450 grams small red potatoes, cut into 1-cm pieces
- 150 grams frozen peas
- 150 grams frozen sweetcorn

To make the crust: Have a deep 25-cm pie dish standing by. Line a baking sheet with parchment paper or a silicone baking mat.

In a large bowl, mix together the flour and salt. Using a pastry cutter or two forks, cut in the butter and shortening until the mixture is sandy and there are no pieces larger than a pea. Slowly add the ice water, a little at a time, gently working the mixture until the dough just comes together. You may need a bit more or less water.

Halve the dough and, on a lightly floured surface, roll out one half until it's large enough to cover the pie dish, about 40 cm in diameter. Fit the dough into the pie dish, gently pressing it into the bottom and sides. Trim the edge until it only overhangs by about ½ cm. Fold it under to create a finished edge and gently crimp. Refrigerate until needed.

Roll the second half of dough out on to the prepared baking sheet and, using a plate that is slightly bigger than the top of your pie dish, cut a perfect circle. Find the centre and create the centre of the waterwheel by gently pressing a glass into the dough, creating a deep indent. Use a ruler and a pastry cutter or knife to cut the spokes, creating vents for the pie. Refrigerate the top crust until needed.

To make the filling: Preheat the oven to 220°C.

In a large, deep sauté pan over a medium-high heat, heat the oil and butter until the butter foams. Add the leeks and celery and sauté until soft and beginning to brown, 4 to 5 minutes. Stir in the salt, sumac, thyme and white pepper. Stir to combine. Sprinkle in the flour and cook, continuing to stir, for 2 minutes, or until the flour smells nutty.

continued on page 76

Main Dishes

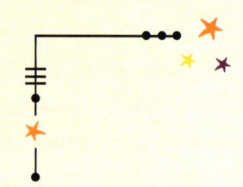

continued from page 75

Slowly add the stock and stir to incorporate, using the stock to deglaze the pan.

Add the carrots and potatoes. Simmer for 10 to 15 minutes, or until the potatoes are just tender and the stock has thickened. Remove from the heat and add the frozen peas and corn. Stir to combine.

To assemble, remove the pie dish and the top crust from the refrigerator. Fill the pie dish with the vegetable mixture and shake gently to settle. Use a second baking sheet to flip the top crust, then peel away the parchment paper and invert the crust, right-side up, on to the pie dish. Gently press the edges together. Bake for 35 to 40 minutes, or until the crust is golden brown and crisp. Allow to cool for 10 minutes, slice and serve.

Sanderson Sisters Barbecue Fillet

The cat most definitely does *not* have Thackery's tongue when he calls Winifred Sanderson a hag. Mary suggests the boy be barbecued and filleted as punishment. It sounds extreme, but one mustn't judge her *too* harshly. No doubt scheming to suck the lives out of Salem's children has left poor Mary – and her sisters – absolutely *famished*. But the proper ingredients can bring an enterprising witch right up to speed. This savoury grilled fillet practically melts in the mouth. With red and black pepper, lime juice and a tangy chimichurri, this dish is sure to fuel a trick-or-treater – or would-be witch – all the way through Halloween night!

Yield: 4 servings | GF

For the Brisket

120 ml red wine vinegar

1 tablespoon rock salt

Juice of 1 lime

6 cloves garlic, crushed

1 shallot, chopped

½ teaspoon dried oregano

¼ teaspoon red pepper flakes

Freshly ground black pepper

Stems from 1 bunch fresh coriander (leaves reserved for chimichurri)

Stems from 1 bunch fresh parsley (leaves reserved for chimichurri)

1.35 kilograms brisket, trimmed of excess fat but otherwise left whole

For the Chimichurri

2 cloves garlic, peeled

1 shallot, cut into chunks

60 grams fresh parsley leaves

60 grams fresh coriander leaves

60 ml red wine vinegar

Juice of 1 lime

¾ teaspoon rock salt

Pinch red pepper flakes

120 ml olive oil

Freshly ground black pepper

To make the brisket: In a well-sealing container large enough to hold the piece of meat, combine the vinegar, 120 ml water, salt, lime juice, garlic, shallot, oregano and red pepper flakes. Season with black pepper to taste. Stir to combine.

Roughly chop the coriander and parsley stems, then add them to the marinade, stirring to combine. Add the brisket and turn to coat. Marinate in the refrigerator for at least 4 hours or up to 8 hours.

To barbecue the brisket, let the meat come to room temperature before grilling. Remove the meat from the marinade and discard the marinade.

Heat a grill to medium-high, around 200°C. Sear the meat on all sides, until well browned, about 4 minutes, then move the meat away from a direct flame. Cook for 30 to 45 minutes, turning every 10 minutes and checking the internal temperature. When an instant-read thermometer inserted into the thickest part of the meat registers 60°C remove from the grill, tent it with foil, and let it rest for at least 10 minutes before carving. You can also cook this recipe using your preferred grilling or roasting method.

To make the chimichurri: In the bowl of a food processor fitted with a blade attachment, or a blender, chop the garlic and shallot by pulsing until a fine consistency is reached. Add the parsley leaves and pulse again until most of the leaves are chopped. Add the coriander leaves and pulse again until everything is chopped.

Add the vinegar, lime juice, salt and red pepper flakes, then pulse again several times to combine. With the motor running, slowly add the olive oil until it is all incorporated. Season with black pepper to taste. Transfer to an airtight container and refrigerate until about 30 minutes before serving.

Allow to come to room temperature, then serve with the brisket.

Main Dishes

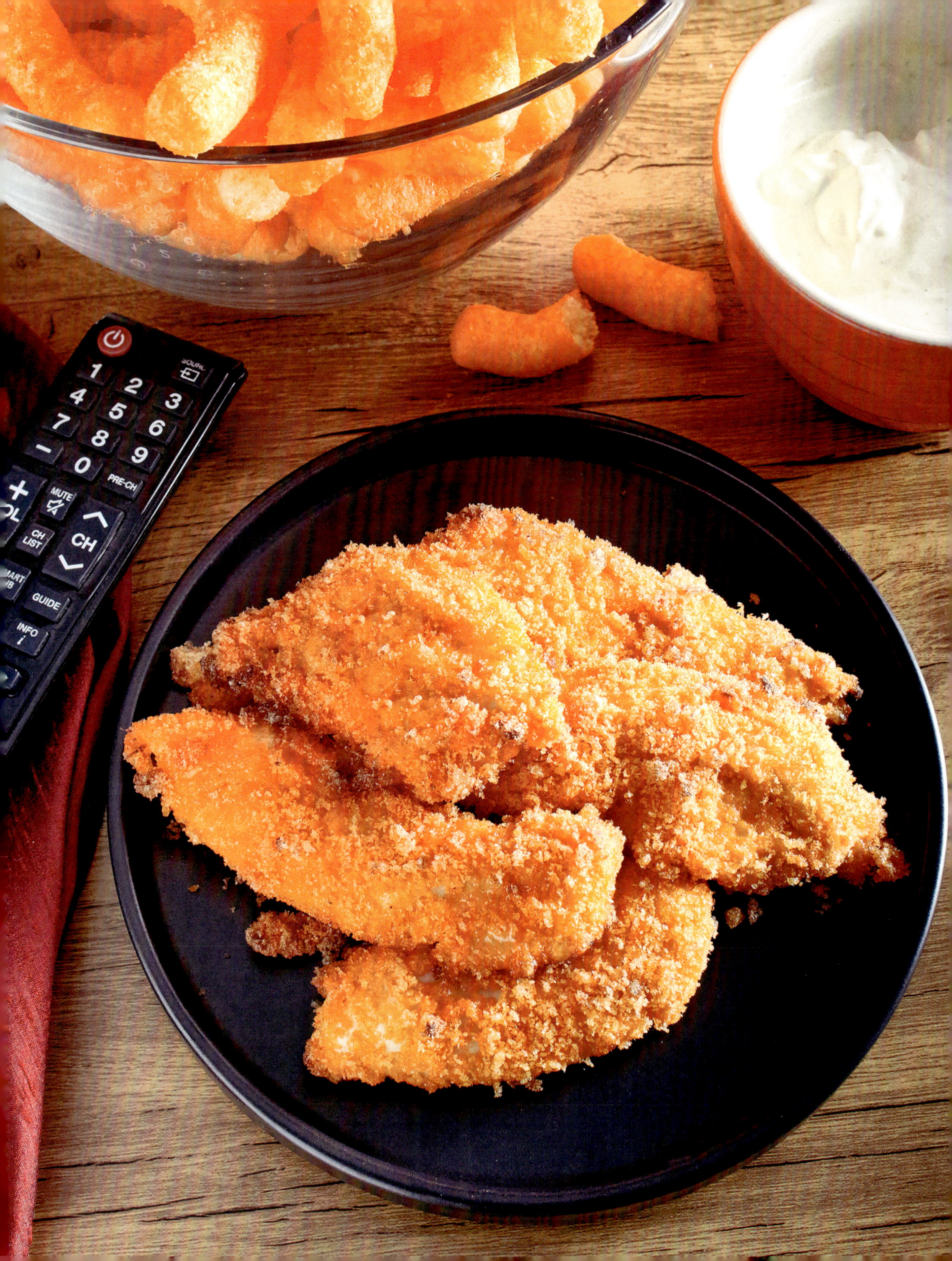
1 2 3
4 5 6
7 8 9
0
PRE-CH
MUTE
CH
CH LIST
GUIDE
INFO

Cheese Puff Chicken Tenders

Mary makes herself *quite* at home in Master's house. She curls up in his favourite easy chair and happily stuffs her face with a bowl of cheese puffs she finds on the table. Although Master's wife is unimpressed – and, in fact, develops an immediate loathing for the snack-happy witch – these cheesy, crunchy chicken tenders will be beloved by young and old alike. The littlest witches may enjoy them plain, while those with more adventurous palates might serve them over salad … or with a side of Dead Man's Toes (page 33)! However one prefers them, these chicken tenders are a staple in any Salem household. No witchcraft necessary!

Yield: 6 servings | **GF***

For the Sauce

- 180 ml sour cream
- 60 grams mayonnaise
- 1 tablespoon mustard
- ½ teaspoon onion powder
- ¼ teaspoon salt
- Freshly ground black pepper
- Dash hot sauce (optional)

For the Chicken Tenders

- 480 ml buttermilk
- ½ teaspoon rock salt
- ½ teaspoon paprika
- ¼ teaspoon onion powder
- 1 tablespoon mustard
- 1.8 kilograms chicken breast fillets
- 400 grams cheese puffs, pulverised

Note

This recipe can be easily made gluten-free by using a gluten-free cheese puff.

To make the sauce: In a small bowl, combine the sour cream, mayonnaise, mustard, onion powder and salt. Season with black pepper to taste and add hot sauce (if using). Mix well and refrigerate until serving.

To make the chicken tenders: In a large container that seals well, combine the buttermilk, salt, paprika, onion powder and mustard. Add the chicken and turn until well coated. Refrigerate for 30 minutes.

Preheat the oven and two baking sheets to 220°C. Line a third baking sheet with parchment paper.

Set up a dredging station by covering a large plate with about a third of the cheese puffs. One at a time, remove the chicken tenders from the marinade and dredge in the cheese puff coating, pressing gently to help it adhere. Place the coated tender on the third prepared baking sheet. When the parchment paper is full, carefully transfer the chicken on its parchment to one of the baking sheets in the oven. Line the third baking sheet with another piece of parchment. Repeat this process, adding more cheese puff coating to the plate as needed, until all the tenders are coated and in the oven.

Bake for 15 to 18 minutes, or until crisp and golden brown and an instant-read thermometer inserted into the thickest part of the chicken registers 75°C.

Allow to rest on the baking sheets for 2 to 3 minutes, then serve with the sauce on the side.

Main Dishes

Graveyard Gnocchi Grubs

When Max, Dani, and Allison run off into the graveyard, they know the Sanderson sisters won't be able to follow. But while witches cannot set foot on hallowed ground, other dangers lurk beneath the dirt – like long-dead zombie ex-boyfriends or even grubs! This ghoulish dish offers a cheeky nod to those underground inhabitants of Salem's infamous graveyard. And with hints of mushroom in both the gnocchi *and* the sauce, it's been known to leave fungi-lovers absolutely screaming with joy.

Yield: 6 servings | GF, V

For the Gnocchi

1.125 kilograms gold potatoes, scrubbed well

200 grams rice flour, plus more for dusting

2 teaspoons salt

4 dried shiitake mushrooms, pulverised

2 tablespoons olive oil

2 large eggs

For the Mushroom Sauce

450 grams cremini mushrooms, stemmed and halved

2 tablespoons olive oil

30 grams salted butter

7 grams stemmed fresh sage leaves

3 cloves garlic, peeled

½ teaspoon salt

240 ml double cream

50 grams grated Parmesan cheese

Specialist Tools

Potato ricer or food mill

To make the gnocchi: Preheat the oven to 190°C.

Pierce the potatoes in a few places with a fork. When the oven is preheated, place the potatoes directly on the oven rack in the centre of the oven. Bake for 45 to 50 minutes, or until fork-tender.

While the potatoes are still hot, use a tea towel to handle them and halve them lengthwise. Scoop out the flesh and leave it on the chopping board to release steam. Discard the skins or reserve them for a later use.

Using a potato ricer or food mill, process the potatoes into a large bowl. Set aside. In a medium bowl, mix the rice flour with the salt and shiitake. Set aside.

Make a well in the centre of the potatoes and add the olive oil and eggs. With a fork, whisk the eggs and olive oil together and then begin to incorporate the potato. Once most of the egg mixture has disappeared, start adding the flour mixture. Continue to add the flour mixture and mix until the dough comes together and is smooth.

Dust a baking sheet with rice flour. On a surface dusted with rice flour, divide the dough into six equal parts. Working with one piece of dough at a time, roll it into a 1-cm-thick rope. Cut each rope into pieces that are about 4 cm long. Place a large serving fork with its prongs touching and pressing down on the chopping board. Use the side of your thumb to roll each piece of dough down the back of the fork, pressing the grooves into the piece and creating the fold. Place the finished piece on the prepared baking sheet and continue this process until all the dough has been used. Refrigerate until needed.

To make the sauce: Working in batches, pulse the mushrooms in a food processor until minced. Set aside.

Bring a large pot of salted water to the boil.

Meanwhile, line a plate with paper towels. In a large sauté pan over a medium-high heat, heat the oil and butter until the butter foams. Add the sage leaves and fry until crisp, about 2 minutes. Use a slotted spoon to transfer the sage to the prepared plate.

Add the garlic to the pan, still over a medium-high heat, and sauté until fragrant, 1 to 2 minutes. Add the minced mushrooms and salt, stirring to combine. Cook, stirring occasionally, until the mushrooms are tender and have released their liquid, 5 to 7 minutes.

Turn the heat to medium-low and slowly add the cream, stirring continuously until the cream is incorporated and slightly reduced, 3 to 5 minutes. Stir in the Parmesan cheese and remove from the heat.

Working in batches, cook the gnocchi in the boiling salted water, being careful not to overcrowd, for 2 to 3 minutes. Using a spider or large slotted spoon, transfer the cooked gnocchi to the sauce and gently stir to coat. Repeat until all the gnocchi are cooked and coated in the sauce. If needed, thin the sauce a bit with a ladle of cooking water. Transfer to a serving platter and scatter the fried sage over the top. Serve immediately.

Notes

The gnocchi can be made up to a day ahead and covered and refrigerated. They can also be frozen on the baking sheet and then transferred to a freezer container once solid. They can be kept frozen for up to one month.

In a rush? Pre-made gnocchi can often be found in both the dried and fresh pasta sections of your local supermarket.

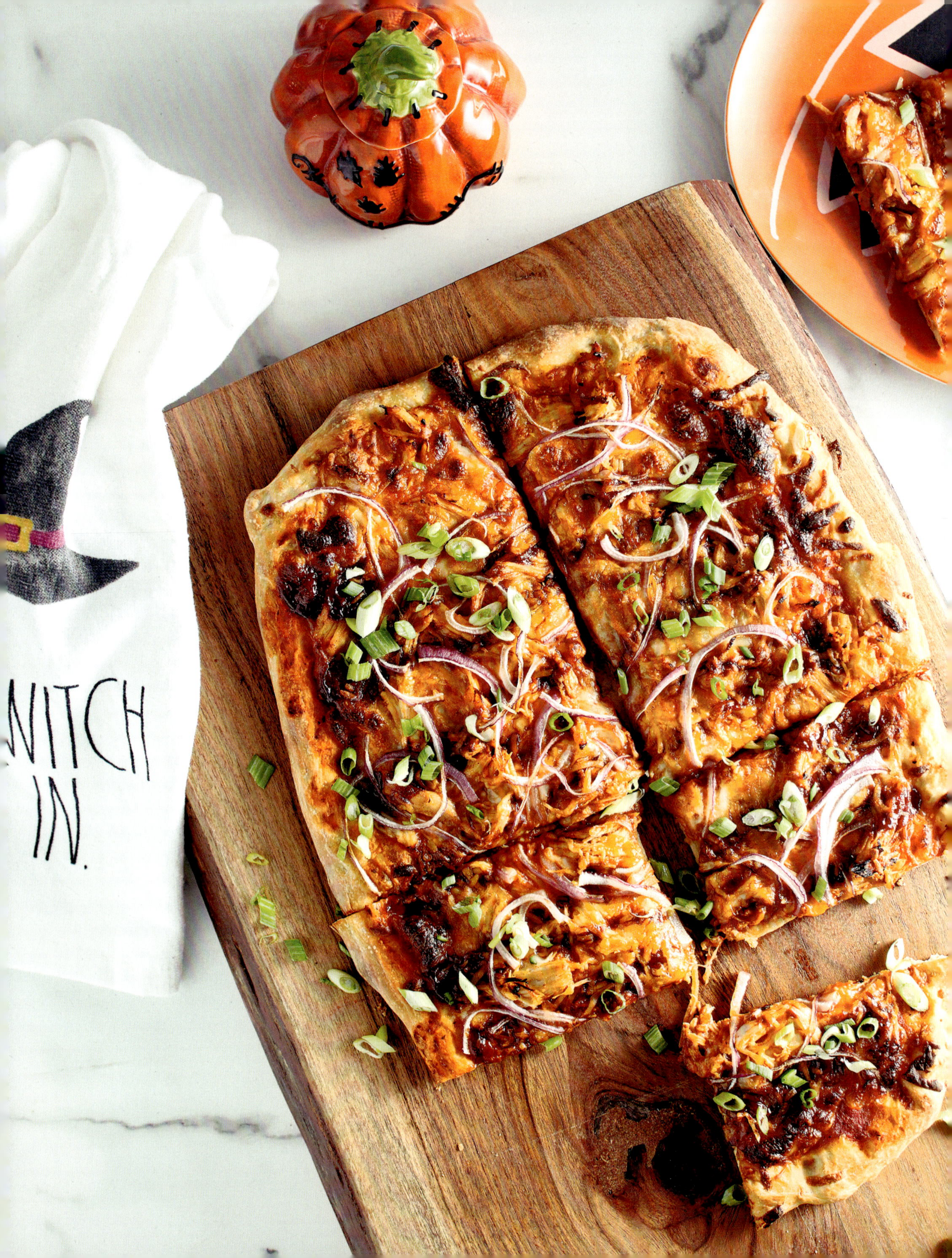
WITCH
IN.

Hollywood Barbecue Chicken Pizza

When the graveyard bullies find out Max is from California, they immediately give him a snarky nickname: Hollywood. But even these bullies would have nothing but praise for Hollywood's protein-packed signature dish. A tasty twist on a popular party favourite, this chicken pizza blends the traditional doughy base with a fiery barbecued topping. Tangy, savoury and quintessentially Californian, this slice of Hollywood is sure to please any hungry high schooler – or a trio of kindly old spinster ladies!

Yield: 2 pizzas or about 6 servings | **GF***

For the Pizza Sauce

- 1 tablespoon olive oil
- 1 tablespoon balsamic vinegar
- One 800 gram can chopped tomatoes
- 1 teaspoon salt
- ½ teaspoon dried oregano
- Freshly ground black pepper

For the Barbecue Sauce

- 60 ml apple cider vinegar
- 2 tablespoons dark brown sugar
- 1 teaspoon salt
- ½ teaspoon ground cayenne
- ½ teaspoon onion powder
- 425 grams tomato sauce
- 70 grams pomegranate syrup

For the Pizza

- Two 400 gram shop-bought pizza doughs
- 900 grams grated mozzarella
- 675 grams grilled boneless skinless chicken thighs or precooked chicken, shredded
- 240 grams grated Cheddar
- ½ red onion, thinly sliced
- 4 spring onions, white and light green parts only, thinly sliced

To make the pizza sauce: In a medium saucepan over a medium-high heat, combine the olive oil, balsamic vinegar and chopped tomatoes. Add the salt and oregano and season with black pepper to taste. Bring to a rolling boil, then turn the heat to low and simmer until the sauce is reduced by a third, 20 to 30 minutes.

To make the barbecue sauce: While the pizza sauce simmers, in a medium saucepan over a medium heat, combine the apple cider vinegar, brown sugar, salt, cayenne and onion powder and stir. Add the tomato sauce and pomegranate syrup, stirring to combine. Bring to a simmer, then turn the heat to low and continue to simmer until the sauce reduces by a third, about 20 minutes.

To make the pizza: Preheat the oven and two baking sheets to 220°C.

On a lightly oiled piece of parchment paper big enough to cover the baking sheet, roll or stretch out one piece of the dough into a rough rectangle. Spread half of the pizza sauce over the dough and top with half of the mozzarella. Scatter half of the chicken over the cheese and drizzle with half of the barbecue sauce. Scatter half of the Cheddar, half of the red onion and half of the spring onion over that. Repeat the process with the second piece of dough and the remaining ingredients.

Use an extra baking sheet or large chopping board to transfer the pizza on its parchment paper to the oven. Gently slide the parchment and pizza on to the preheated baking sheets. Bake, rotating halfway through, for 10 to 12 minutes, or until the cheese is bubbly and the crust is golden brown.

Notes

Leftover Roasted Red Spice Chicken (page 61) works well for the chicken in this dish.

This recipe can be easily made gluten-free by using gluten-free or cauliflower pizza crusts.

Main Dishes

Tie-Dye California Smoothie Bowl

There's a lot to be said for the Californian laid-back, tie-dyed point of view. Those who embrace it have been known to be less stressed, holistically balanced and uncompromisingly health-conscious. This fruit-filled smoothie bowl summons the spirit of a signature snack from Max's home state. With Greek yogurt, raspberries and blue spirulina, it's sure to make even a Hollywood expat feel right at home.

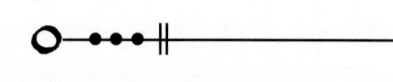

Yield: 2 smoothie bowls | GF*, V, V+*

240 ml Greek yogurt

2 teaspoons honey

½ teaspoon blue spirulina powder

60 grams frozen raspberries

120 ml coconut water

130 grams frozen mangoes

75 grams granola

120 grams fresh raspberries

140 grams fresh blueberries, plus more for garnish

2 tablespoons chia seeds

In a small bowl, combine the yogurt, honey and blue spirulina. Refrigerate.

In a small blender, combine the frozen raspberries with 60 ml of the coconut water and puree. Transfer to a small jug or measuring jug and refrigerate. Starting with a clean blender, puree the remaining 60 ml of coconut water and the mango, then refrigerate.

Evenly divide the granola between two large, shallow bowls. Top with the fresh raspberries and blueberries. Divide the yogurt evenly between the two bowls, carefully spreading it out to reach the rim of the bowl.

Pour or spoon the raspberry puree into the middle of each bowl, being careful to leave a border of yogurt. Repeat with the mango puree, placing it in the centre of the raspberry. Use a knife to drag through the colours, creating a fun pattern (or you can let your guests create their own).

Decorate with more blueberries around the edge, if desired, and sprinkle the chia seeds to create a peace symbol in the centre.

Note

This recipe can be easily made gluten-free by choosing your favourite gluten-free granola, and vegan by using a plant-based yogurt.

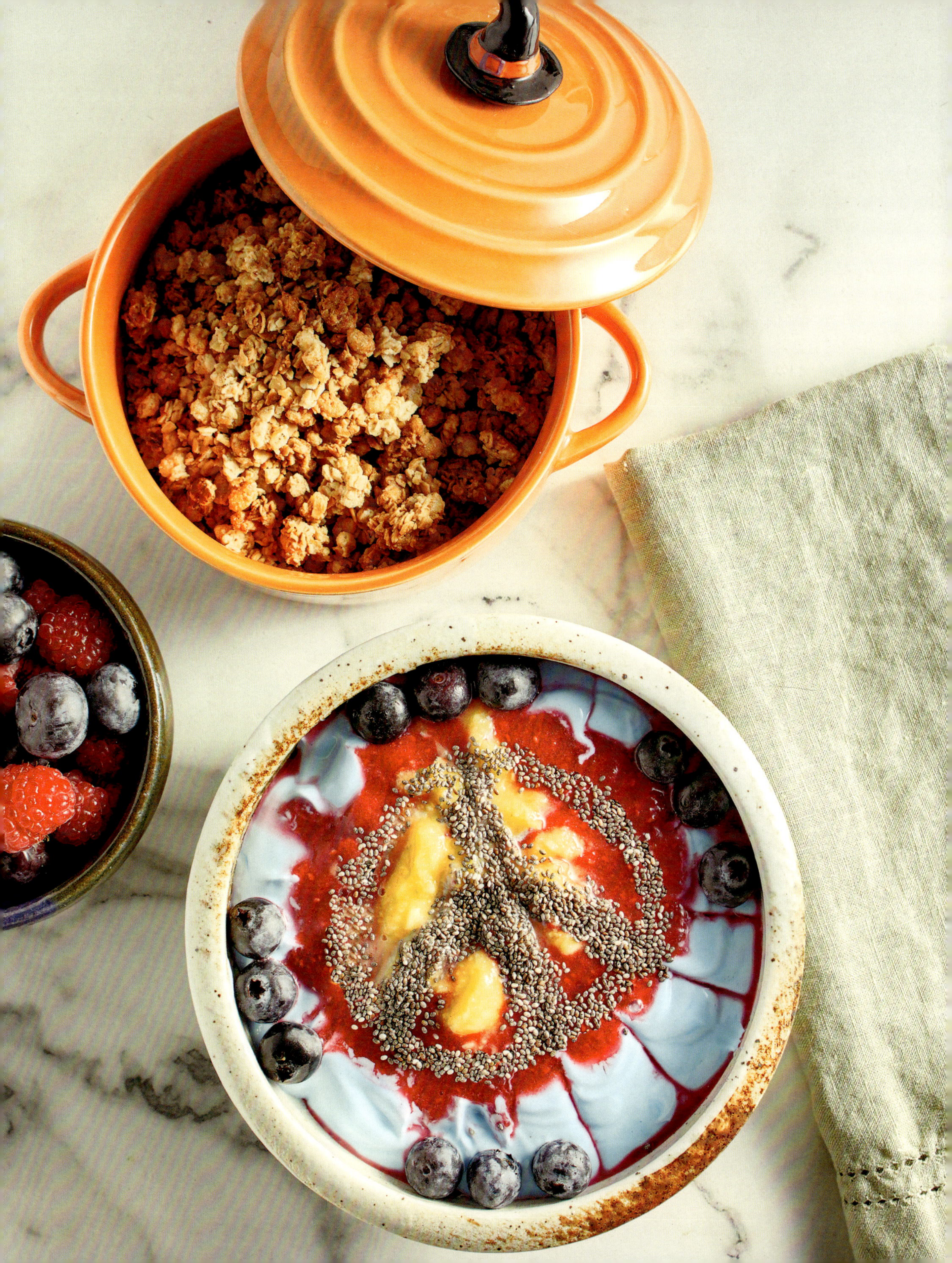

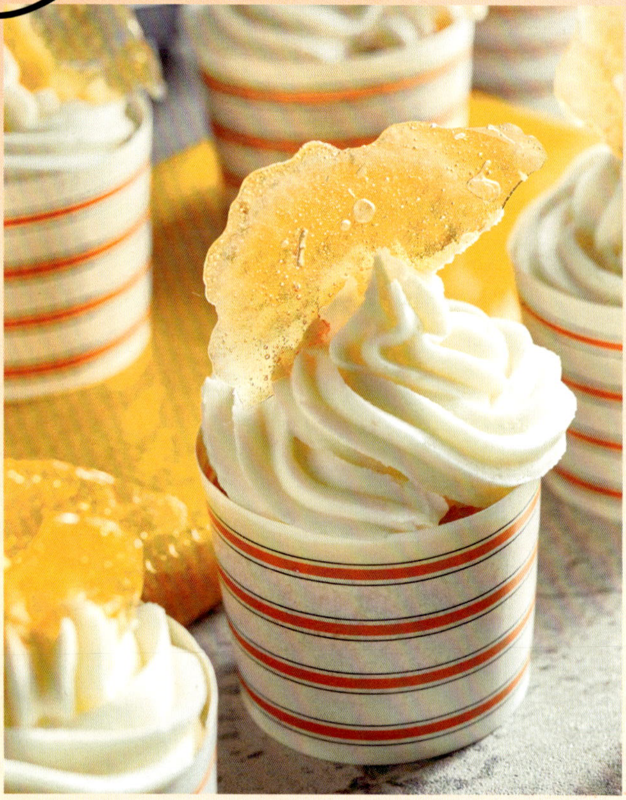

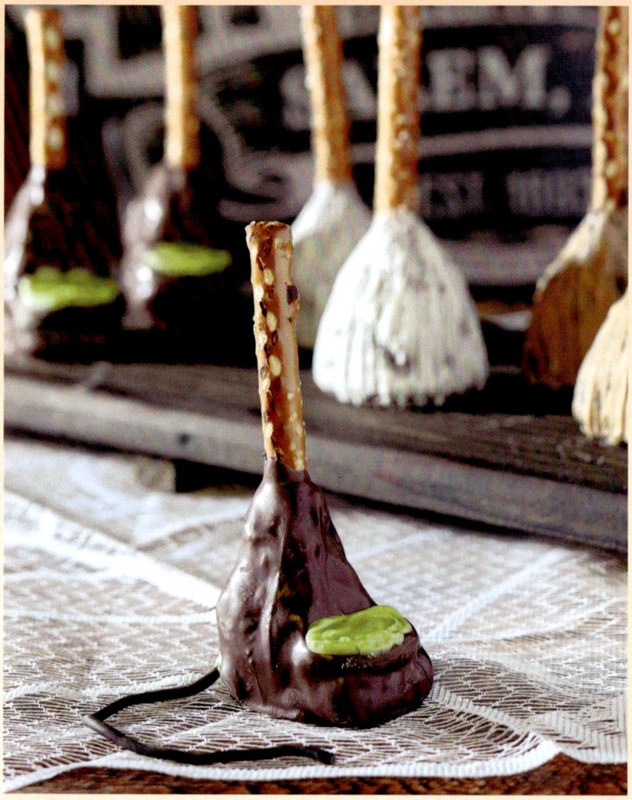

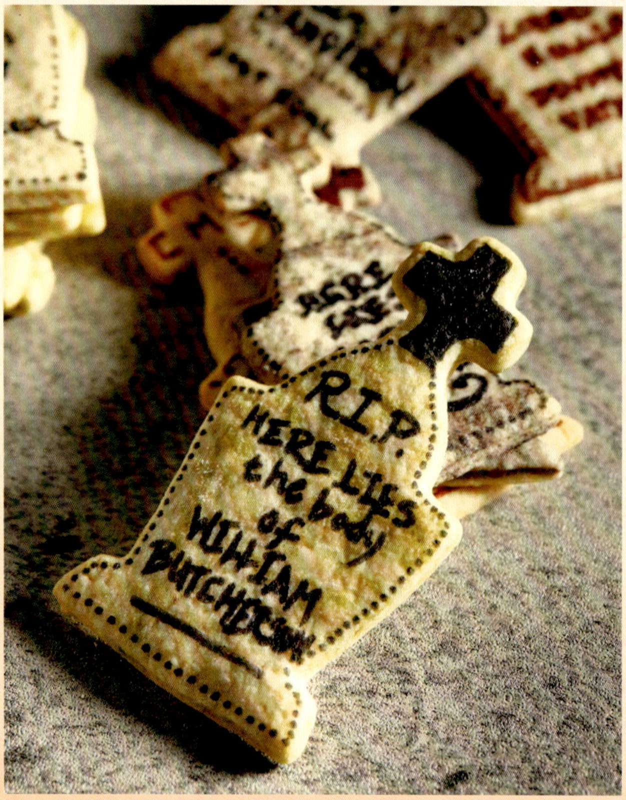
R.I.P.
HERE LIES
the body
of

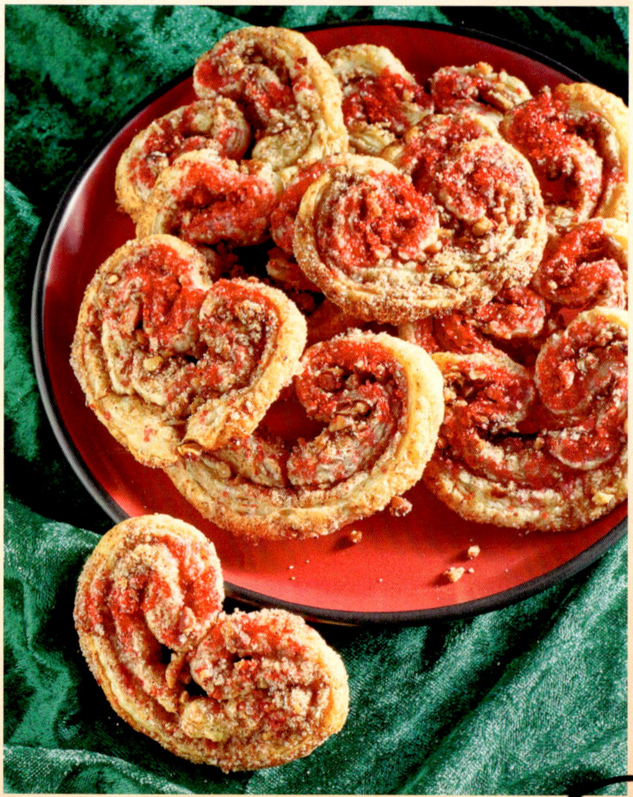

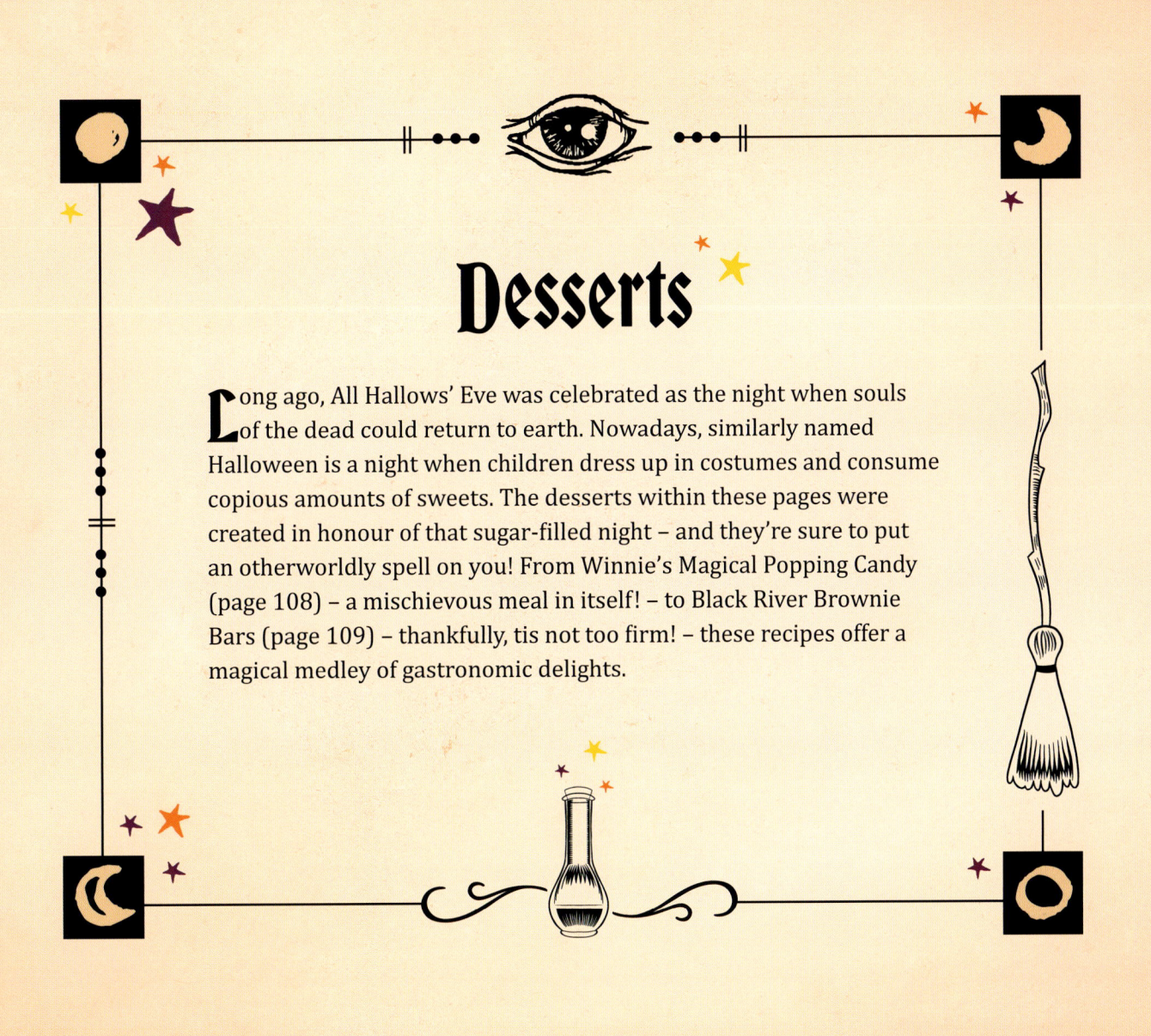

Desserts

Long ago, All Hallows' Eve was celebrated as the night when souls of the dead could return to earth. Nowadays, similarly named Halloween is a night when children dress up in costumes and consume copious amounts of sweets. The desserts within these pages were created in honour of that sugar-filled night – and they're sure to put an otherworldly spell on you! From Winnie's Magical Popping Candy (page 108) – a mischievous meal in itself! – to Black River Brownie Bars (page 109) – thankfully, tis not too firm! – these recipes offer a magical medley of gastronomic delights.

Blood Orange Jack-O'-Lantern Tarts

*All Hallows' Eve: a haunted night,
When black flame candles burn.
And witches cackle with delight
Awaiting youth's return.*

*As jack-o'-lanterns glow so bright,
The evening takes a turn.
These blood orange tarts will cause a fright
With faces oh so stern!*

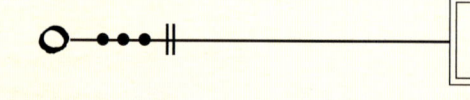

Yield: 6 tarts | GF*, V

For the Filling
150 grams sugar
2 tablespoons cornflour
60 ml fresh lemon juice
120 ml orange juice
Zest of 1 orange
3 egg yolks
15 grams unsalted butter

For the Crusts
200 grams chocolate cookie crumbs
90 grams salted butter, melted
2 tablespoons sugar

For the Garnish
110 grams dark chocolate

Specialist Tools
Six 10 cm tart tins
Pastry bag

To make the filling: In a medium, heavy-bottomed saucepan, whisk together the sugar, cornflour, lemon juice, orange juice, orange zest and egg yolks until fully incorporated. Place over a medium heat and, whisking constantly and making sure to reach the edges of the pan, cook until the mixture thickens, 3 to 5 minutes. The mixture should resemble a loose pudding. Stir in the butter and continue to whisk until the butter is melted. Remove from the heat immediately.

Over a container with a tight-fitting lid, press the mixture through a fine-mesh sieve. Place a piece of parchment paper over the surface of the mixture and seal with the lid. Refrigerate for at least 2 hours.

To make the crusts: While the filling is chilling, preheat the oven to 180°C.

In a medium bowl, stir together the cookie crumbs, butter and sugar. Scoop about ¼ cup of the crumb mixture into each of six 10 cm tart tins and use a glass to press the bottoms flat. Use your fingers to gently press the crumb mixture against the sides and into the fluted edges. Place the tart tins on a rimmed baking sheet and bake for 10 to 15 minutes, or until firm and just starting to crisp. Remove from the oven and allow to cool completely.

To make the garnish: Line a baking sheet with parchment paper. Gently melt the chocolate in a small microwave-safe bowl in 30-second bursts, stirring in between until smooth. Add the chocolate to a pastry bag or sealable bag and snip a small opening in the end. Pipe six sets of jack-o'-lantern faces on the parchment paper and allow to set in the refrigerator for about 5 minutes.

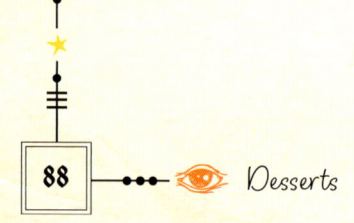

Desserts

All the components can be made up to three days ahead. Keep the filling in the refrigerator, the crusts in an airtight container and the garnish in a container on its parchment paper (cut into squares for easier storage). When ready to serve, fill each crust with about a quarter of the filling, use a spatula to smooth, and decorate with the chocolate face pieces. Once assembled, the tarts can be refrigerated for about 1 hour. To serve, carefully unmould the tart by pressing up from the bottom, then place on a small plate.

= Notes =

This recipe can be easily made gluten-free by using your favourite gluten-free cookie in the crusts.

The cookies should be processed in a food processor until they are evenly crushed and sandy in texture. Measure out 200 grams for the tart crust. You may have extra cookie crumbs.

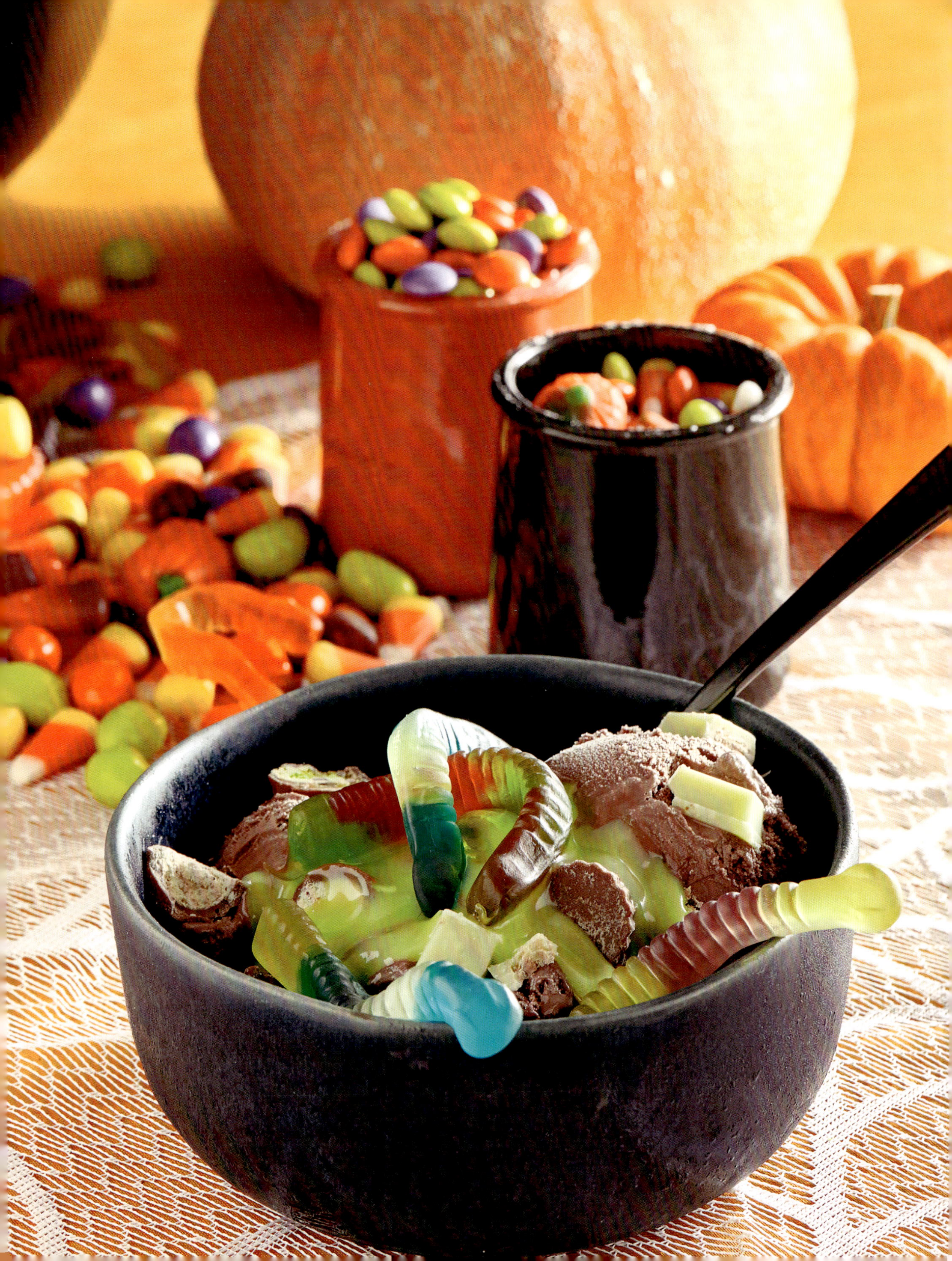

Halloween Candy Ice Cream with Gummy Worm Ganache

Billy Butcherson may have once been deep asleep in his wormy bed, but the tight-lipped corpse would no doubt leap from his grave if offered a bowl of this candy-filled treat. Rich, chocolatey ice cream is topped with an unexpected ganache that's sure to please the young, the old and the dearly departed alike. With several kinds of chocolate and a hidden contingent of worms, this sweet treat is sure to enchant *anyone* brave enough to gobble it up!

Yield: About 1 litre | **GF*, V***

For the Ice Cream
- 300 ml double cream
- 60 grams unsweetened cocoa powder
- One 400 gram can sweetened condensed milk
- 60 grams chocolate Halloween candy of choice, roughly chopped into bite-size pieces

For the Gummy Worm Ganache
- 120 ml double cream
- 1 small bag gummy candy
- 60 grams white chocolate chips

To make the ice cream: In the bowl of a food mixer fitted with the whisk attachment, combine the double cream and cocoa powder by whisking on a low speed until well blended. Turn the mixer to high and beat the cream mixture until stiff peaks form.

Add the condensed milk and fold in until no streaks remain. Add the Halloween candy and fold again. Put the mixture into a large airtight container and freeze for a minimum of 8 hours or overnight.

To make the ganache: Just before serving, add the cream and gummy candy to a small saucepan over a medium-low heat. Cook, stirring, until the gummy candy is completely melted.

Put the white chocolate chips into a medium bowl. Pour the cream mixture over the white chocolate chips and allow to stand for 5 minutes. Stir until smooth.

Serve the ganache over the ice cream and top with gummy worms.

Note

This recipe can be easily made gluten-free and vegetarian by using only gluten-free and vegetarian sweets.

Desserts

Thackery Binx Treats

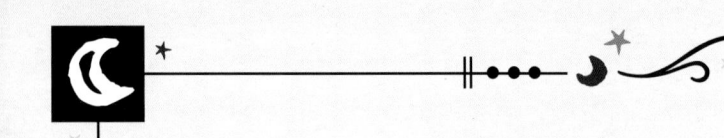

In his life as a cat, Binx has spent years hunting mice down in the old Salem crypt. After all, one does what one must to survive a Sanderson curse! But there's nothing cursed about these Binx-inspired treats. Perfectly sweetened cherries are dipped in chocolate and topped with almonds to create the most adorable critters that Salem's ever seen. As Dani might say, hunting mice just got a lot more fun!

Yield: 12 to 16 mice | GF, V

- One 370 gram jar natural maraschino cherries, stem on and pitted
- About 30 grams sliced almonds
- 16 wrapped chocolate kiss-shaped candies
- 120 grams dark chocolate chips
- 15 grams vegetable fat
- Small decorative balls for eyes

Pour the jar of cherries and their juices into a large bowl. Sort through and find 12 to 16 cherries with nice long stems and good shapes, not crushed or broken. Return the rest of the cherries and their syrup to the jar and reserve for future use.

Rinse the selected cherries in a fine-mesh sieve and turn out on to paper towels to thoroughly dry.

While the cherries are drying, line a baking sheet with parchment paper or a silicone baking mat. Sort the almonds and create pairs of ears and unwrap enough chocolate candies for each cherry.

Melt the chocolate chips in a chocolate melting pot or a small microwave-safe bowl in 30-second bursts, heating as few times as possible and stirring to complete the melting. Stir in the vegetable fat until the mixture is smooth.

Dip each cherry, holding on to the stem, into the chocolate and make sure it covers all the way to the stem. Shake off excess chocolate and then press the bottom of the cherry to the flat side of the kiss. Lay the pair down on its side, with the stem at one end and the point of the kiss at the other. Press two almond slices into the chocolate just behind the kiss, creating the ears. Continue until all the cherries have been dipped.

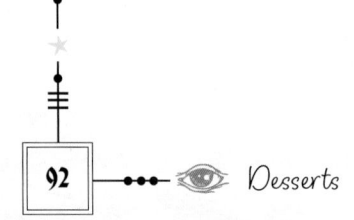

continued on page 94

Desserts

Hame Candle

...at of a hanged man.
...at on a full moon.
... spirits of the dead
...in on Halloween night.

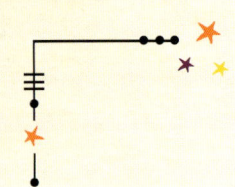

continued from page 92

Using a toothpick or skewer, dot each kiss right in front of the ears with two dots of chocolate and stick the decorative balls on to make eyes. Allow to set for 10 to 15 minutes at room temperature or for 5 minutes in the refrigerator.

Serve immediately or store carefully between layers of parchment paper in an airtight container for up to three days.

"Hey, Cupcake" Cupcakes

Be careful what you wish for! When an enthusiastic bus driver greets Sarah with an appreciative, "Hey, cupcake," he thinks he's greeting a gorgeous creature – one he very much hopes he'll be seeing again. These vanilla cupcakes offer a happy nod to that unwitting driver. With brown butter buttercream and crushed butterscotch candies, these cupcakes have been known to disappear lickety-split. In no time at all, you'll be bidding farewell to the entire batch … *and* a certain "mortal bus boy"!

Yield: About 24 cupcakes | V

For the Cupcakes

- 240 grams plain flour
- 2 teaspoons baking powder
- ½ teaspoon salt
- 400 grams sugar
- 240 grams unsalted butter, softened
- 6 large eggs
- 2 tablespoons vanilla extract

For the Icing and Tuile Garnish

- 240 grams unsalted butter, cut into small pieces
- 1 teaspoon rock salt
- 1 tablespoon vanilla extract
- 600 grams icing sugar
- 80 ml double cream
- 12 unwrapped butterscotch candies (optional)

Specialist Tools

- Pastry bag and large star piping nozzle (optional)

To make the cupcakes: Preheat the oven to 180°C and line two muffin trays with cases.

In a medium bowl, whisk together the flour, baking powder and salt and set aside.

In the bowl of a food mixer fitted with the paddle attachment, cream together the sugar and butter on a medium speed until light and fluffy, about 3 minutes. Add the eggs, one at a time, beating well after each addition to keep the mixture light and fluffy. With the final egg, add the vanilla.

Working in two batches, fold in the flour mixture, scraping down the bowl as you go. Fill each muffin case two-thirds full. Bake for 20 to 25 minutes, or until a skewer inserted into the centre comes out clean. Rotate the pans halfway through baking. Allow to cool in the pan for 10 minutes, then transfer the cupcakes to a wire rack to cool completely before icing.

To make the icing and tuile garnish: In a large, heavy-bottomed saucepan over medium heat, heat the butter, stirring, until completely melted. Continue stirring until the butter clarifies and begins to brown. The butter will foam and bubble, but continue stirring. When the butter has reached a deep golden brown and has a nutty scent, 5 to 7 minutes total, remove from the heat. Decant to a large bowl and allow to cool completely.

Add the salt and vanilla, stir to combine. Add the icing sugar, 100 grams at a time, beating with a hand mixer on a medium-high speed after each addition. The mixture will eventually become stiff and crumbly.

continued on page 96

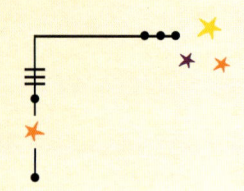

continued from page 95

Continue beating while slowly adding in the double cream until the mixture has reached a smooth consistency. Note that you may need 1 tablespoon less or 1 tablespoon more of double cream to achieve an easily spreadable consistency.

Ice each cupcake with a spatula or a pastry bag fitted with a large star piping nozzle.

Start the butterscotch tuile garnish (if using) by preheating the oven to 180°C.

On a baking sheet lined with a silicone baking mat, place the butterscotch candies at least 5 cm apart.

Bake for 8 minutes, or until just starting to spread. Place a piece of parchment paper over the candies and press down with a heavy glass or jar. Twist gently to create the sheer edges. Allow to cool completely. Remove the parchment, break each candy in half and store in between pieces of parchment paper in an airtight container until needed. Don't worry if they don't break perfectly in half; the organic shapes and shards are what make this a fun garnish.

Top the cupcakes with the tuiles and serve.

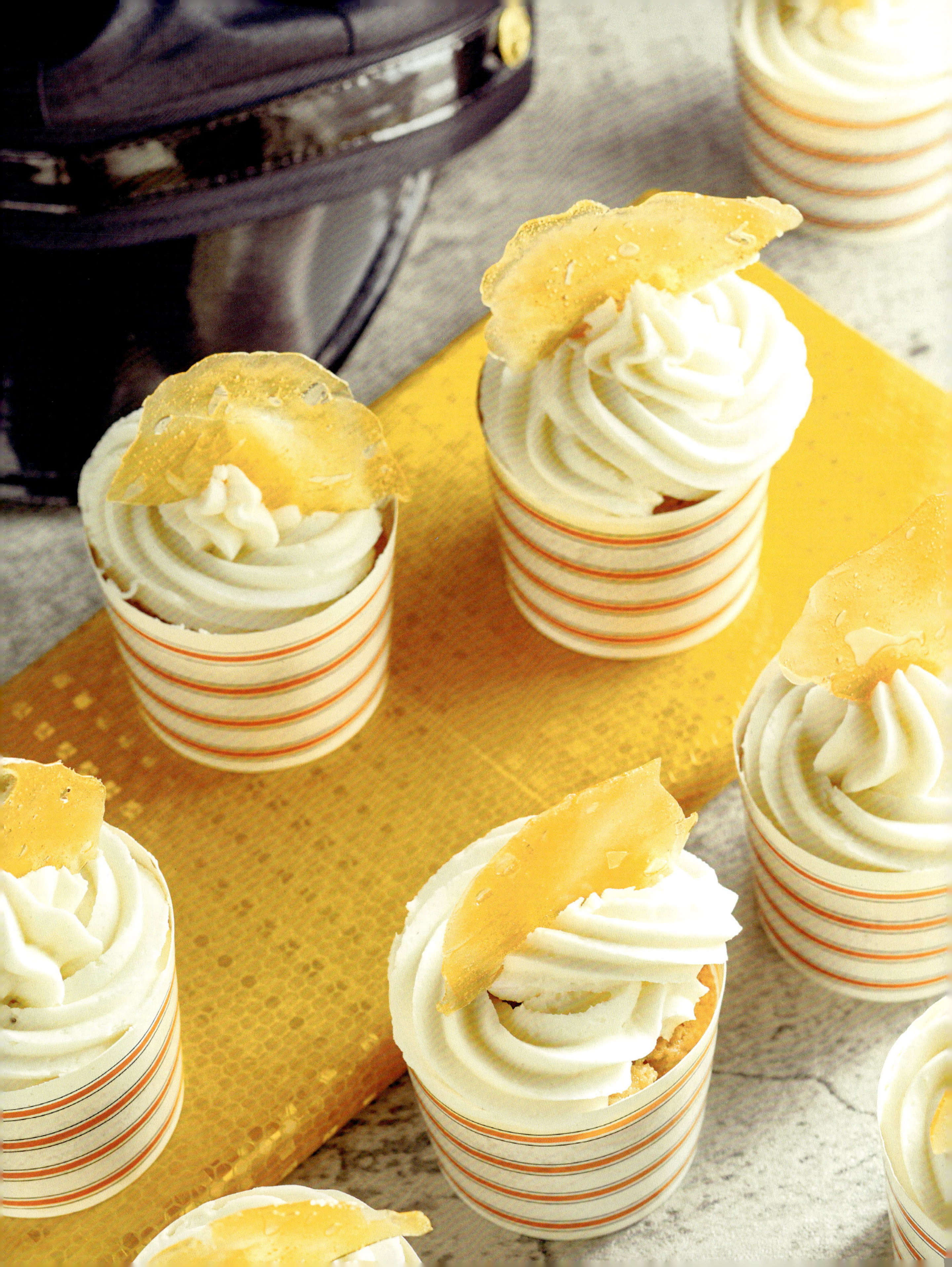

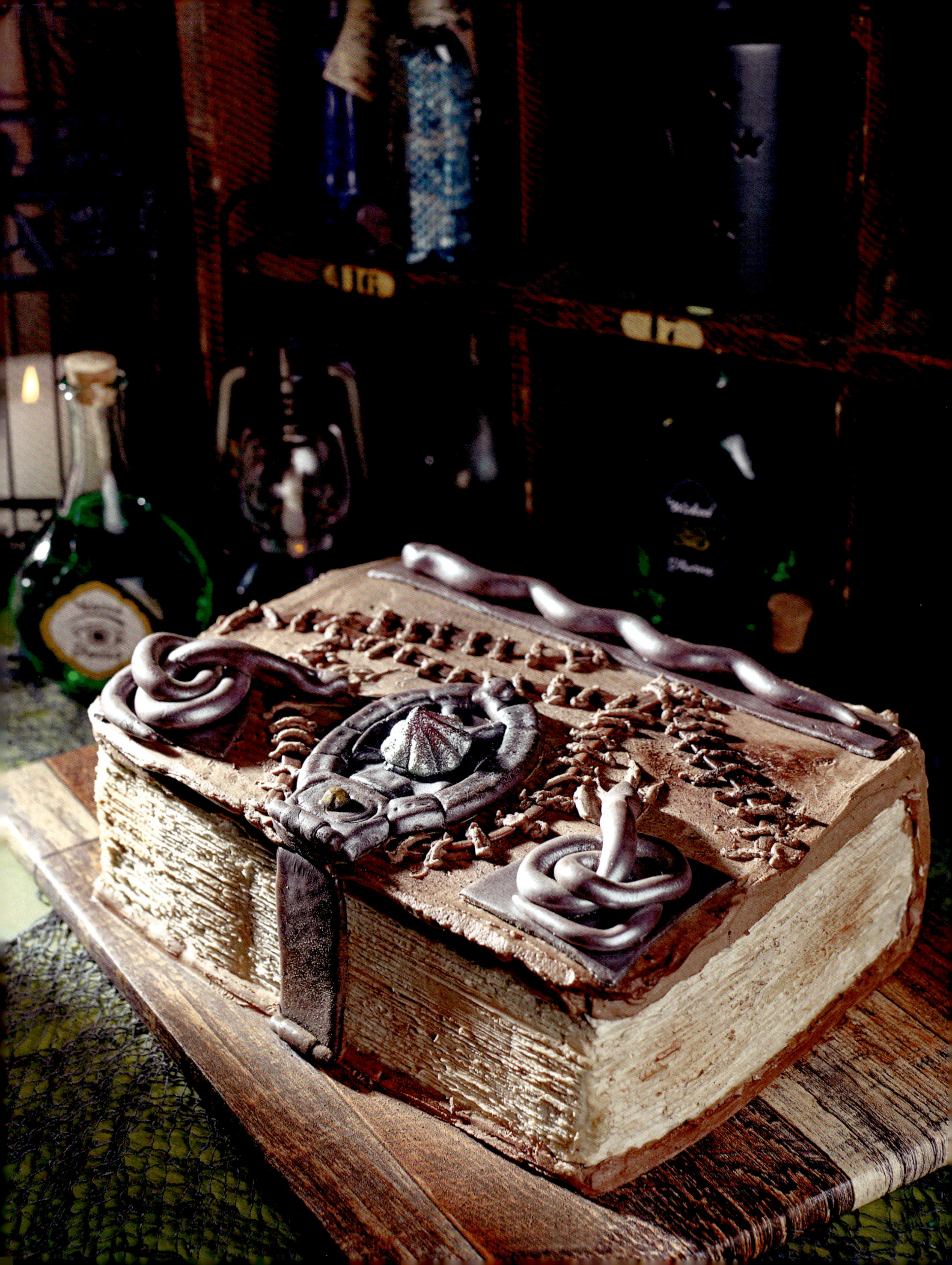

Winnie's Spellbook Cake

Winifred Sanderson's beloved book was given to her by Master himself. Its contents are said to contain her "most powerful and evil spells", and it's feared throughout the community of Salem. Although this dessert requires no dark magic, its dark chocolate base and buttercream filling make it a flavourful favourite. Just be sure to keep it away from magic candles – black flame or otherwise!

Yield: 12 to 14 servings | V

For the Cake

- 120 grams unsalted butter
- 165 grams light brown sugar
- 150 grams granulated sugar
- 2 large eggs
- 2 teaspoons vanilla extract
- 120 grams cocoa powder
- 180 grams plain flour
- 2 teaspoons baking powder
- ¼ teaspoon salt
- 120 ml sour cream
- 240 ml hot water

continued on page 100

To make the cake: Line a 28-by-35-cm cake tin with parchment paper and set aside. Preheat the oven to 180°C.

In the bowl of a food mixer fitted with the paddle attachment, cream together the butter and both sugars on a medium-high speed until light and fluffy, about 3 minutes. Add the eggs and vanilla. Beat again until well combined. Add the cocoa powder and mix again until completely incorporated.

In a small bowl, mix together the flour, baking powder and salt.

Add half of the flour mixture to the butter mixture and mix until incorporated. Scrape down the sides of the bowl and add the sour cream all at once. Mix until completely incorporated. Add the remaining flour mixture, mix again and scrape down the sides of the bowl.

With the mixer running on a low speed, slowly drizzle in the hot water. Continue to mix until all of the water is incorporated and the batter is smooth, 2 to 3 minutes.

Pour the batter into the prepared cake tin and bake for 25 to 30 minutes, or until a skewer inserted into the centre comes out clean. Allow to cool in the tin for 15 minutes before turning on to a wire rack and removing the parchment. Allow to cool completely.

continued on page 100

Desserts

continued from page 99

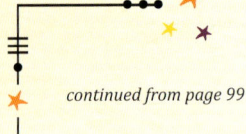

For the Filling and Icing

6 egg whites

¼ teaspoon salt

440 grams dark brown sugar

1 teaspoon fresh lemon juice

720 grams unsalted butter, cut into cubes, plus more for greasing

2 teaspoons vanilla extract

170 grams dark chocolate, melted

150 grams crushed chocolate wafer cookies (optional)

About 30 chocolate chew candies

About 2 teaspoons silver lustre dust

¼ teaspoon gold or bronze lustre dust

About 1 tablespoon black cocoa, cocoa, or black petal dust

Specialist Tools

Sugar thermometer

continued from page 99

To make the filling and icing: Add the egg whites and salt to the bowl of a food mixer fitted with a whisk attachment. In a medium, heavy-bottomed saucepan over a medium-high heat, combine the brown sugar with 240 ml of water and bring to the boil. Set the mixer on a medium speed and whisk until the eggs are frothy, about 1 minute. Add the lemon juice and whisk until soft peaks form, 2 to 3 minutes more, then turn off the mixer.

Grease a heatproof 1 litre measuring jug with butter and set aside. Fit the saucepan with a sugar thermometer and, when the sugar mixture reaches 115°C, decant it to the measuring jug.

Slowly add the sugar syrup to the egg whites in small batches, whisking after each addition. When all the syrup is added, beat the mixture on a high speed until the meringue is completely cool (the outside of the bowl should be cool to the touch), 3 to 5 minutes.

Add the butter, one to two cubes at a time, beating well on a medium speed after each addition. Once all the butter has been incorporated, add the vanilla and briefly beat on a high speed until smooth.

Reserve 4 cups of the icing to fill the cake and create the pages and add the melted chocolate to the rest. Beat again until smooth, about 1 minute.

To assemble the cake: Cut the cake exactly down the middle horizontally, creating 2 smaller layer cakes of equal size. Place one layer on to your desired cake or serving board. Use 2 cups of the plain icing to fill the cake by icing a thick layer on to this cake layer with an offset spatula. If using, sprinkle the crushed cookies on top of the icing. Top with the second cake layer and use the offset spatula to "seal" the edges by pushing icing into the space. Chill in the refrigerator as is for 10 minutes.

Remove from the refrigerator and ice the top of the cake and the back edge (this will become the spine of the book) with the chocolate icing. Use the offset spatula to create neat edges along the front and sides of the cake to create the book cover. Reserve about ½ cup of the chocolate icing, storing in an airtight container at room temperature. You will need this to attach the embellishments. Chill again for 15 to 20 minutes.

Remove from the refrigerator and use the remaining 2 cups of plain icing to pipe the exposed front and side edges, creating the pages. Be careful not to touch the "book cover". Chill again for 10 minutes, or more, before using a long knife or metal ruler to "cut" pages into the edges. As straight as possible, firmly press the edge of the knife or ruler into the icing, over and over, until you have created lines

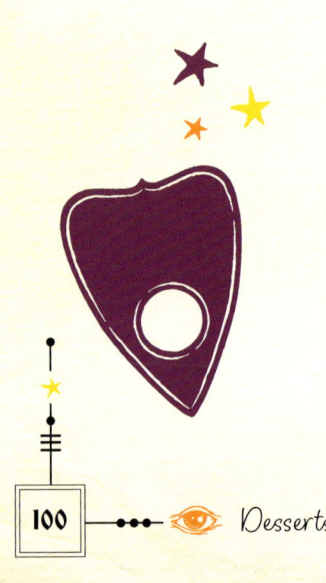

Desserts

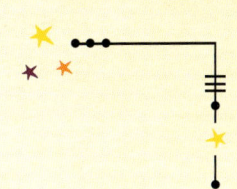

representing the pages from top to bottom. Repeat on the sides, lining up the lines as best you can. Keep in mind the spellbook is a very old book, so imperfections just make it more realistic. Return the cake to the refrigerator while you create the embellishments.

You will need a non-stick surface such as a silicone baking mat or parchment paper, wooden skewers and a microwave-safe plate. Place 3 unwrapped chocolate chews on the plate and microwave for 5 to 10 seconds, until just pliable. Knead together until they are a smooth ball. Roll out the ball on the non-stick surface until you have a 30- to 33-cm snake, making sure to thin out one end for the tail. Gently pinch and flatten the other end to create the head. Coil the snake and set aside. Repeat for one more coiled snake and then make one snake for the top of the spine. Measure the length of your iced cake to make sure it will fit.

Use about 1½ candy chews each, again gently heated, to create 5 fingers for the book spine, using the skewer to create details such as nails and knuckles. Gently heat another 6 candies, knead them together, and roll them out to about 3 mm thick. From this, cut the rounded triangles that sit under the coiled snakes, and the straight strip that sits under the third snake. Use 5 candies to sculpt the lock pieces. For the base of the stitches, use another 2 candies and roll them out to thin ropes of varying lengths, fold each rope in half, creating a double strand, and then gently flatten it.

Use the silver lustre dust and a small, clean brush to "paint" the snakes, snake bases and lock pieces. Age the pieces with the black cocoa or black petal dust. Age the fingers with the cocoa as well.

Remove the cake from the refrigerator and use little dabs of the reserved icing to attach all the embellishments. Do the stitches last, fitting them in around the other decor as desired. Place the remaining icing in a disposable pastry bag, snip a small hole in the tip and pipe the stitches, then pipe perpendicularly over the base stitch lines. For the final step, use the black cocoa to age the rest of the book and pages by gently dusting it on with a pastry brush.

The cake can be made up to a week ahead, wrapped and frozen. Do not defrost before decorating. The decorated cake can be made a day ahead and should be kept in the refrigerator until about 45 minutes before serving.

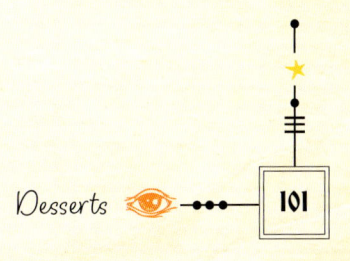

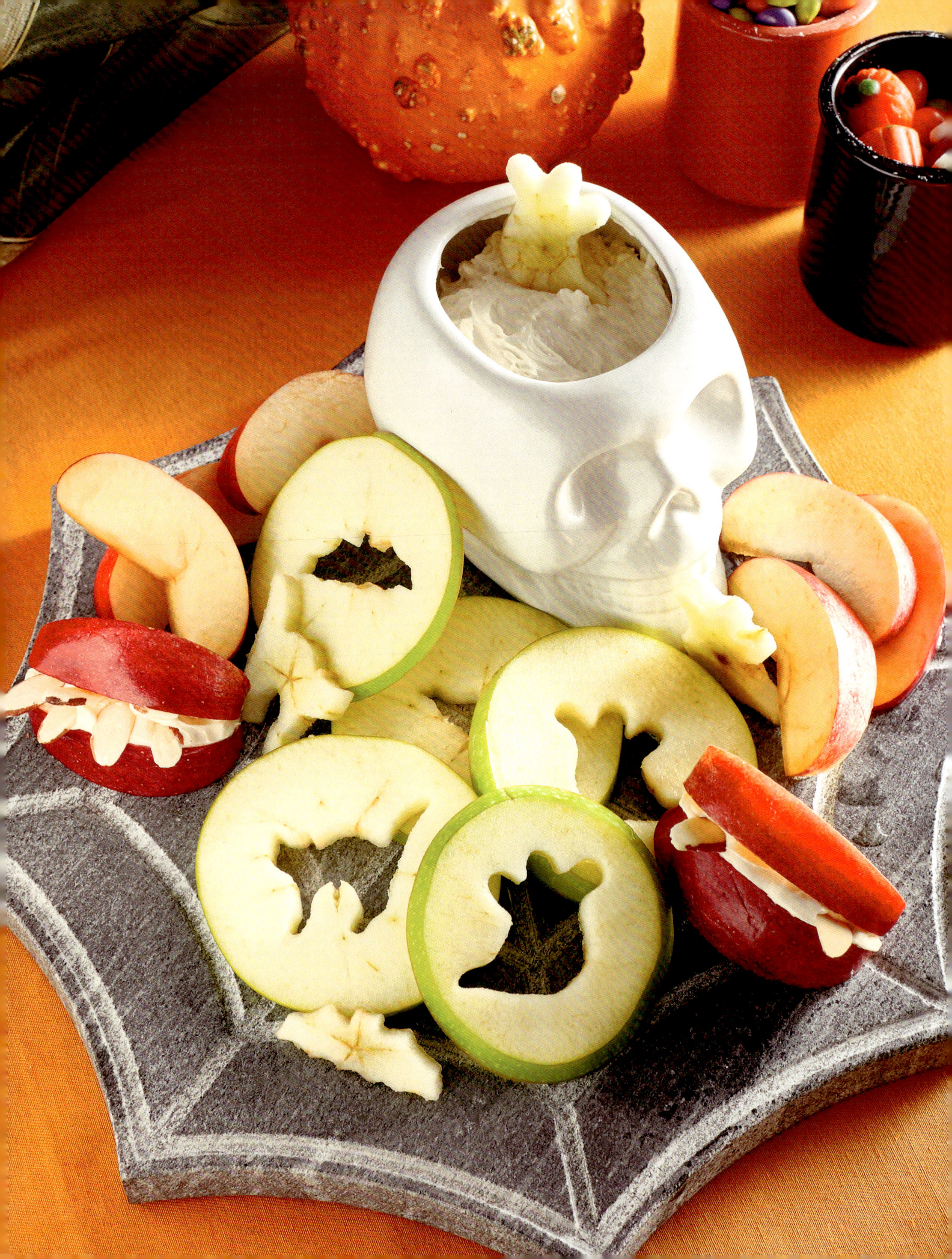

Classic Caramel Apple Dip

Bobbing for apples is a time-honoured tradition. And this tangy twist on a sweet classic will have Halloween revellers bouncing with excitement. A light, creamy whip offers a delightful dipping sauce for thin apple slices – and their bat, cat or ghost cut-outs! Packed with vitamins (and just a sprinkle of sugar), this appley snack is sure to be the hit of any party – no bobbing required!

Yield: *8 servings* | GF, V

225 grams cream cheese, softened

60 ml Greek yogurt

55 grams dark brown sugar

½ tablespoon vanilla extract

4 large apples

1 tablespoon apple cider vinegar, plus more as needed (optional)

Sliced almonds (optional)

Specialist Tools

Small Halloween cookie cutters, such as bats, cats and ghosts (optional)

In a medium bowl, using a hand mixer on a medium speed, combine the cream cheese and yogurt until light and fluffy. Add the brown sugar and beat until completely incorporated. Add the vanilla and mix again. Store in an airtight container in the refrigerator until ready to serve.

The apples can be prepared a few ways:

1. Quarter, core and slice apples into wedges. Toss all cut apples with the apple cider vinegar to coat them. Serve alongside the dip.

2. Slice the apples from end to end into thin rounds and use the cookie cutters to core and make fun shapes. Serve alongside the dip.

3. Quarter, core and slice the apples into wedges. Use two wedges to create a monster mouth. Spread about 2 teaspoons of the dip on to one slice of apple and top with a second slice, making sure the peel sides are facing the same way. Insert almond slices as fangs and serve.

Desserts

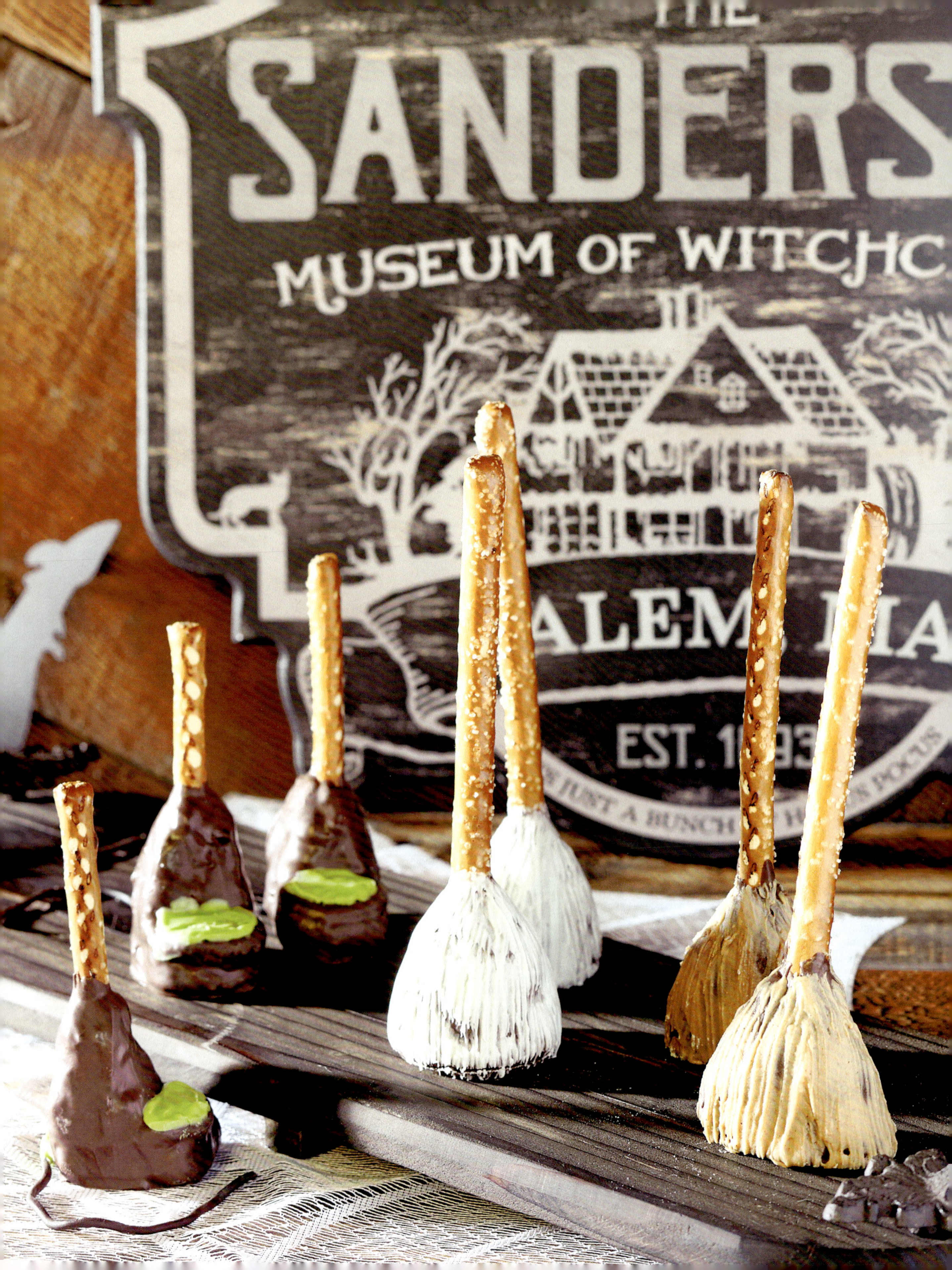
SANDERS
MUSEUM OF WITCHC

Broomstick, and Other Transport, Treats

Common household cleaning tools are the Sanderson sisters' preferred means of travel. But after three hundred years, many things have changed – and not always for the better. While Winnie and Sarah are able to fly into the night on a trusty old broomstick and mop, respectively, poor Mary must make do with a thoroughly modern vacuum. But no matter the vehicle, each of these enchanting broomstick treats is filled with peanut butter cups and moulded to resemble one of the Sanderson sisters' trusty old (or new!) rides. Into the night!

Yield: About 12 treats | V

For the Cake

- 60 grams unsalted butter
- 165 grams light brown sugar
- 1 large egg
- 1 teaspoon vanilla extract
- 60 grams cocoa powder
- 90 grams plain flour
- 1 teaspoon baking powder
- ⅛ teaspoon salt
- 160 grams smooth peanut butter
- 120 ml hot water

continued on page 106

Line a 20-by-20-cm baking sheet with parchment paper and set aside. Preheat the oven to 180°C.

To make the cake: In a large bowl using a hand mixer on a medium speed, cream together the butter and brown sugar until light and fluffy, about 3 minutes. Add the egg and vanilla and beat again until well combined. Add the cocoa powder and mix again until completely incorporated.

In a small bowl, mix together the flour, baking powder and salt.

Add half of the flour mixture to the butter mixture and mix again until incorporated. Scrape down the sides of the bowl and add the peanut butter all at once. Mix until completely incorporated. Add the remaining flour mixture, mix again and scrape down the sides of the bowl.

With the mixer on a low speed, slowly drizzle in the hot water. Continue to mix until all of the water is incorporated and the batter is smooth, 2 to 3 minutes.

Pour the batter on to the prepared baking sheet and bake for 10 to 15 minutes, or until a skewer inserted into the centre comes out clean. Allow to cool on the sheet for 30 minutes, then break the cake up and transfer it to a large bowl. Refrigerate until completely cool, at least 1 hour.

continued on page 106

Desserts

continued from page 105

For the Icing

120 grams unsalted butter, softened

65 grams icing sugar

40 grams cocoa powder

1 teaspoon vanilla extract

2 tablespoons double cream

For Assembly

12 to 14 pretzel rods

8 unwrapped thin peanut butter cups (dark chocolate is a nice touch here)

560 grams dark melting chocolate

140 grams white melting chocolate

1 to 2 drops bright green food colouring

60 cm black liquorice lace (optional)

90 grams peanut butter baking chips

continued from page 105

To make the icing: In a large bowl, using a hand mixer on a low speed, mix together the butter, icing sugar and cocoa powder until well combined but still crumbly. Add the vanilla and double cream. Continue to mix on a medium speed until light and fluffy, about 2 minutes.

Add the icing to the cake crumbles and use the mixer on a low speed to combine until a dough forms.

To assemble: Line a baking sheet with a silicone baking mat. Assemble the pretzel rods and the unwrapped peanut butter cups on the sheet. Halve four of the peanut butter cups and set aside.

Working with about 3 tablespoons of cake dough, use your hands to form it into a broom shape around the end of a pretzel rod. Press the base of the "broom" over a peanut butter cup half, covering it partly with the cake dough and creating a firm, stable base. Lay the broom down on the baking sheet and continue until you have four brooms. Reserve the remaining peanut butter cup halves.

Again working with about 3 tablespoons of cake dough, form a round "mop" shape around one end of a pretzel rod. Press the bottom of the mop over a whole peanut butter cup, partially covering it with dough and creating a firm base. Lay the mop down on the baking sheet and continue until you have four mops.

To make the vacuums, break two pretzel sticks roughly in half (don't worry, you have a few extra) and use 3 tablespoons of dough to form a vacuum shape on the broken end of a pretzel stick. Use a reserved peanut butter cup half to create a firm base, rounded edge facing front, by pressing the cake pop gently over the cup and using the shape to help form the front of the vacuum. Leave the vacuums standing up on the tray.

Freeze all the cake pops for 1 hour.

When the hour is almost up, melt the dark chocolate in a chocolate melting pot or medium microwave-safe bowl in 30-second bursts. Remove the cake pops from the freezer. Dip each cake pop into the melted chocolate, making sure to coat the joint between cake and pretzel rod. You may need a small spatula to help cover the whole cake pop. Gently shake off excess chocolate and set it, base-side down, standing up on the baking sheet. Repeat until you have covered all the cake pops.

Desserts

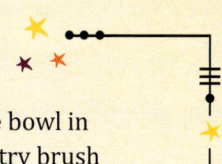

Next, using a clean melting pot or small microwave-safe bowl in 30-second bursts, melt the white chocolate. Using a pastry brush (a silicone one works best for this job), brush the "mop" bases with streaks of white chocolate to create the strings of the mops. Repeat with all four mops, setting them back on the baking sheet as you go.

Once all the mops have been decorated, take a small amount of leftover white chocolate, about 1 tablespoon, and dye it green with the green food colouring. Use a small spatula or demitasse spoon to decorate the front of the vacuum with the green white chocolate. Use a small dot of the green chocolate to stick a 15-cm piece of liquorice (if using) to the back as the cord.

Using the remaining white chocolate as a base, add the peanut butter chips and melt in the microwave in 30-second bursts, stirring until combined and smooth. Use a clean pastry brush (again silicone is best in this case) to brush on the broom bristles. Refrigerate all the cake pops for 5 to 7 minutes, or until all the chocolate is set.

The cake pops can be stored in an airtight container between layers of parchment paper for up to four days. They can also be wrapped in cellophane bags and given as gifts.

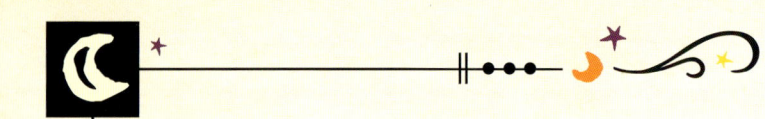

Winnie's Magical Popping Candy

Winifred Sanderson has countless spells up her sleeve. She can turn a boy into a cat ... or steal the youth from an unsuspecting child. And she's been known to put on quite the show by using her magic to create all kinds of fantastical explosions! With shocking bursts of sweetness, this popping candy conjures up the spirit of a firecracker of a witch. It's destined to be a true crowd-pleaser – one that's absolutely bubbling with flavour!

Yield: 480 ml | GF, V, V+

1 teaspoon baking soda (see note)
200 grams sugar
2 tablespoons golden syrup
½ teaspoon rock salt
2 to 3 drops bright green food colouring
¼ teaspoon orange extract

Specialist Tools
Sugar thermometer

Note
Make sure your baking soda is active and not expired.

Line a rimmed baking sheet with parchment paper and set aside.

In a medium, heavy-bottomed saucepan, carefully pour the sugar into the centre of the pan. Pour 2 tablespoons water and the golden syrup around the edge. Place the pan over a medium heat and use a wooden spoon to gently pull the moisture through the sugar. Once all the sugar is moistened, clip a sugar thermometer to the side of the pan and let the mixture boil without stirring until it reaches 150°C.

Remove from the heat, add the baking soda all at once, and stir. Be careful as the mixture will bubble and foam! Keep stirring until all the powder has been incorporated. Add the food colouring and orange extract and stir until even in colour. Pour out on to the prepared baking sheet, and spread into an even layer. You will not necessarily cover the whole sheet. Allow to cool completely and then immediately break into small chunks and store in an airtight container for up to one week.

Desserts

Black River Brownie Bars

The Sanderson sisters haven't been around for the past three hundred years. In that time, the world has witnessed many advances – cars, buses and the roads necessary to convey gorgeous creatures, such as the sisters, from here to there. But while those roads may look a fair bit like a black river, their namesake brownies are far from firm as stone. With black cocoa, dark chocolate chips and a black river cream cheese swirl, these brownie bars are a mouthwatering treat!

Yield: About 12 bars | V

- 110 grams dark cooking chocolate, broken into small pieces
- 180 grams salted butter
- 250 grams granulated sugar
- 220 grams dark brown sugar
- 4 large eggs
- 1½ teaspoons vanilla extract
- 120 grams plain flour
- 120 grams dark chocolate chips
- 3 tablespoons black cocoa powder (see note)
- 225 grams cream cheese, softened

Preheat the oven to 180°C.

Line a 22-by-28-cm baking sheet with parchment paper so that the paper hangs over the ends.

In a large microwave-safe bowl, combine the cooking chocolate and butter. Microwave for 1 minute and stir to completely melt chocolate and butter. If needed, microwave 30 seconds more. Add 200 grams of the granulated sugar and the brown sugar, stirring to combine.

Add three of the eggs, one at a time, stirring briskly after each addition. Add 1 teaspoon of the vanilla, stirring to combine. Add the flour and stir to completely combine.

Remove about ½ cup from the batter and set aside. Mix the chocolate chips into the remaining portion of brownie batter, then spread the mixture evenly on the bottom of the prepared baking sheet.

In a clean medium bowl, use a hand mixer on a medium speed to beat the cream cheese, remaining 50 grams of sugar, remaining ½ teaspoon of vanilla, remaining 1 egg and the black cocoa until light and fluffy, 1 to 2 minutes.

Spread the cream cheese mixture over the brownie mixture. Dot the cream cheese mixture with the remaining brownie mixture and use a knife to swirl. Bake for 35 to 40 minutes, or until a skewer inserted into the centre comes out fudgy but not wet.

Allow to cool completely before cutting and serving. Store in an airtight container for up to three days.

Notes

Black cocoa powder is available online and in specialist stores. It will give your brownies an extra dark colour and unique depth of flavour. However, regular cocoa powder can be substituted.

For the cleanest cuts, chill the brownies on the baking sheet in the refrigerator for about 30 minutes.

Desserts

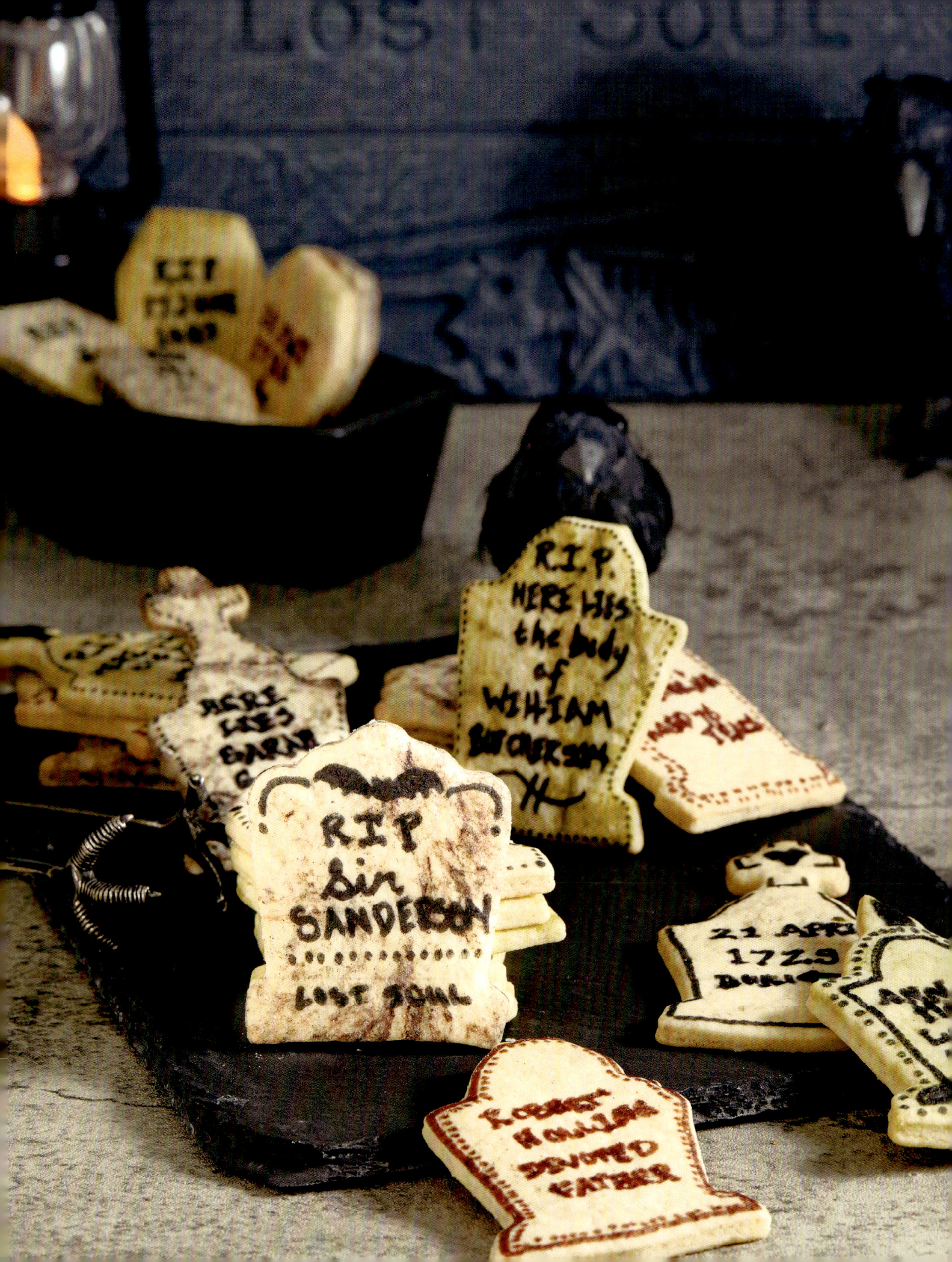

Gravestone Sugar Cookies

"Three hundred years ago, the Sanderson sisters bewitched people … and now they've returned from the grave!" While Max's declaration was met with derision, these graveyard-inspired desserts will tickle the fancy of even the most hostile crowd. With black cocoa, matcha and allspice, and a clever marble technique that evokes the essence of the *grave* beyond, these sugar cookies will be a huge Halloween hit.

Yield: *About 36 cookies* | V

240 grams plus 1 tablespoon plain flour

2 teaspoons baking powder

½ teaspoon rock salt

120 grams unsalted butter, softened

100 grams sugar

1 teaspoon vanilla extract

2 large eggs

½ teaspoon black cocoa powder

½ teaspoon matcha powder

¼ teaspoon ground allspice

Specialist Tools

Gravestone-shaped cookie cutters

Edible ink markers

In a small bowl, mix together 240 grams of the flour, the baking powder and salt. Set aside.

In a large bowl, using a hand mixer on a medium speed, cream together the butter and sugar until light and fluffy, 1 to 2 minutes. Add the vanilla, stir to combine, then add the eggs, one at a time, beating after each addition. Add the flour mixture all at once and beat until it resembles soft crumbles.

Add a third of dough crumbles to each of two small bowls. Add the cocoa powder to one bowl and knead until just mixed but so the dough is still marbled. Repeat this process with the matcha powder and the other bowl of dough.

Add the remaining 1 tablespoon flour and the allspice to the remaining dough. Form each dough into a disc, wrap it in parchment paper and refrigerate for at least 1 hour.

Preheat the oven to 190°C. Line two baking sheets with parchment paper or silicone baking mats.

Roll out each flavour of dough to about ½ cm thick and cut with gravestone-shaped cookie cutters, placing them on the prepared baking sheets as you go, spacing them about 1 cm apart. Refrigerate the scraps of each dough. Once you've cut cookies out from all three doughs, use the scraps to create a marble of all three flavours. Cut out additional gravestones. Chill the cookies in the refrigerator for at least 15 minutes before baking.

Bake for 7 to 9 minutes, or until just beginning to brown at the edges and firm to the touch. Allow to cool completely on a wire rack.

To decorate the cookies, use edible ink markers to write and draw gravestone details.

Desserts

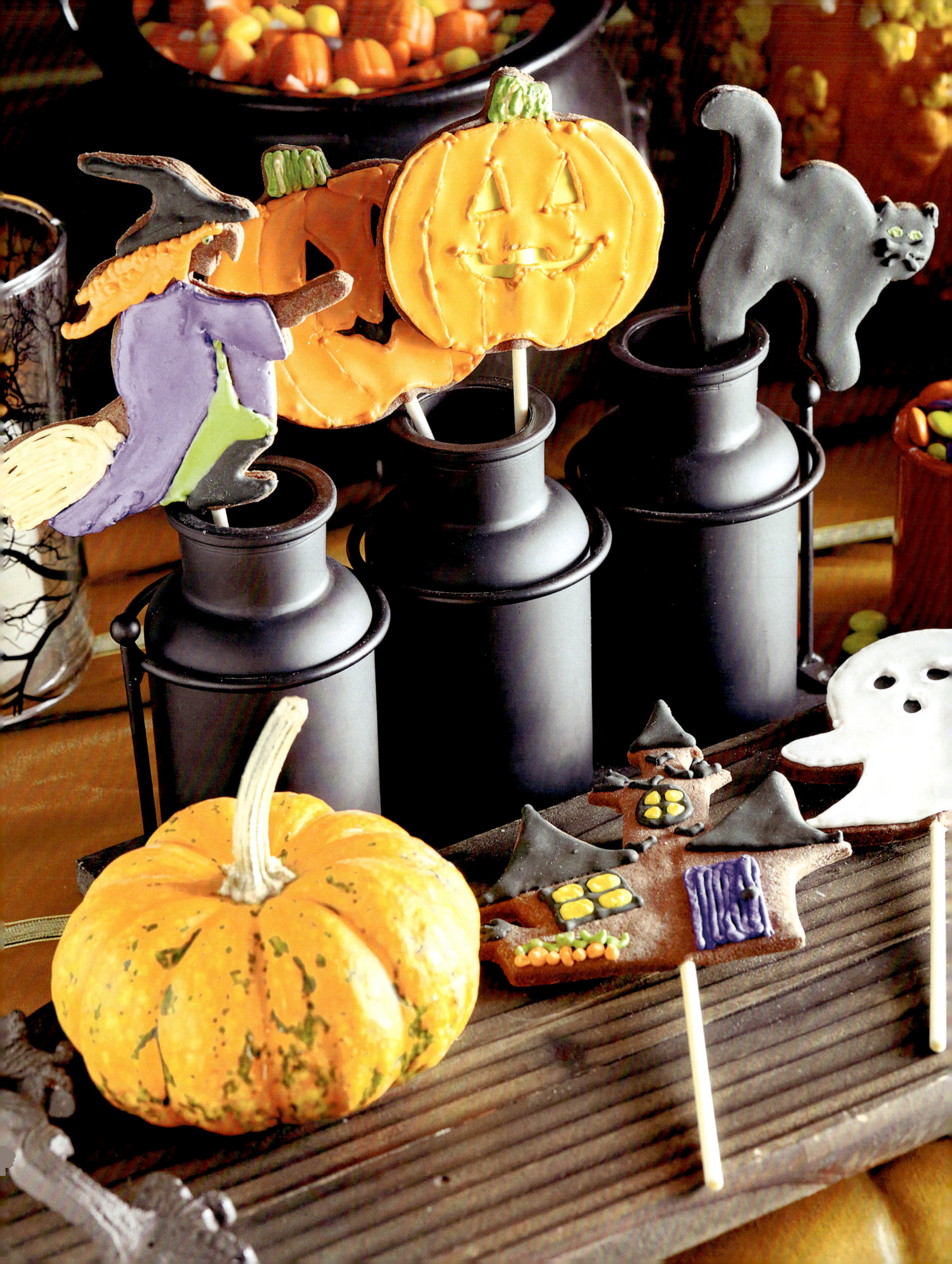

Witch Cookie Lollies

The sisters three are somewhat fair,
With warty skin and wild hair.
But come the morning they'll reclaim
Their youth and looks – in Master's name.
This witchy lolly will bring them glee –

Their likeness on a grand cookie!
'Twas loved by Dani when she tried
A lolly while at Allison's side.
So make a batch. Look to the sky
Where broomsticks soar. "Sisters! We fly!"

Yield: About 16 cookie lollies | V

For the Cookies

180 grams salted butter, softened
110 grams cream cheese, softened
150 grams sugar
60 grams cocoa powder
1 teaspoon vanilla extract
1 large egg
300 grams plain flour

For the Royal Icing

400 grams icing sugar, sifted
3 tablespoons egg white powder
1 to 2 drops black, green, purple, yellow and/or orange food colouring

Specialist Tools

Halloween cookie cutters
Sixteen 15-cm paper lollipop sticks
Pastry bags and writing tips

To make the cookies: In a large bowl, using a hand mixer or the bowl of a food mixer fitted with the paddle attachment, beat the butter on a medium-high speed until light and fluffy, 1 to 2 minutes. Add the cream cheese and beat again until the mixture is smooth, fluffy and pale. Add the sugar and mix until completely incorporated. Add the cocoa powder and vanilla and mix again until completely incorporated. Add the egg and mix again. Add the flour in two batches, mixing after each addition, until completely incorporated.

Split the dough into two pieces, flatten into discs, wrap in parchment paper and chill in the refrigerator for at least 1 hour.

Working with one disc at a time, roll out the dough to about 3 mm thick on a lightly floured silicone baking mat (see note). Using Halloween cookie cutters, cut out the desired shapes and peel off the excess dough. Rewrap and chill scraps to roll out more cookies.

Using an offset spatula, gently lift the bottom half of each cookie and place a lollipop stick under it. Make sure the stick has lots of cookie coverage, at least 5 cm, even if it needs to be at an angle for some shapes. Set the cookie back down on to the stick and use your fingers to gently press the dough on to the stick. Slide the baking mat on to a baking sheet and chill in the refrigerator for 15 minutes before baking.

While the cookies are chilling, preheat the oven to 180°C. Roll out more dough on another baking mat and cut out more cookies, repeating the steps above. Chill each batch for at least 15 minutes before baking.

When the cookies have chilled, bake them for 9 to 11 minutes, or until firm in the middle and starting to barely crisp around the edges. Allow to cool on the baking mat on a wire rack.

continued on page 114

Desserts

continued from page 113

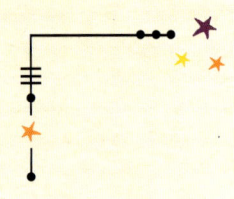

To make the icing: In the bowl of a food mixer fitted with the whisk attachment, combine the icing sugar, egg white powder and 6 tablespoons water. Whisk on a low speed for 7 to 10 minutes, or until the icing holds stiff peaks. (If using a hand mixer, whisk on a high speed for 10 to 12 minutes.) Divide the icing into small bowls and use the food colouring to create your desired colours. Transfer the icing to pastry bags fitted with writing tips.

To decorate, turn each cookie over, exposing the lollipop stick, and pipe a thin stripe of icing in your desired colour over the stick. Allow to dry for 30 to 40 minutes before turning over and decorating as desired. Allow the cookies to dry completely before serving, packaging or storing, at least 3 hours. Store in an airtight container between layers of parchment paper or place each cookie in a cellophane bag for gifting.

Notes

Rolling out your cookies directly on the baking mat means you won't need to move delicate shapes. Just lift away the excess dough, leaving behind your cutouts.

While black icing is a go-to choice for Halloween, it can also stain fabrics. If serving cookies to small children, you may want to let the chocolate dough stand in for the black icing or use other creative colours! After all, the Sanderson sisters never wear basic black! Black icing can also temporarily stain tongues and lips, but this can add to the Halloween fun!

Desserts

Desserts   115

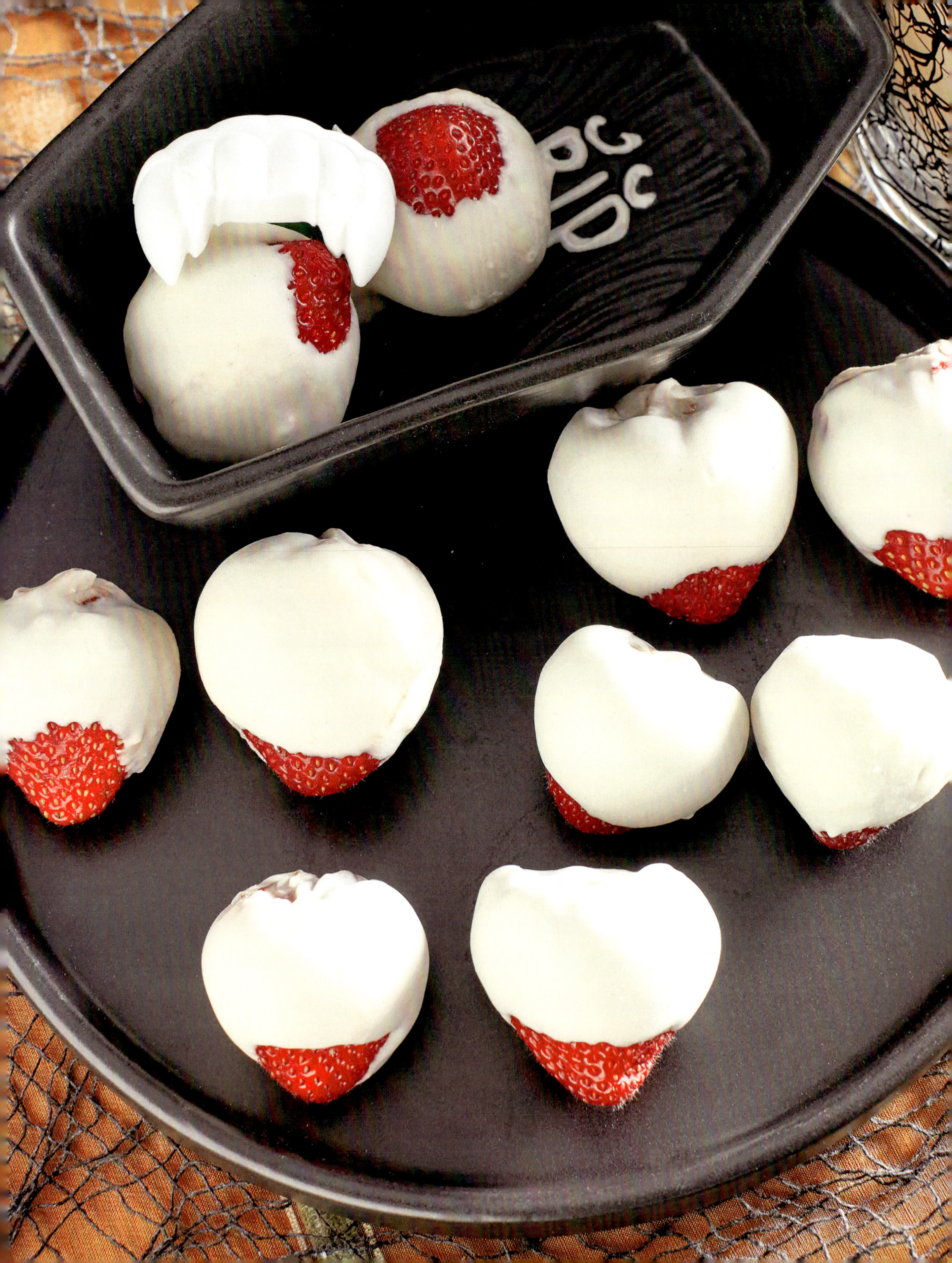
RIP

Dad-cula Fang Strawberries

Only the coolest dads can pull off a *dad*-cula vampire costume. But *anyone* can whip up these treats, which are inspired by the truly incomparable Mr Dennison. Fresh strawberries pair gloriously with a dark chocolate filling and white chocolate coating, yielding a succulently sweet creation that's sure to have dads, mums and children alike dancing with joy.

Yield: *About 24 fangs* | GF, V

- 450 grams strawberries, rinsed and hulled
- 2 tablespoons double cream
- 60 grams dark chocolate chips
- About 425 grams white chocolate melting wafers

Dry the strawberries well. Have a mini muffin tray standing by.

In a medium microwave-safe bowl, pour the double cream over the chocolate chips. Microwave in 30-second bursts for 1 minute, let the ganache stand for 3 minutes, then stir until well melted.

Using a small spoon, fill each strawberry cavity with ganache and rest in a mini muffin hole. Once all the strawberries have been filled with ganache, put the mini muffin tray in the refrigerator for 15 minutes to set.

Line a baking sheet with parchment paper and keep it close by. In a separate small, microwave-safe bowl, melt the white chocolate in 30-second bursts two to three times, stirring after each time, until completely smooth.

Dip each strawberry, chocolate-filled-side down, leaving the tip of each strawberry exposed. Work quickly so as not to melt the chocolate. Shake off excess chocolate and place the strawberry on the prepared baking sheet. Once all the strawberries have been coated, refrigerate for 5 minutes to set.

Serve immediately or store in an airtight container between layers of parchment paper for up to 24 hours.

Desserts

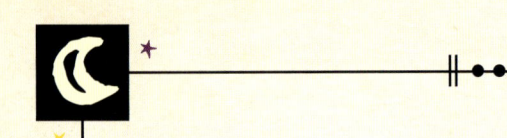

Twisted Winifred Spirals

Winifred Sanderson's towering crimson buns that playfully sit atop her head lend an air of mischief to her formidable persona. Just like the witchy sister herself, these spirals combine a dash of sweetness with a dose of spice. Cinnamon, cayenne and a few spoonfuls of sugar melt into a buttery puff pastry to create the ultimate mini palmier – no spells required!

Yield: *About 40 spirals* | V

150 grams finely chopped pecans, toasted (see note)

100 grams sugar

1 tablespoon ground cinnamon

¼ teaspoon ground cayenne

One 480 gram packet puff pastry, thawed

30 grams salted butter, melted

Red sanding sugar for decorating (optional)

> **Note**
>
> To toast nuts, heat a small stainless-steel or cast-iron pan on the stove over a medium-high heat for about 1 minute. Add the nuts, stir and then remove the pan from the heat. Continue to stir the nuts until fragrant, about 2 minutes.

In a small bowl, combine the cooled toasted nuts with the sugar, cinnamon and cayenne and set aside.

Roll out each piece of puff pastry on a lightly floured surface into a 30-by-30-cm square.

On a large piece of parchment paper or silicone baking mat, sprinkle about a quarter of the nut mixture on the surface, covering approximately a 30-by-30-cm space. Cover the mixture with one of the pastry squares. Roll over the square with a rolling pin to press the pastry into the nut mixture. Brush the top of the pastry piece with half of the melted butter and scatter another quarter of the nut mixture on to the top of the pastry, spreading out evenly and to the edges. Roll the rolling pin over the top one more time to press the nut mixture on to the dough.

Fold each side towards the middle so the two edges meet dead centre, gather nut mixture from underneath, and press it into any blank parts of the pastry. Fold each side in half again and then fold the entire piece in half at the centre seam. You should have a long rectangle made of eight layers of pastry. Some nut mixture may be left behind; use this for the next piece. Place the dough on a baking sheet and place it in the freezer for 15 minutes. Repeat with the second piece of pastry.

While the pastry is chilling, preheat the oven to 200°C. Line a baking sheet with parchment paper or a silicone baking mat.

Remove the pastry from the freezer and slice into ½-cm-thick slices. Place them on the prepared baking sheet, spaced 2.5 cm apart. Sprinkle with red sanding sugar (if using) and bake for 12 to 15 minutes, or until golden brown and crisp.

Allow to cool on the baking sheet and then serve or store in an airtight container for up to three days.

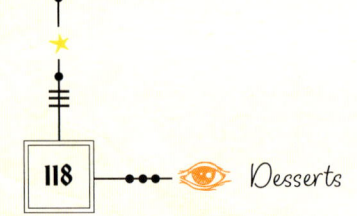

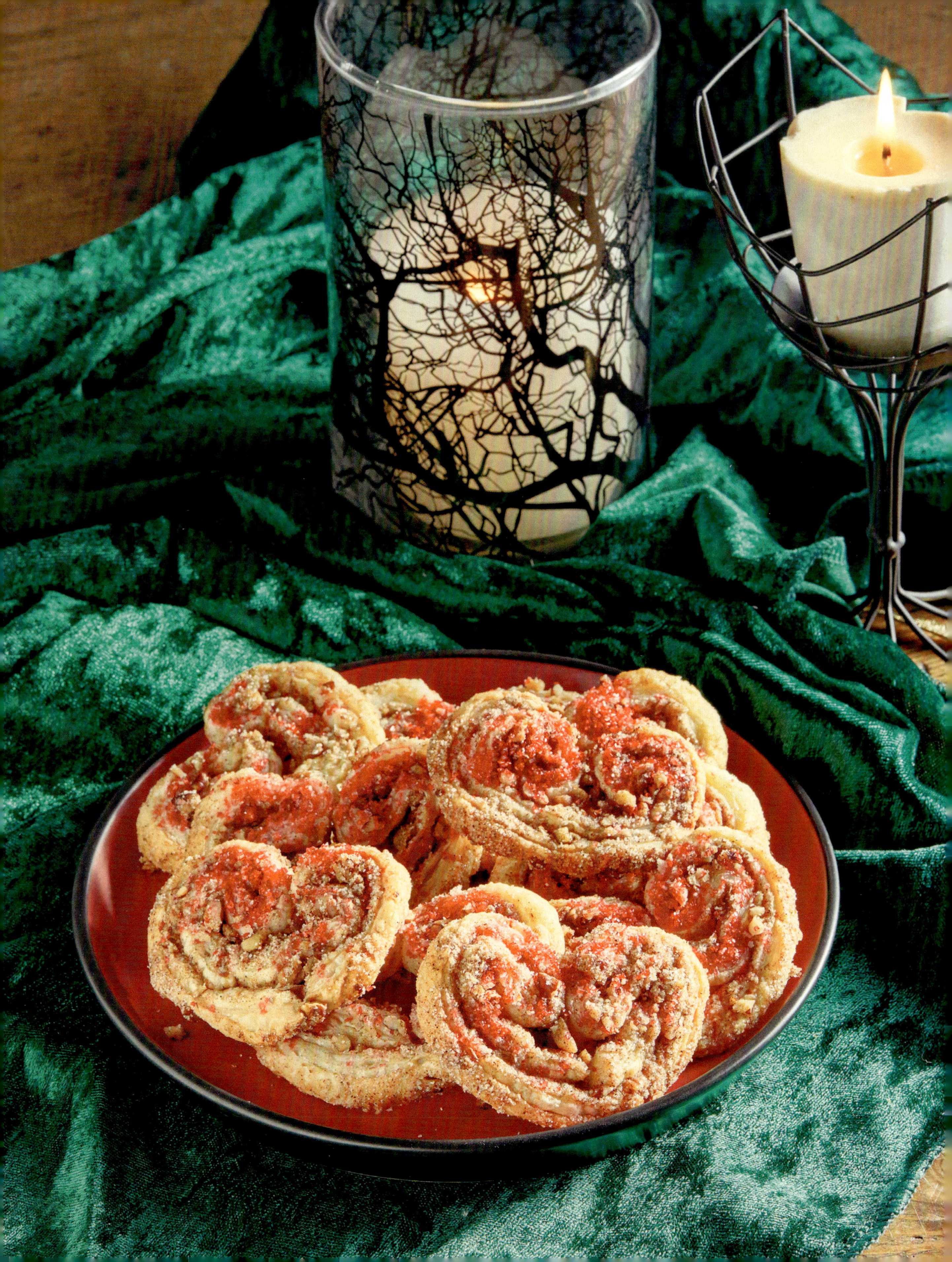

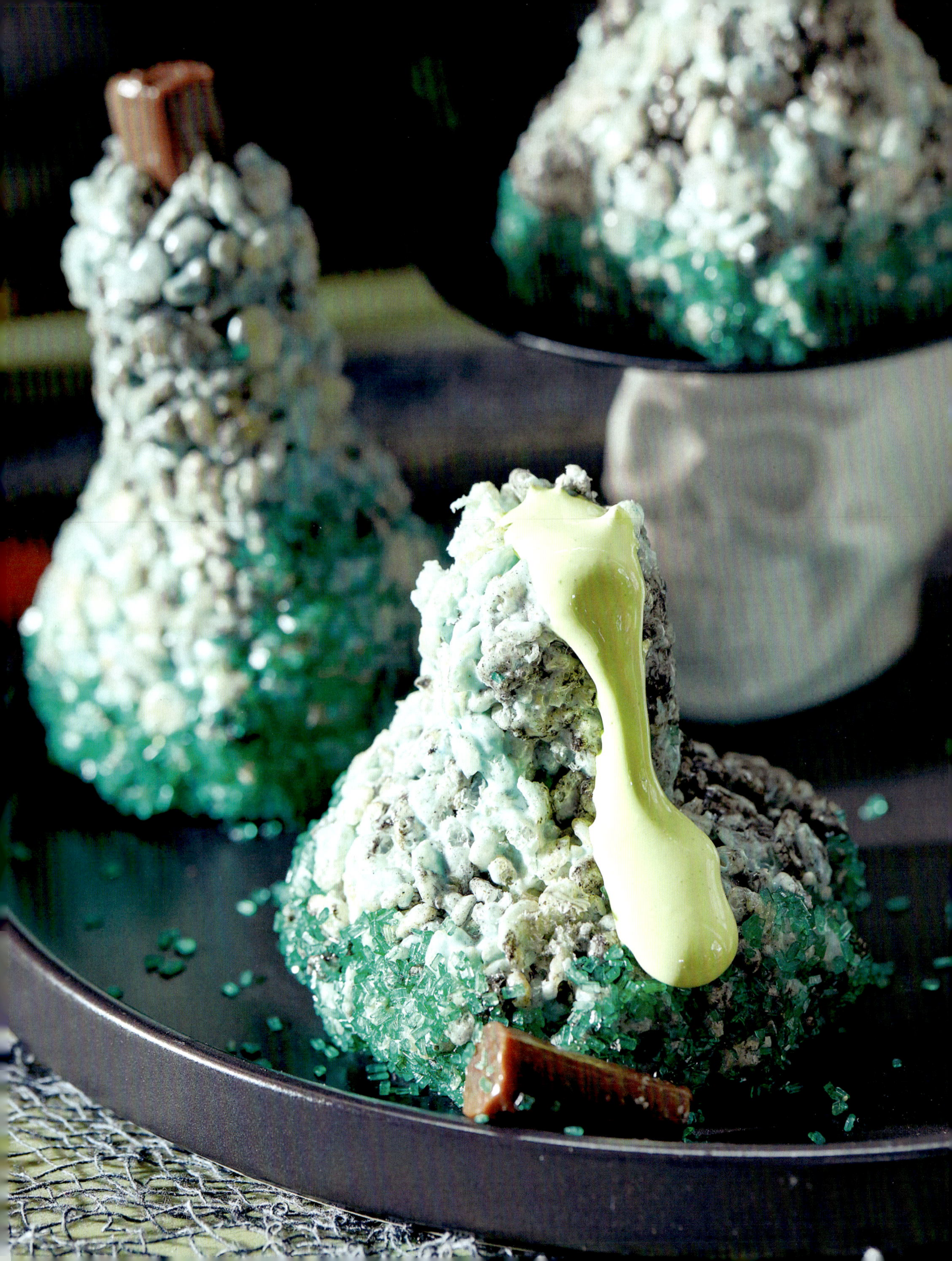

Puffed Rice Potion Bottles

Some potions steal youth. Some strip children of their baby fat. And others exist for the sole purpose of bringing lots and lots of happiness. These blue and green potion bottles cheerfully camp in the happiness category. With rich butter, fluffy marshmallows and a sprinkle of cocoa powder, this potion is sure to enchant even the most wayward of witches.

Yield: About 8 potion bottles | **GF***

- 150 grams puffed rice cereal
- 280 grams marshmallows
- 30 grams salted butter, plus more for greasing marshmallow bowl and hands
- 1 to 2 drops light blue food colouring
- 1 to 2 drops bright green food colouring
- 200 grams marshmallow fluff
- 2 teaspoons black cocoa powder
- 200 grams sugar crystals
- 8 chocolate chew candies, unwrapped

Specialist Tools
Pastry bag

Note: This recipe can be easily made gluten-free by using gluten-free rice cereal.

Place the rice cereal in a large bowl. Grease a large microwave-safe bowl with butter and melt the marshmallows and 30 grams butter in 30-second bursts. Stir until completely melted. Add the blue food colouring and stir until well incorporated.

Add the marshmallow mixture to the rice cereal and stir until completely combined.

In a small bowl, add the green food colouring to the marshmallow fluff, then transfer to a pastry bag. Set aside.

Add the cocoa powder to the cereal mixture and stir until incorporated. Do not overmix so you have a mottled colouring.

Place the sanding sugar on a shallow plate and have the chocolate chew candies standing by. Snip a small hole in the bottom of the pastry bag.

On a non-stick surface, such as parchment paper or a silicone baking mat, start to mould your "potion bottles". Grease your hands with a little butter and, using a 1-cup scoop of cereal mixture, mould it into a rough ball shape. Make a well in the middle and fill with about 1 tablespoon of marshmallow fluff. Close the cereal mixture over the marshmallow fluff and start building up to create the neck of the potion bottle. Keep compacting as you go but be careful not to squish out the marshmallow fluff. Use the parchment to flatten the base of the bottle so it will stand upright on its own.

To finish off your bottle, create a small hole in the top to place the chocolate chew candy (the "cork"). Press the cereal mixture around it.

Place the finished potion bottle bottom into the sanding sugar and push sugar up the sides about 2 or 3 cm to create the "potion". Repeat this process until all of the rice cereal mixture is gone, greasing your hands as necessary.

These can be stored in an airtight container for up to five days or in sealed cellophane bags to give as gifts.

Desserts | 121

Tart Face Tart

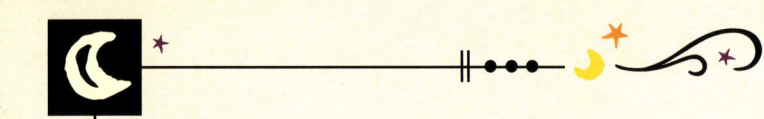

Master's wife is *not* impressed when the tantalising trio appears in her living room. Between Sarah's enchanting dance, Winifred's wicked sass and Mary's overly familiar approach of making herself at home, the "little woman" quickly sours on her company. But it's her nickname for her unwanted guests that inspires this perfectly prickly treat. Berries fold neatly into a no-bake biscuit crumb crust, making these tarts the ultimate dish to serve to company – invited or otherwise!

Yield: *8 servings* | GF*, V

For the Filling
225 grams cream cheese, softened
100 grams sugar
1 tablespoon sour cream
1 tablespoon fresh lime juice
120 ml double cream

For the Crust
200 grams shortbread crumbs
Zest of 1 lime
50 grams sugar
90 grams salted butter, melted

For the Berry Topping
170 grams golden or red raspberries
Juice from 1 lime
2 tablespoons superfine sugar
110 grams blueberries
110 grams strawberries (optional)

Specialist Tools
22-cm tart tin

To make the filling: In a medium bowl, using a hand mixer or in the bowl of a food mixer fitted with the paddle attachment, cream together the cream cheese, sugar, sour cream and lime juice on a medium speed until light and fluffy, 1 to 2 minutes. Set aside. In another medium bowl, whip the cream on a high speed until stiff peaks form and then fold it into the cream cheese mixture. Cover and refrigerate while making the crust.

To make the crust: Preheat the oven to 180°C.

In a medium bowl, mix together the biscuit crumbs, lime zest, sugar and melted butter. Pour the crumb mixture into a 22-cm tart tin and press it evenly on the bottom and up the sides.

Bake for 10 to 12 minutes, or until slightly golden. Remove from the oven and allow to cool completely on a wire rack. Baking the crust briefly makes for the easiest slicing, but for a truly no-bake version, freeze the crust for 15 or 20 minutes, until firm, before filling.

Once the tart shell is cool, spread the filling mixture into the pan and smooth it out evenly. Refrigerate for at least 2 hours or overnight.

continued on page 124

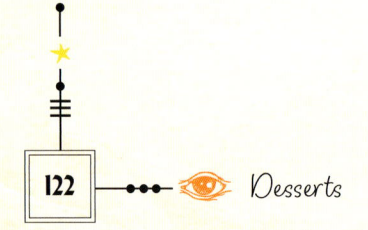

Desserts

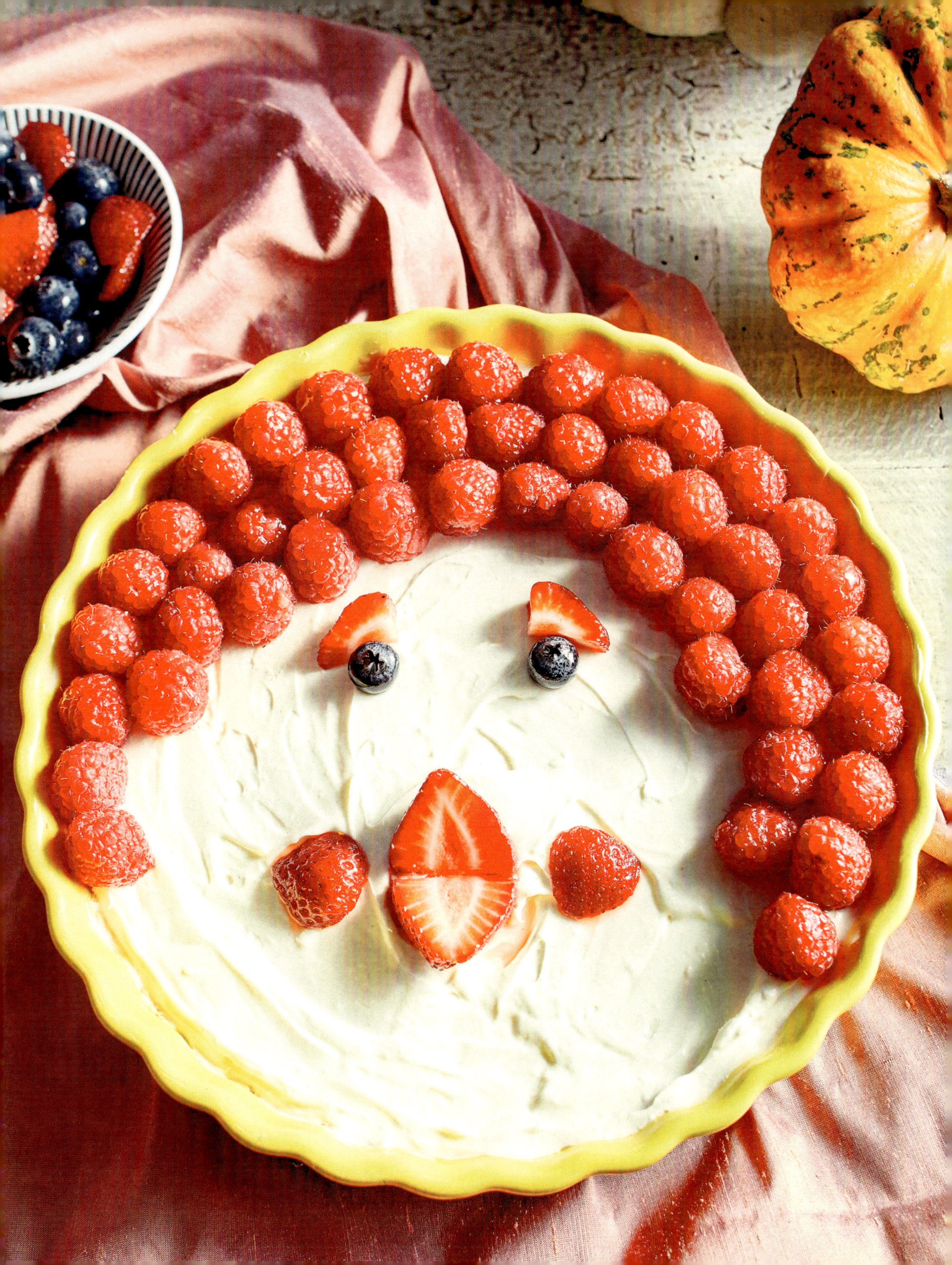

continued from page 122

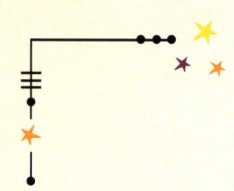

To make the topping: When ready to serve, rinse the raspberries and place them on layered paper towels to dry completely. In a small bowl, mix together the lime juice and sugar, then set aside. Rinse the blueberries, drain thoroughly and add them to the lime mixture, stirring to coat. Rinse, hull and slice the strawberries (if using), then add them to the lime mixture, stirring to combine.

Arrange the raspberries along the top edge of the tart in two or three rows, creating "hair". Use a pastry brush to brush the berries with some of the juices from the bowl. Create eyes, blushing cheeks and lips with some of the blueberries and strawberries. When serving, ladle extra berries and juice over each slice.

Notes

The shortbread should be processed in a food processor until they are evenly crushed and sandy in texture. Measure out 200 grams for the tart crust. You may have extra crumbs.

This recipe can be easily made gluten-free by using your favourite gluten-free biscuits in the crust.

Desserts

Cat Tongue Cookies

When Thackery Binx goes missing, his father is beside himself. He demands that Winnie tell him what she's done, but Winnie slyly declares that the cat's got her tongue. These classic cookies offer a cheeky nod to Winnie's coy comment. Thin French cookie crisps with black tahini make this dessert so delicious, they won't stay a secret for long. Looks like the cat's out of the bag!

Yield: About 36 cookies | V

120 grams unsalted butter
2 tablespoons black tahini
1 teaspoon vanilla extract
50 grams icing sugar
¼ teaspoon ground cardamom
3 egg whites
1 large egg
90 grams plain flour

Specialist Tools
Pastry bag

Note
These cookies have a delicate flavour that pairs with your favourite cup of brew or Pumpkin Spiced Golden Milk (page 142).

Preheat the oven to 180°C. Line two baking sheets with parchment paper or silicone baking mats.

In a medium bowl, using a hand mixer on a medium-high speed, cream together the butter, tahini and vanilla, until light and fluffy. Add the icing sugar and cardamom and mix until incorporated. Slowly add the egg whites, mixing continually until completely incorporated, and then add the egg, mixing until the mixture is light and fluffy. Slowly add the flour, folding it in with a rubber spatula and scraping down the sides of the bowl as you go.

Load the batter into a pastry bag, then snip a 1-cm hole into the bottom. With the tip of the pastry bag raised off the surface of the baking sheet by approximately ½ cm, pipe 6- to 7-cm strips of batter spaced at least 7.5 cm apart. Repeat until both prepared baking sheets are full.

Bake, rotating halfway through if necessary, for 6 to 8 minutes, or until the edges are crisp and the centres are set. Allow to cool on the baking sheets before removing and storing in an airtight container for up to two days.

Desserts

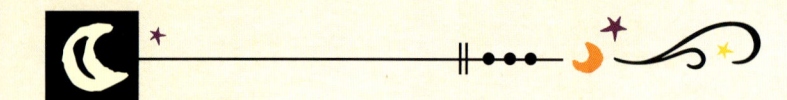

"Bonjour!" Crème Brûlée

Jacob Bailey High School offers a well-rounded education. From maths and science to history and French, its students are guaranteed to graduate with an expanse of academic experiences. Those with artistic proclivities may wish to avail themselves of the ceramics studio – where a blazing kiln fires completed pieces … or unwitting witches. And while a pairing of French immersion and pottery is an undoubtedly unusual choice, even the Sandersons would appreciate this gently flamed crème brûlée – especially if it's being served alongside a certain book of spells! *Bonjour, je veux mon livre!*

Yield: 6 servings | GF, V

3 large eggs

100 grams granulated sugar

480 ml double cream

1 teaspoon vanilla extract

60 grams "No Witches Here" Pumpkin Butter (page 30)

165 grams coarse sugar, such as raw or turbinado

1 teaspoon ground cinnamon

Specialist Tools
Kitchen torch (see note)

Preheat the oven to 150°C. Place six 110 gram ramekins in a roasting tray.

In a medium bowl, combine the eggs and granulated sugar until just blended. Gradually stir in the cream until everything is well blended and smooth. Strain through a fine-mesh sieve into a large measuring jug. Stir in the vanilla and gently swirl in the pumpkin butter.

Split the batter evenly between the ramekins. Place the roasting tray in the oven and use a clean measuring jug to fill the tray with water until it reaches three-quarters of the way up the ramekins.

Bake for 30 to 40 minutes, until the custards are set but still slightly quivering in the centre. Remove the custards from the water bath and allow to cool to room temperature. Cover and refrigerate for at least 2 hours or up to two days.

When ready to serve, mix together the coarse sugar and cinnamon in a small bowl. Sprinkle the sugar mixture over the top of each custard until it covers it completely. Use a kitchen torch to brûlée the sugar until completely melted. Allow the custards to sit for 5 minutes before serving.

> **Note**
>
> Don't have a torch? Place the oven rack in its highest position and turn the grill on high. Place all the custards on a baking sheet and place in the oven, watching carefully until the sugar is completely melted and browning in spots, about 1 minute.

Desserts

Fly Ice Cream

It's a generally known fact that witches have rather peculiar tastes. Foods that humans might consider to be repulsive are often considered quite the witchy delicacy. But witches and mere mortals can *all* scream – in a good way, of course – for fly ice cream! With sugar, cream and rum raisins, this particular dessert is positively out of this world.

Yield: 8 servings | GF, V

- 120 ml spiced rum
- 110 grams brown sugar
- 300 ml double cream
- 400 grams can sweetened condensed milk
- 400 grams black raisins, plus more for garnish

In a small saucepan over a medium heat, bring the rum and brown sugar to a simmer. Cook, stirring often, for 5 to 7 minutes, or until the mixture thickens and the sugar is dissolved. Allow to cool and set aside.

In the bowl of a food mixer fitted with the whisk attachment, whip the cream on a high speed until stiff peaks form,. Fold in the condensed milk and transfer to a large, shallow container with an airtight lid. Freeze for 2 hours, then fold in the rum syrup and raisins.

Return to the freezer and let freeze for a minimum of 4 hours, but overnight is preferable. To serve, scoop into dishes and top with more raisin "flies" if desired.

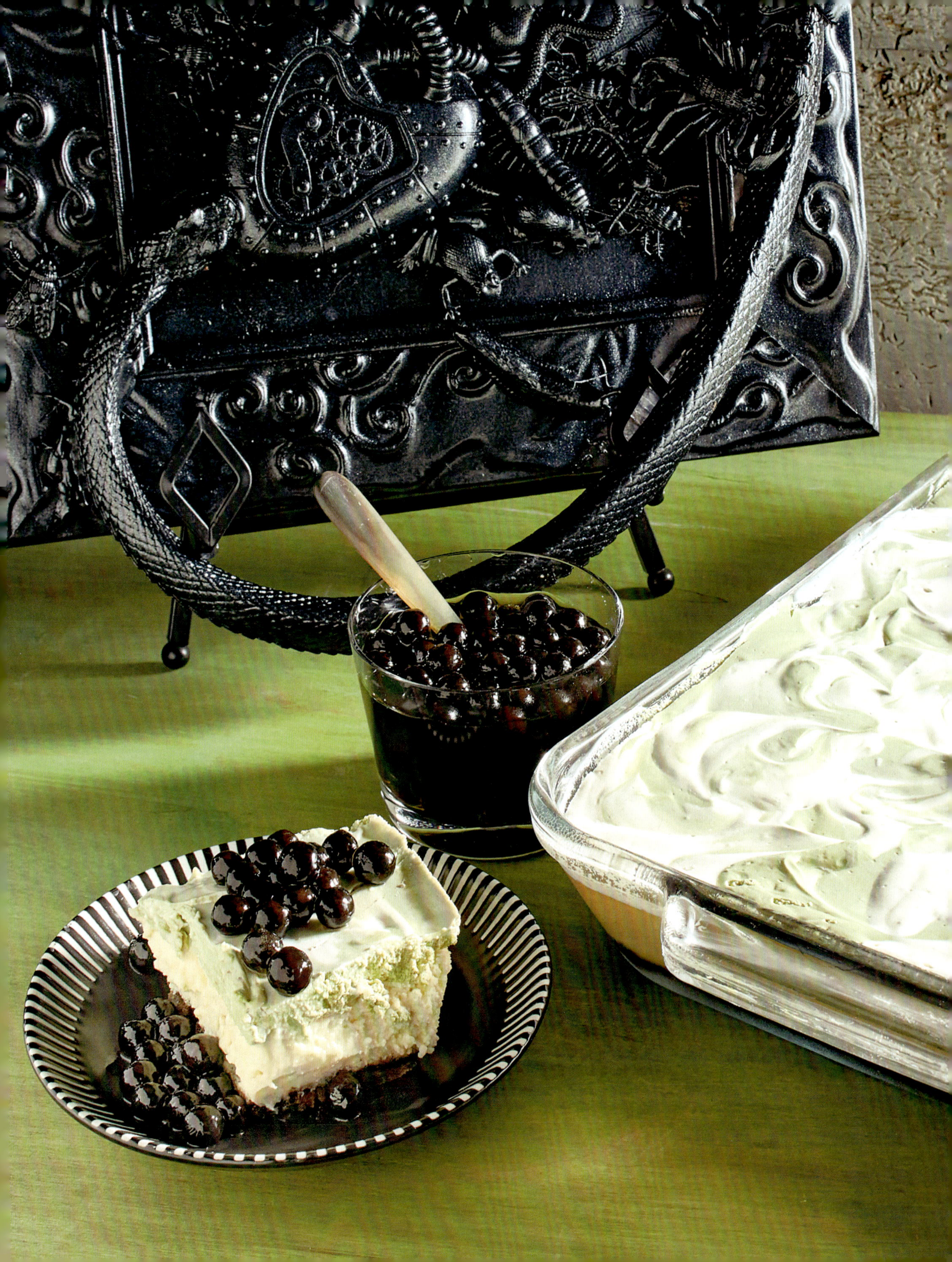

Frogspawn Boba Matcha Cheesecake

Eye of newt and spawn of frog . . .
Wait – no newt! That's for the glogg.
Substitute some cream cheese, then
Add in eggs, sugar (again),

Magic too – lest it be bland.
(Don't get banished from the land!)
With a swirl, you too shall make
A boba matcha cheesecake!

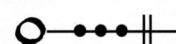

Yield: 1 cheesecake or 14 to 16 servings | GF*, V

For the Crust
- 280 grams crushed ginger biscuits
- 120 grams unsalted butter, melted
- 3 tablespoons granulated sugar
- 1 tablespoon black cocoa powder

For the Cheesecake
- Four 225 grams blocks cream cheese
- 2 tablespoons fresh lemon juice
- 1 tablespoon vanilla extract
- 300 grams granulated sugar
- 5 large eggs

For the Matcha Topping
- 960 ml sour cream
- 100 grams granulated sugar
- 1 teaspoon vanilla extract
- 1½ tablespoons matcha

For the Boba and Syrup
- 100 grams granulated sugar
- 110 grams dark brown sugar
- 200 grams prepared brown sugar boba pearls

> **Note**
> This recipe can be easily made gluten-free by using your favourite gluten-free biscuits in the crust.

Preheat the oven to 180°C and have an 28-by-38-cm glass casserole dish standing by.

To make the crust: In the casserole dish, mix the crushed biscuits, melted butter, sugar and cocoa powder until well combined. Press the mixture until it evenly covers the bottom of the dish. Bake for 8 to 10 minutes, or until crisp and fragrant.

To make the cheesecake: While the crust bakes, combine the cream cheese, lemon juice and vanilla in the bowl of a food mixer fitted with the paddle attachment. Beat on a medium speed until light and fluffy. Add the sugar and beat again until well combined. Add the eggs one at a time, beating to combine after each addition.

Pour the batter on to the crust and spread out evenly. Return the dish to the oven and bake for 30 to 40 minutes, or until the edges are puffed and the centre is firm but wobbly.

To make the matcha topping: While the cheesecake bakes, have two medium bowls standing by. Divide the sour cream and sugar evenly between each bowl and stir to combine. Add the vanilla to one bowl and stir to combine. Add the matcha to the other bowl and stir to combine.

When the cheesecake base is done and out of the oven, use separate spoons to spoon generous dollops of each sour cream topping, alternating between the two flavours. Use a knife to swirl the two flavours together. Return the cheesecake to the oven and bake for 7 to 9 minutes more, or until the topping has set. Allow to cool completely on a wire rack, then cover and refrigerate until serving.

continued on page 130

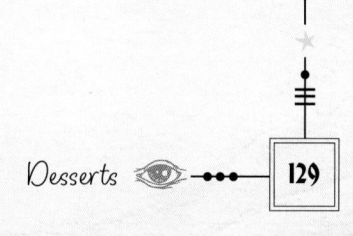

Desserts

continued from page 129

To make the boba syrup: In a small saucepan over a medium-high heat, add 240 ml water, granulated sugar and brown sugar. Bring to the boil, then turn the heat to medium-low and simmer for 1 minute. Remove from the heat and add the prepared boba pearls. Cover and allow to cool.

This syrup can be stored at room temperature for up to 4 hours or in the refrigerator overnight. Refrigerated boba pearls will have a firmer texture.

To serve, slice the chilled cheesecake into 7.5-by-7.5-cm squares and, using a slotted spoon, top with boba pearls.

Dust Bombs

Allison is well versed in the story of the Sandersons. While the black flame candle has brought the witches back to Salem for one night only, unless they can steal the life force of children, they'll be dust when the sun comes up. And when Winnie, Mary and Sarah ultimately depart our earthly realm, they're desprongd to do so in a burst of glitter – a veritable dust bomb! This sparkling orb – concocted with edible glitter, sprinkles and a handful of mini marshmallows – is perfect for breaking over ice cream ... or any dessert that could benefit from just a touch of magic.

Yield: 3 bombs | GF

200 grams dark chocolate melts

2 tablespoons purple sprinkles (see note)

1 teaspoon purple sparkle sugar

2 tablespoons red sprinkles

1 teaspoon red sparkle sugar

2 tablespoons green sprinkles

1 teaspoon green sparkle sugar

15 grams mini marshmallows

Lustre dust in purple, red and green (optional)

Note

Have fun with the sprinkle sugar combos. The method is just a suggestion. Create a custom mix for each sister using their signature colours and even a tiny spider, rat or bone. These are great to serve with two scoops of your favourite ice cream. Crack them open to "explode" sprinkles over the top.

Place one sphere mould on a baking sheet. In a medium microwave-safe bowl, melt the chocolate melts in 30-second bursts, stirring in between, for up to 90 seconds, until smooth.

Use a pastry brush to paint a thick layer of the melted chocolate into each mould. Be sure to go all the way up the side of the mould, to avoid any sheer spots. Refrigerate for 5 to 10 minutes, until set.

When the chocolate has set, carefully remove each half from the mould. (Don't worry if the edges chip a bit.)

Heat a microwave-safe plate (without anything on it) in the microwave for 30 to 45 seconds, until it's hot to the touch. Carefully remove the plate and cover it with a piece of parchment paper. Place half a sphere on the plate, rim-side down. Gently press and twist the sphere to clean up and flatten the edge. Place this half sphere back on the baking sheet and fill it with 2 tablespoons of purple sprinkles, 1 tablespoon of purple sparkle sugar, and 6 to 8 mini marshmallows.

Repeat the process with the second half sphere, again cleaning and heating up the edges. Gently press the two halves together, sealing in the sprinkles and marshmallows. Use melted chocolate from the plate to close any gaps.

Repeat this process with the remaining two sphere moulds, chocolate, marshmallows, sprinkles and sugar, using the different colours for each. Reheat the plate as necessary.

Dust each bomb with the coordinating lustre dust (if using). Store in an airtight container for up to two weeks or package in cellophane bags for gift giving.

Desserts

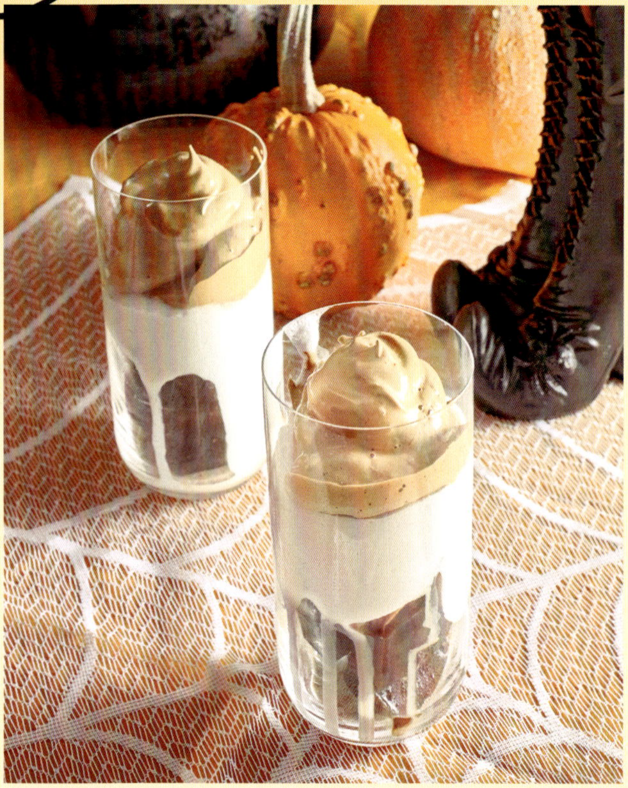

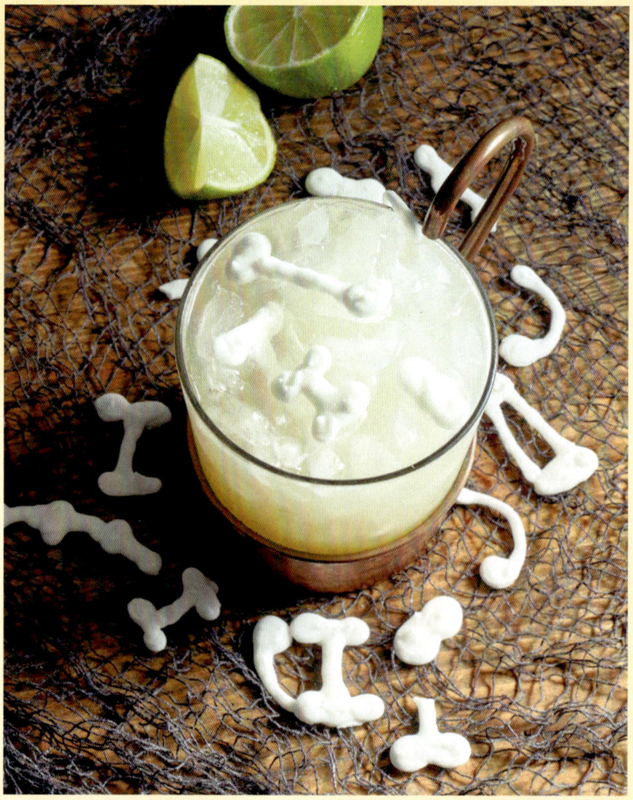

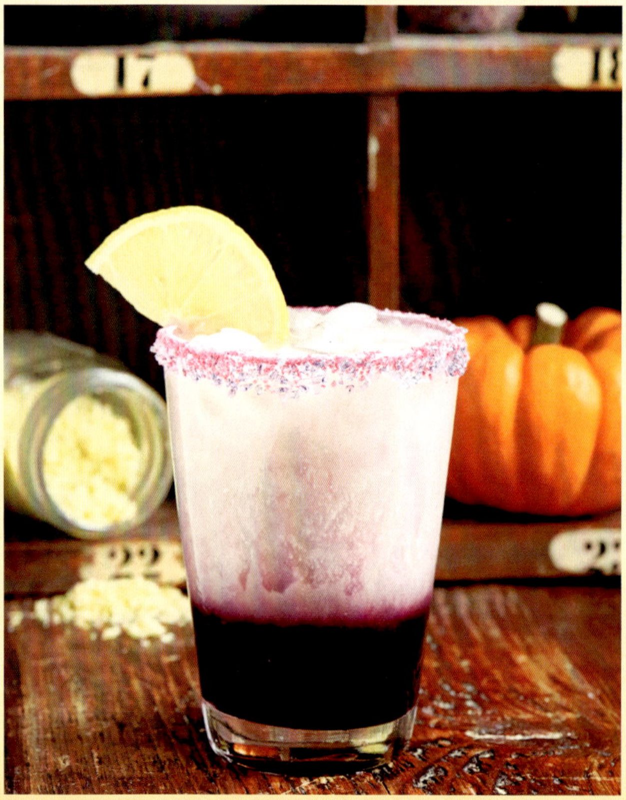
17

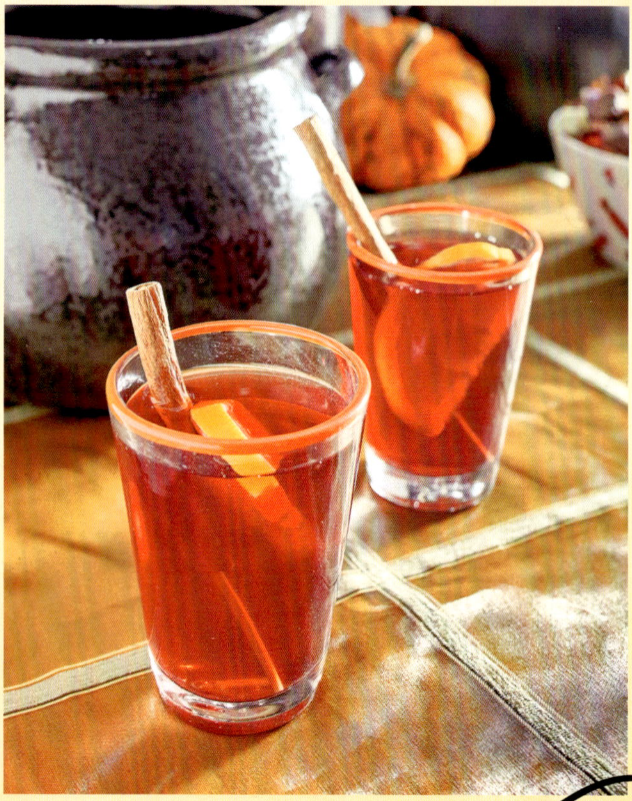

Drinks

Bubbling brews and creamy floats make up the final section of our witchy menu. From drinks inspired by each of the Sandersons – and beautifully reflecting their unique personalities – to the signature beverage of Salem's elite, the concoctions within these pages truly offer something for everyone. Most refreshing indeed!

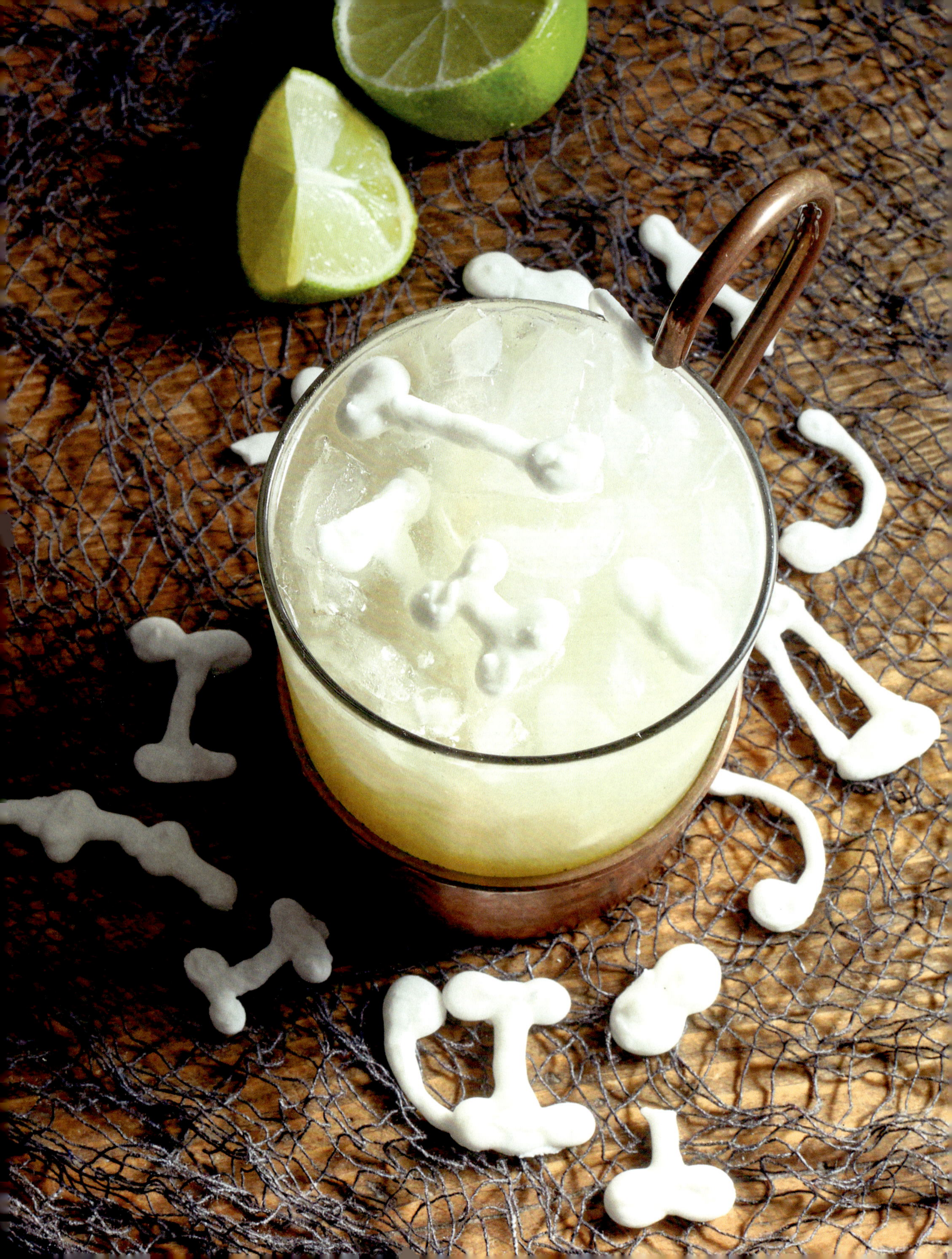

Most Refreshing Drink

When Max summons the burning rain of death, the Sanderson sisters are quick to take cover. But this drink will have any witch – or even your average Salemite – crawling out of their grave to steal but a single sip. Lemon, lime and a splash of the dreaded Burning Rain of Death syrup give this sparkling beverage its ghoulishly good flavour. And a meringue-made bone serves as a reminder of the fate that may befall those who cross the wrong witch ... or her sisters!

Yield: 8 servings | GF, V, V+*

For the Meringue Bones
1 tablespoon egg white powder
130 grams icing sugar

For the Drink
1 cup fresh lime juice (about 12 limes)
1 cup fresh lemon juice (about 6 lemons)
120 ml syrup from Burning Rain of Death Drink (page 143), or more as desired
960 ml still or 240 ml sparkling water

Specialist Tools
Piping bag with medium writing tip

Note
This recipe can be easily made vegan if served without the meringue bones.

To make the meringue bones: In a small bowl, using a hand mixer or the bowl of a food mixer fitted with the whisk attachment, combine the egg white powder, icing sugar and 2 tablespoons water. Mix on a high speed for 4 to 6 minutes, or until stiff peaks form.

Transfer the meringue mixture to a piping bag fitted with a medium writing tip and pipe out different bone shapes on to a piece of parchment paper. Allow to dry completely. Once the bones are dry, gently lift them from the parchment paper with an offset spatula. Store in an airtight container for up to two weeks until ready to serve.

To make the drink: Combine the lime and lemon juice, then strain them into an airtight container through a fine-mesh sieve, discarding the pulp. Combine the juices with the syrup and refrigerate until needed.

To serve, either combine all of the citrus mixture with the 960 ml of still water in a large jug with ice or combine 120 ml of the citrus mixture with 240 ml of sparkling water over ice. Garnish each drink with a few meringue bones or place in a bowl next to the drink station.

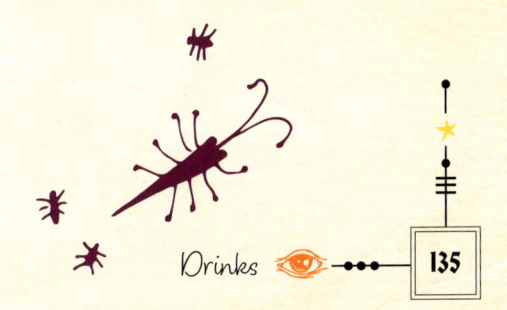

Drinks

"I Put a Spell on You" Brew

Max, Dani and Allison sound the alarm at Salem's most populous Halloween party. The Sandersons have returned ... and they're here to steal the lives of children! But when three dazzling women emerge from the crowd – each the spitting image of a Sanderson sister – they instantly *put a spell* on Salem's unwitting adults. And when these women burst into a toe-tapping, heart-pounding song-and-dance, the only thing that could snap the Salemites out of their trance is an *especially* strong brew. This one is a flavourful coffee beverage that certainly packs a punch ... and it might just be the thing to lift the Sandersons' curse!

Yield: 2 servings | GF, V, V+*

480 ml cold coffee
2 tablespoons instant coffee
2 tablespoons sugar
120 ml single cream or milk

Specialist Tools
Ice cube trays
Milk frothing whisk

Note
This recipe can be easily made vegan by replacing the single cream with your favourite dairy substitute.

Pour the cold coffee into the ice cube trays and freeze overnight.

In a medium bowl or measuring jug, combine the instant coffee, sugar and 2 tablespoons water. Whisk with a milk frother or by hand, about 2 minutes, until it forms a thick icing-like consistency.

In another medium bowl or measuring jug, pour in the single cream and whisk with the milk frother or by hand until light and foamy, about 2 minutes.

Split the coffee ice cubes between two glasses, gently spoon the whipped cream over the ice, and then top with half of the coffee foam.

Serve with spoons for stirring and enjoying.

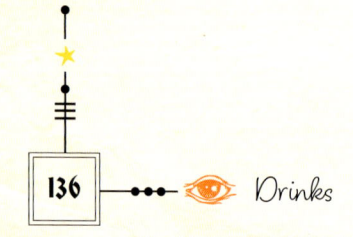

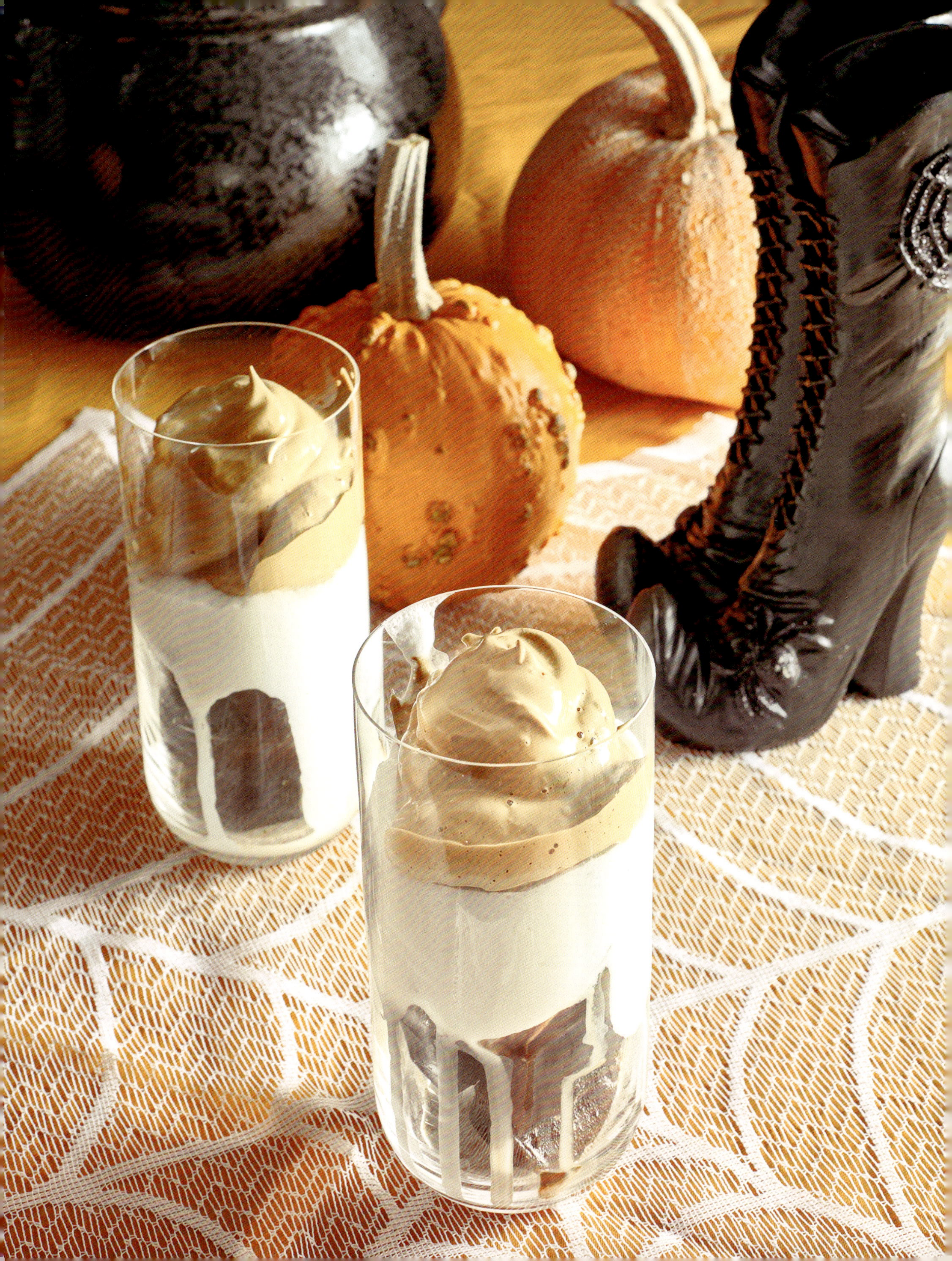

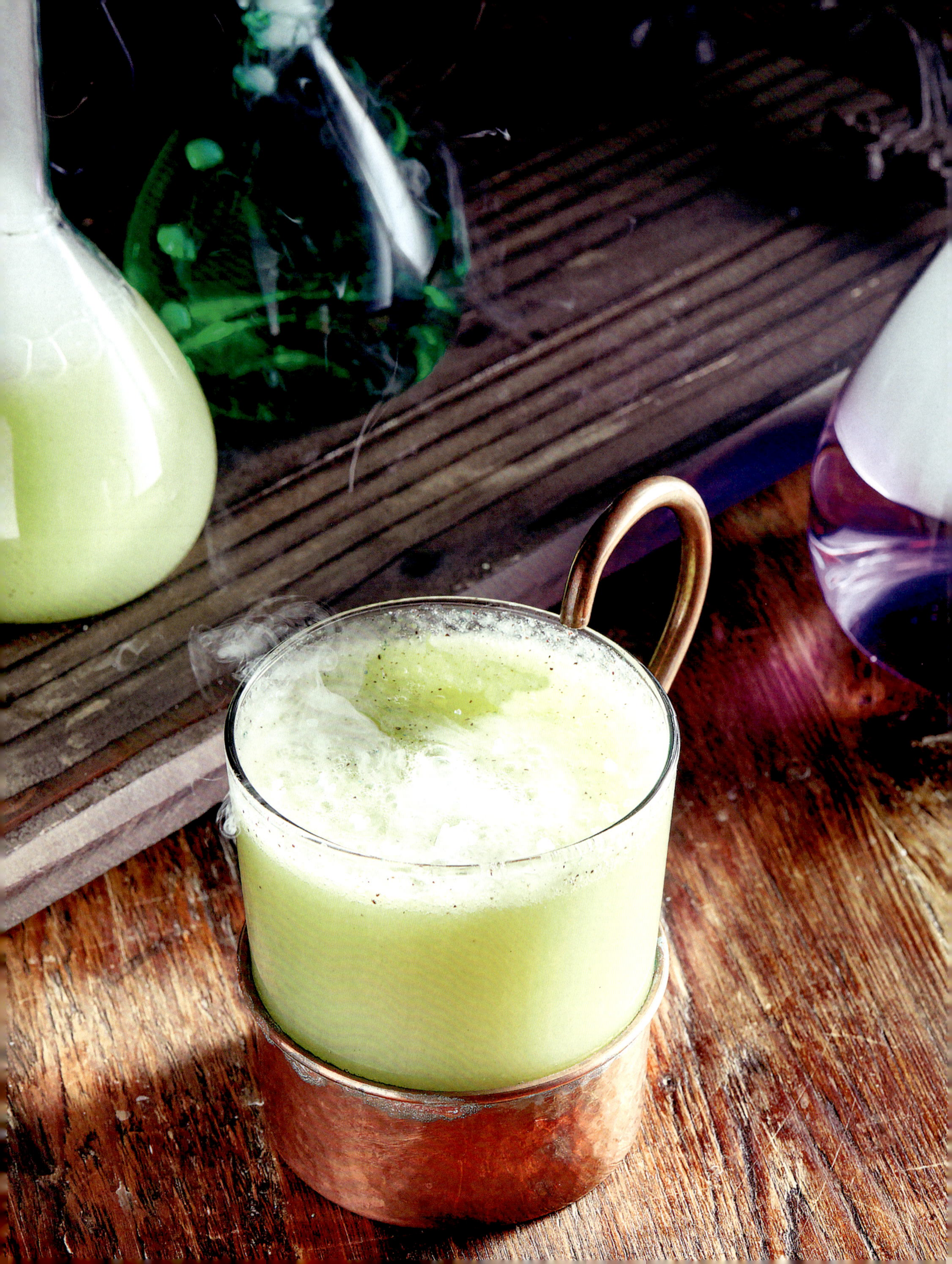

Life Potion Witches' Drink

After capturing Emily Binx, Winnie brews a most devious potion before declaring, "One drop of this and her life will be mine!" With luscious green kiwi and bubbling ginger ale, this potion invokes the essence of Winnie's bewitching brew. (While omitting the less palatable ingredients of newt saliva and a bit of one's own tongue!) So enchanting is this brew, it's sure to have guests declaring, "Thou art divine!"

Yield: 6 servings | GF, V

4 ripe kiwis
120 ml pineapple juice
¼ teaspoon green lustre dust
1 litre ginger ale, chilled

Note

Want to give your potion an extra kick? Use ginger beer instead of ginger ale.

Halve each kiwi and scoop out the flesh. Transfer it to the jug of a blender. Add the pineapple juice and blend until completely pureed. Strain the mixture through a fine-mesh sieve into a large measuring jug, pressing the mixture through. Discard the solids. Strain the mixture again, without pressing, to catch even more seeds.

Return the mixture to the blender, add the lustre dust and blend until completely incorporated. Refrigerate in an airtight container until ready to serve.

To serve, fill each of six glasses with ice, pour in about 60 ml of the kiwi mixture and top with about 170 ml of chilled ginger ale. Gently stir and serve immediately.

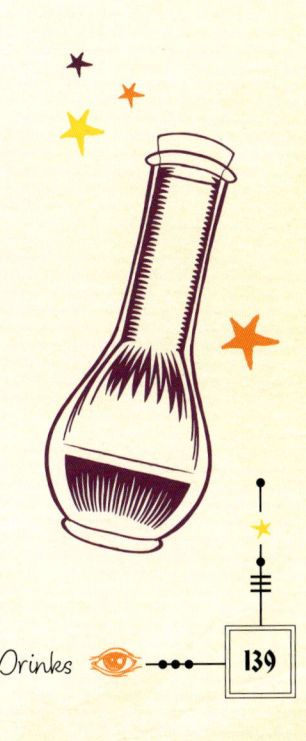

Drinks

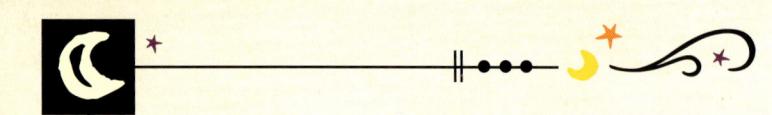

Renaissance Party Cider

Ah, rich people. They're known for fancy parties, bobbing for apples and, of course, their signature beverages. This cider would have been a hit at one of Allison's Halloween parties. Sweet oranges and tangy cranberry juice mingle with spicy cloves and cinnamon sticks in an elegant brew that's sure to impress even the most hoity-toity of Salemites … no hocus pocus about it!

Yield: 10 to 12 servings | GF, V, V+

4 oranges, halved
2 litres apple juice
480 ml pure cranberry juice
1 tablespoon whole cloves
2 cinnamon sticks
1 apple, sliced in rounds (optional)

Juice two or three of the oranges until you have 240 ml of orange juice.

In a medium saucepan, combine the orange juice, apple juice and cranberry juice. Quarter the remaining orange and use a paring knife to score the skin. Insert the cloves into the skin. Add the cloved orange and cinnamon sticks to the saucepan. Bring to a simmer over a medium-high heat. Reduce the heat to medium and cook for 15 minutes.

Serve warm, portioned into heatproof glasses or mugs. Garnish with the apple slices (if using).

Drinks

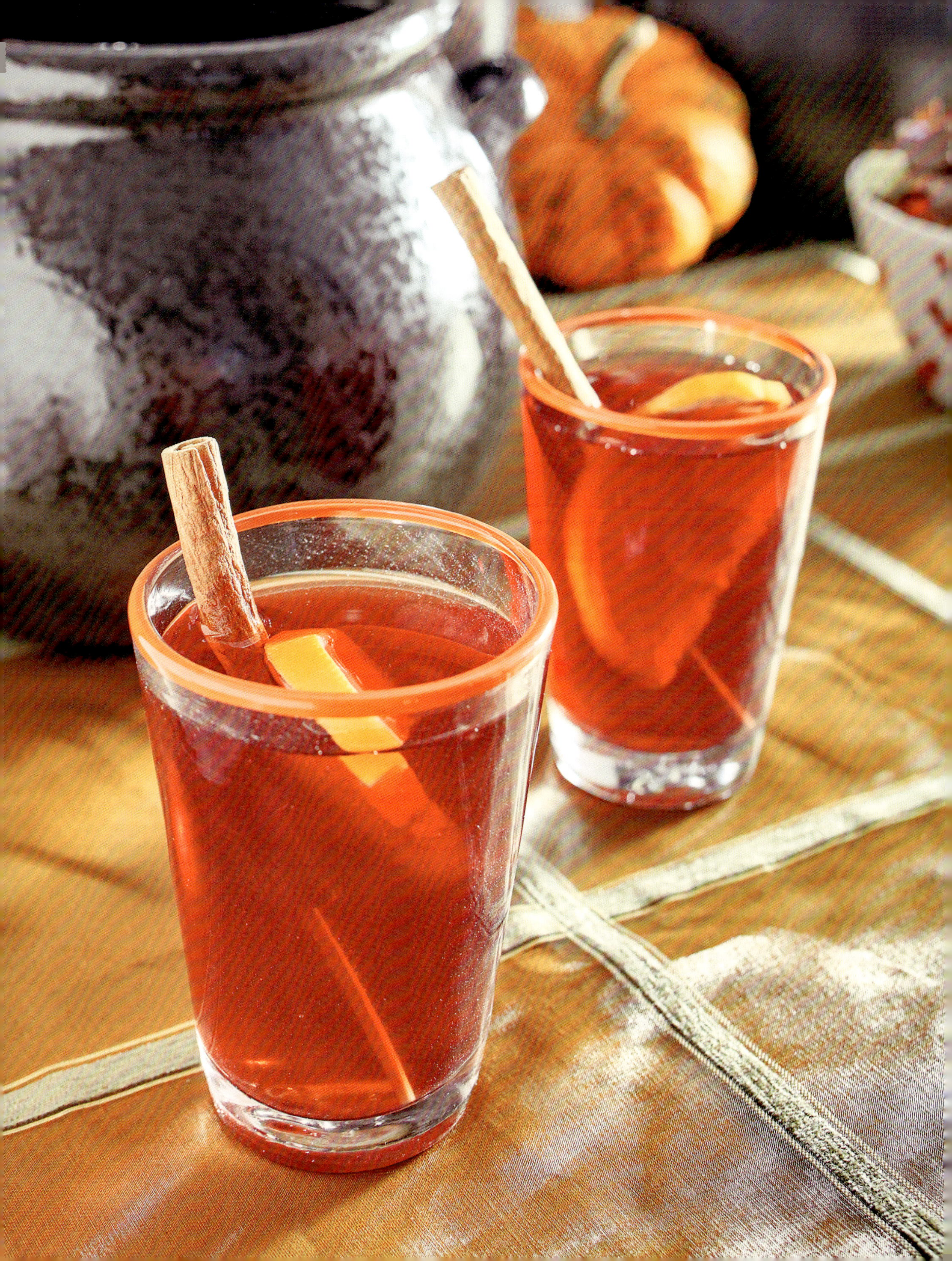

Pumpkin Spiced Golden Milk

Once he's to be Dani's cat,
Binx doth love where he is at.
He will have milk every day!
Prepared in the finest way.
For such spicy autumn brews,

Pumpkin's just the thing to use.
Blend it with some milk of gold
For a flavour that's quite bold.
Summon seasonings most sweet,
Stir lightly, and poof! A treat!

Yield: 2 servings | GF, V, V+*

½ teaspoon freshly ground black pepper

1 teaspoon ground turmeric

480 ml unsweetened almond milk

45 grams "No Witches Here" Pumpkin Butter (page 30) or shop-bought pumpkin butter

1 to 2 tablespoons sweetener of choice, such as honey, agave or maple syrup (optional)

In a medium, heavy-bottomed saucepan set over a medium heat, add the black pepper and turmeric. Stir with a wooden spoon and toast until fragrant, about 1 minute.

Add the almond milk, pumpkin butter and sweetener (if using). Stir to combine and continue to cook until the pumpkin butter and sweetener have completely dissolved and the mixture is hot, 3 to 4 minutes. Decant into two heatproof mugs or glasses. Serve immediately.

Note

This recipe is vegan if using "No Witches Here" Pumpkin Butter, but if using shop-bought, check the ingredients.

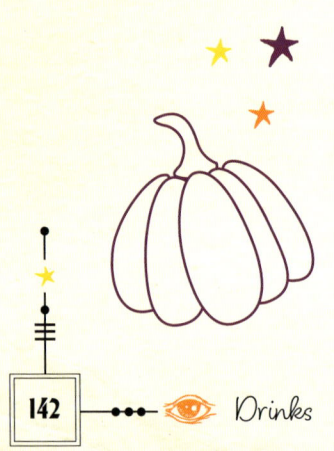

Drinks

Burning Rain of Death Drink

With the Sanderson sisters reawakened, Max knows he has to flee their cottage ... *fast*. Since the witches know nothing of indoor sprinklers, he's able to use this thoroughly modern tool to convince them that he's summoned the sinister, lethal *burning rain of death*. Luckily, there's nothing fearsome about its namesake drink. Winifred, Mary and Sarah are respectively spicy, quirky and sweet – just like this drink. With pink peppercorns, fresh ginger and sugar, *this* Burning Rain of Death won't send one to one's demise. After all, tis but water ... with a tantalising twist!

Yield: 240 ml of syrup, which can be used to flavour up to 12 glasses of beverage | GF, V

- 45 to 60 grams fresh ginger, peeled and thinly sliced
- 200 grams sugar
- 1 teaspoon whole pink peppercorns
- Sparkling water or sparkling apple juice for serving

Combine the ginger, sugar and 240 ml water in a medium saucepan over a medium-high heat and bring to a low boil, stirring often to dissolve the sugar. Turn the heat to medium-low and simmer for 15 minutes.

Remove from the heat, add the peppercorns and allow to cool completely. Strain through a fine-mesh sieve into an airtight container and store in the refrigerator until ready to use or for up to ten days.

To serve, add 2 or 3 tablespoons of the syrup to a tall glass filled with ice and top with about 240 ml of sparkling water.

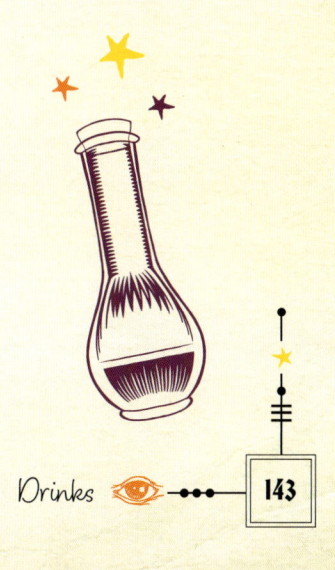

Drinks

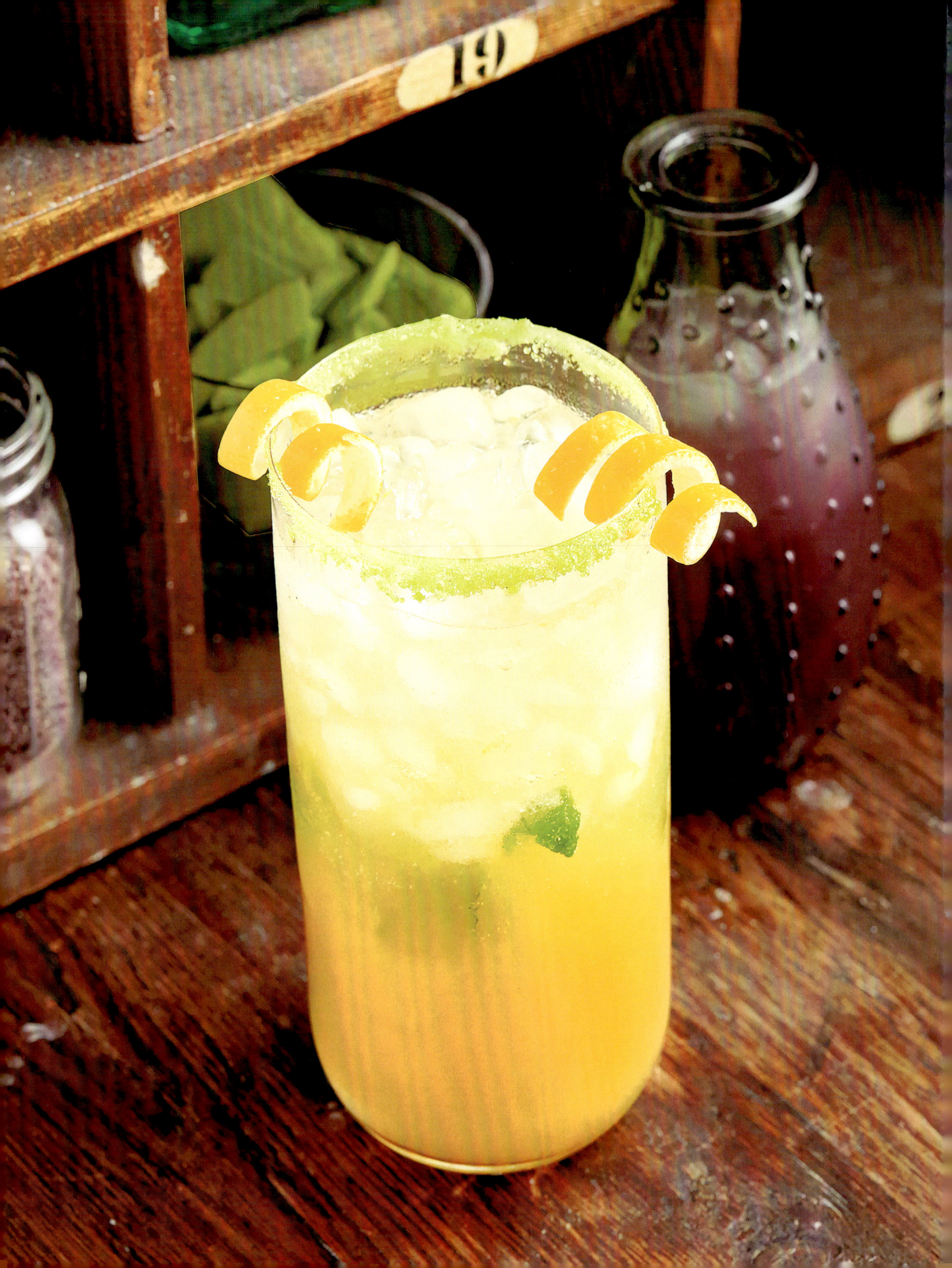

Winnie's Popping Potion

Winifred Sanderson is many things – bold, saucy and altogether unpredictable. It's only fitting that a drink bearing her name would combine all these characteristics … while adding an unexpected twist. This mocktail combines fresh tangy oranges with spicy Burning Rain of Death syrup (page 143) to create a blend that's both devilish and divine. With soothing mint and popping candy, Winnie's drink embraces the unexpected – just like Winnie herself!

Yield: 2 servings | GF, V, V+

2 or 3 oranges

60 grams crushed Winnie's Magical Popping Candy (page 108)

2 lime quarters

4 sprigs fresh mint

240 ml freshly squeezed orange juice (about 2 oranges)

4 tablespoons syrup from Burning Rain of Death Drink (page 143)

About 480 ml sparkling water

Peel wide strips of orange peel from the oranges, leaving the pith behind. Reserve the strips to create the twist garnishes. Juice the oranges. You need 240 ml of juice.

Place the popping candy on a plate or shallow dish. Rim two tall glasses with lime juice by running a lime quarter around the edge, then twist the rims in the popping candy so it sticks.

Add a lime quarter and two mint sprigs to each glass. Use a muddler or wooden spoon to muddle the mint and lime together. Fill each glass with ice. Add 120 ml of the orange juice and 2 tablespoons of the syrup to each glass.

Stir to combine. Top with sparkling water and garnish with the reserved orange twists.

Drinks

Sarah's Sassy Sipper

Sarah Sanderson skips to the beat of her own drum. As flighty as she is formidable, she uses her melodious voice to enchant the children of Salem ... in the hope of sharing their very essence! It's only fitting that her mocktail embodies her sense of whimsy. With notes of hibiscus and a dollop of coconut milk, this drink is sure to take thee away, straight into a land of enchantment. Tis refreshing!

Yield: 4 servings | GF, V, V+

240 ml barista coconut milk
2 hibiscus tea bags
140 grams fresh or frozen blueberries
100 grams sugar
1 lemon
1 tablespoon sparkle sugar (optional)
480 ml sparkling water, chilled

In a small saucepan over a medium-high heat, combine the coconut milk and hibiscus tea bags. Bring the mixture to a simmer, remove from the heat and steep for 15 minutes. Remove the tea bags and refrigerate the flavoured coconut milk in an airtight container until chilled and ready to serve.

In another small saucepan over a medium-high heat, combine the blueberries, sugar and 120 ml water. Bring to the boil, stirring and smashing the berries, and cook for 3 to 5 minutes. Remove from the heat and steep for 15 minutes. Strain through a fine-mesh sieve into an airtight container and discard the solids. Cover and refrigerate until chilled and ready to serve.

To serve, quarter the lemon and run each quarter around the rim of each of four glasses, reserving the lemon quarters for garnish. Place the sparkle sugar (if using) on a rimmed plate and twist each glass rim in the sugar so it sticks. Fill each glass with ice, pour 60 ml of the blueberry syrup into each glass, and top with 60 ml of the coconut mixture. Top off each glass with about 120 ml of sparkling water, garnish with a wedge of lemon and serve.

Drinks

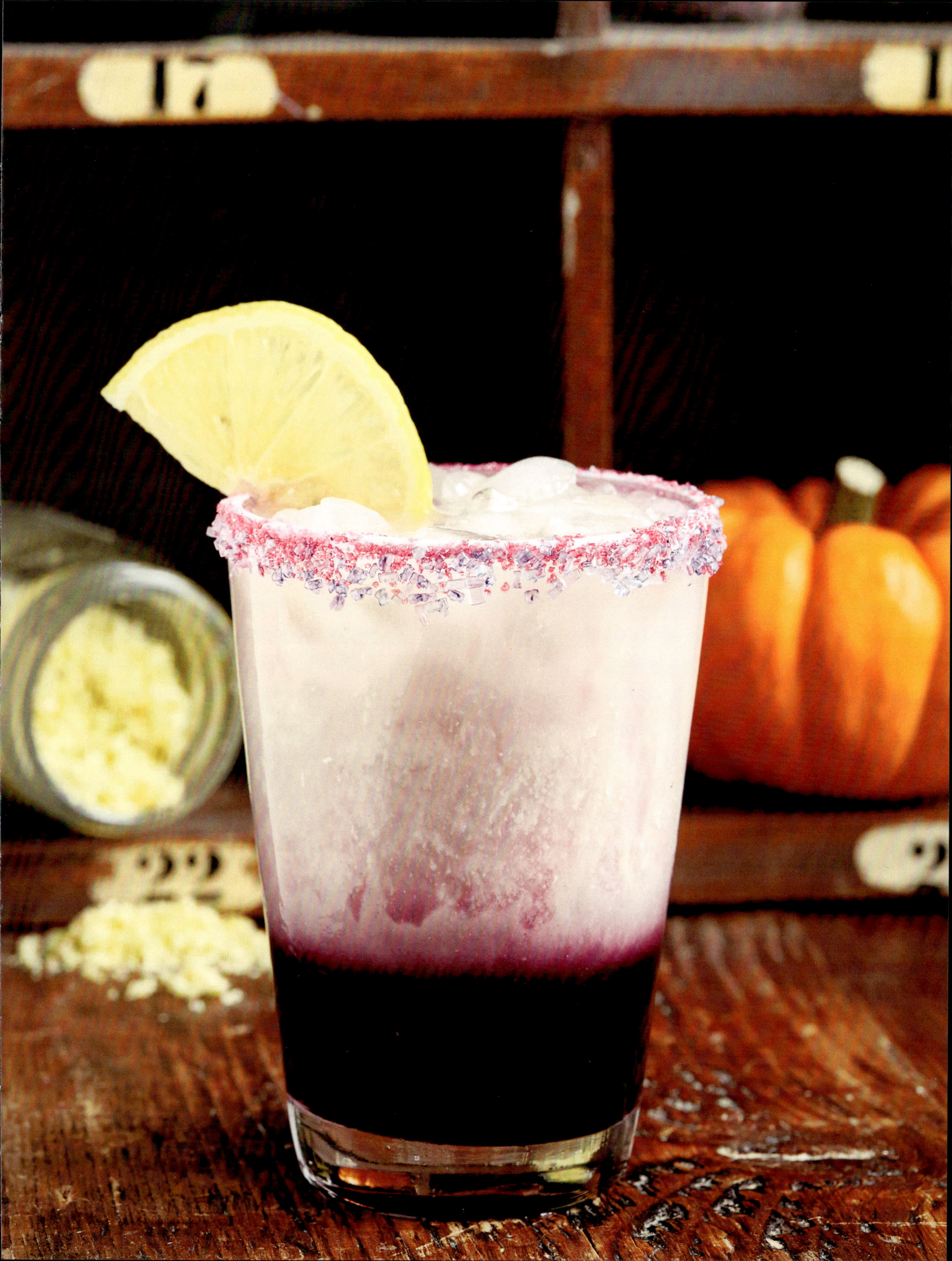
17

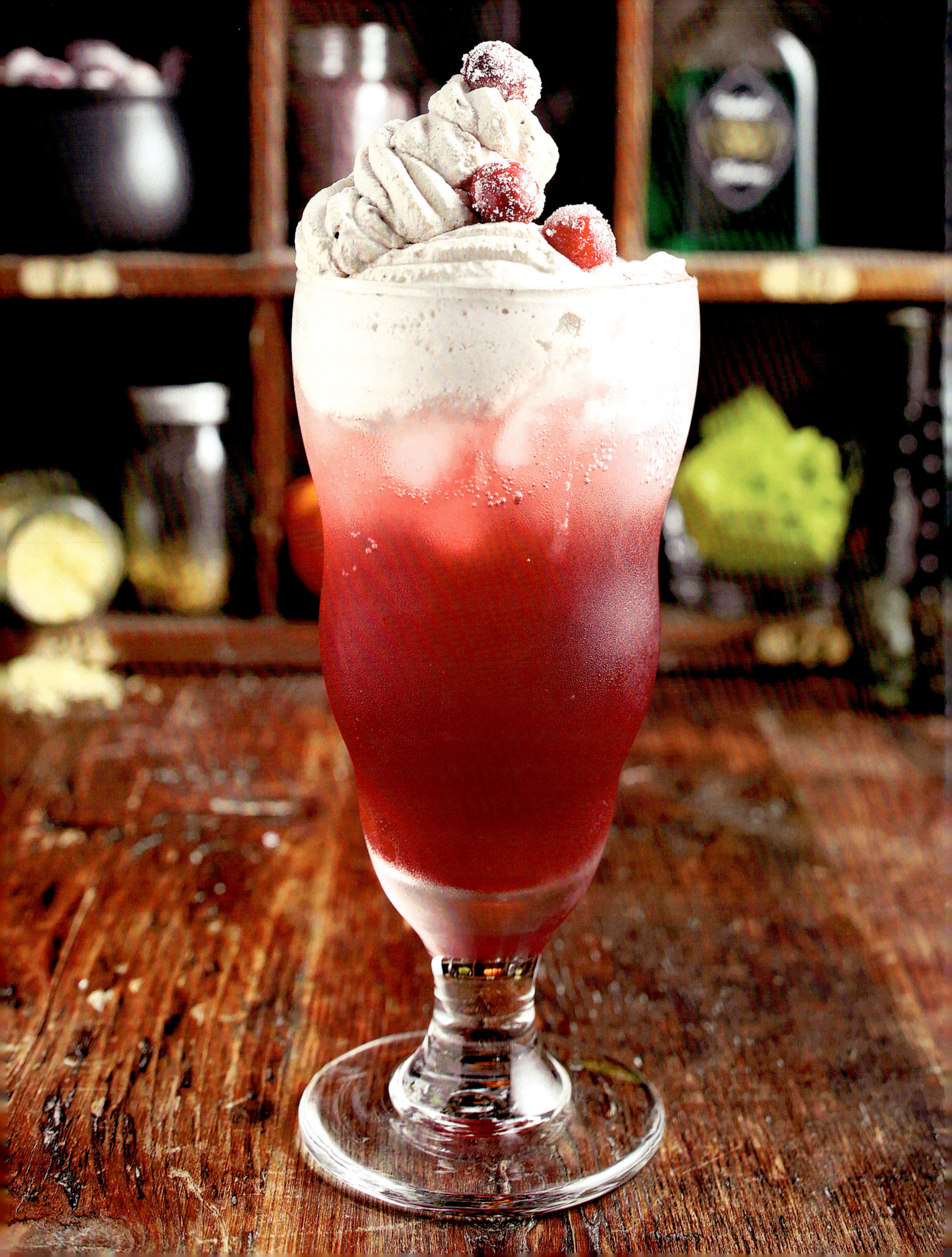

Mary's Magic Elixir

Mary Sanderson is the peacekeeper of the family. When things get stressful, she's the first to suggest a calming circle. And she gently reminds her fierier sister of the importance of being honest with thyself. Her frothy mocktail is as grounded as its namesake, with earthy notes of cherry, a subtle thread of cocoa and a dollop of cranberry syrup drizzled atop cocoa-flavoured whipped cream – a fitting tribute to the crimson streak that graces Mary's hair. After just a few sips, you'll be sure to declare, "I *am* calm!"

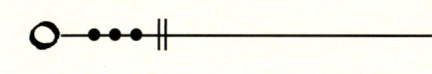

Yield: 2 servings | GF, V

120 ml pure unsweetened cranberry juice

60 ml cranberry syrup from Popping Cranberries (page 35)

120 ml double cream

1 tablespoon chocolate syrup

480 ml sparkling water

6 Popping Cranberries (page 35)

Specialist Tools
Pastry bag and large star tip

In a 240 ml measuring jug, mix together the cranberry juice and syrup. In a medium bowl using a hand mixer on a high speed, whip together the double cream and chocolate syrup until stiff peaks form.

Fill two tall glasses with ice and split the cranberry mixture between them. Fill each glass with about half of the sparkling water. Use a pastry bag fitted with a large star tip or a spoon to pile the chocolate whipped cream on top of each drink. Garnish with the cranberries and serve immediately.

Drinks

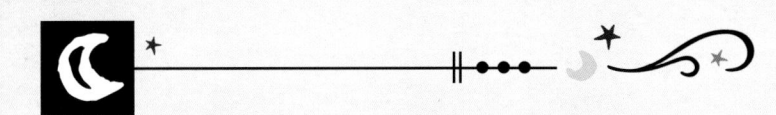

Sunrise Punch

Salem's infamous witchy trio has only until sunrise to enact their sinister spell. If they can usurp the youth from the town's children, immortality will be theirs! But if Winifred, Mary and Sarah can't break their curse before the dawn, they'll be in for a real *punch*. Just like the Sandersons' hour of reckoning, this tasty tropical brew evokes notes of a bright new day. It's just the thing to usher in another glorious morning – whether as youthful, attractive witches ... or mere specks of dust!

Yield: 8 servings | GF, V, V+

280 grams frozen cherries
1 orange, sliced
½ grapefruit, sliced
240 ml cherry juice
240 ml grapefruit juice
480 ml orange juice

In a large jug, layer the cherries, sliced oranges and sliced grapefruit. Pour in the cherry juice.

Fill the jug with ice and then add the grapefruit juice, followed by the orange juice. Serve immediately. Provide tongs to serve fruit with each glass.

Note

Having a party? Double the recipe. Set up two jugs with fruit in each and keep one jug in the freezer. When the second jug is needed, add the juice and ice as above.

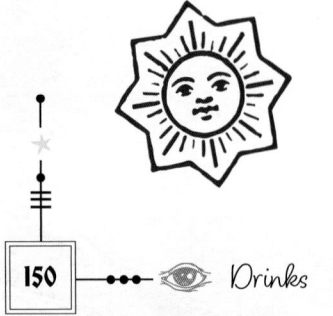

Drinks

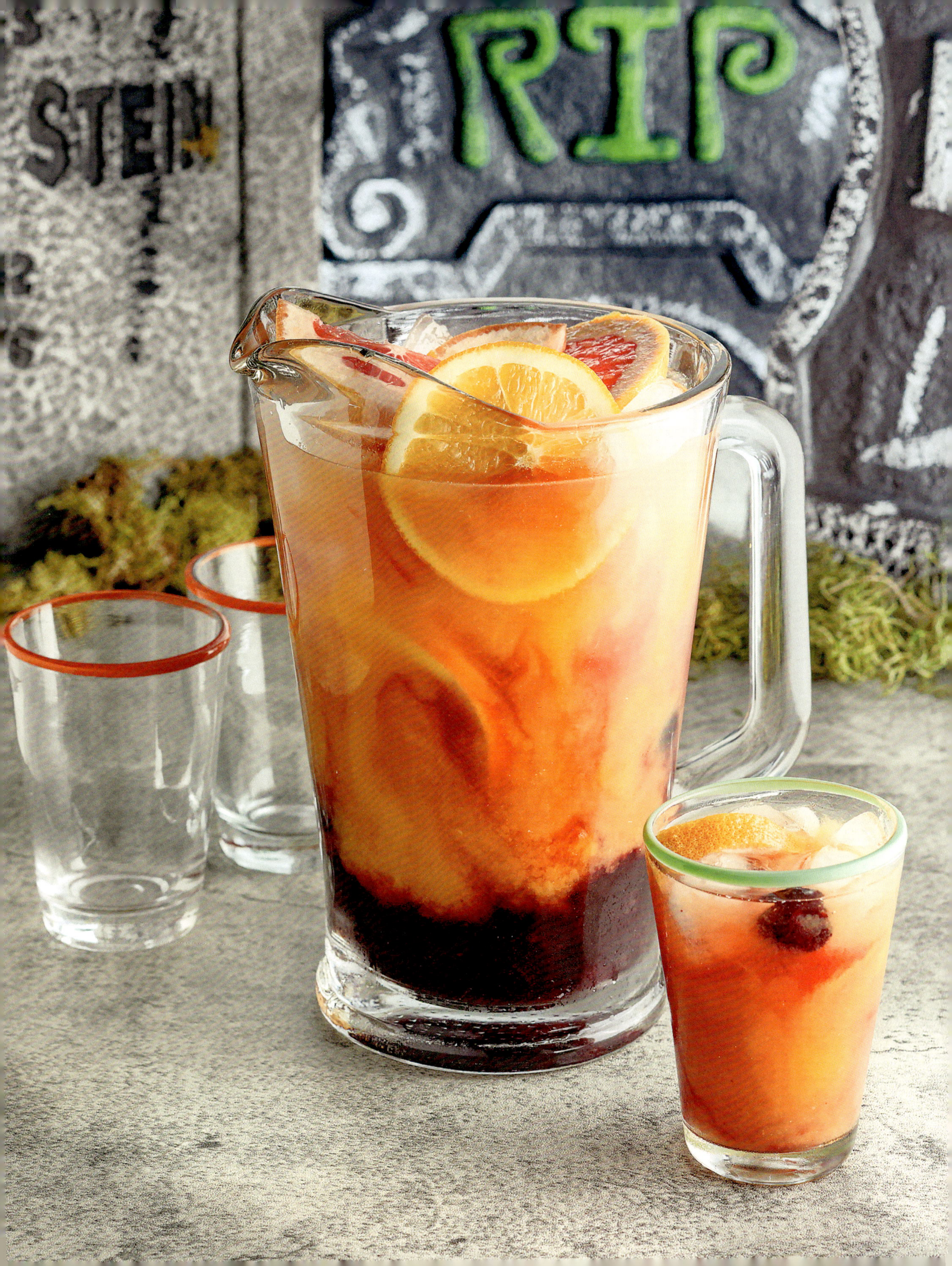

STEIN
RIP

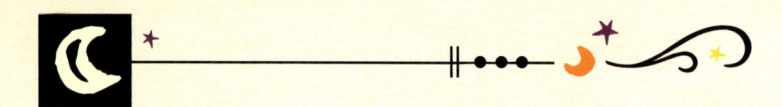

"Ice" Cream Float

With his namesake hair and open-mouthed breathing, Salem's resident bully may not bring much to the table. Ice (don't call him Ernie!) is mean, dim-witted and prone to fits of anger. But even he wouldn't be able to resist this rich, creamy dessert. With vanilla ice cream and blue sanding sugar swirled into a delicious cream soda, this "Ice" Cream Float is worth its weight in gold ... or candy tolls!

Yield: 2 servings | GF, V, V+*

About 1 tablespoon blue sanding or sparkle sugar

¼ teaspoon honey

4 scoops vanilla ice cream

360 ml cream soda, well chilled

Pour the sanding sugar on to a shallow plate. Brush the rims of two 480 ml glasses with the honey. Press the rims of the glasses on to the sugar and twist to coat. Scoop one scoop of ice cream into each glass, sprinkle with more sanding sugar and freeze for at least 1 hour.

When ready to serve, remove the glasses from the freezer, fill each with about 120 ml of the soda, pouring down the side to reduce foaming, and add another scoop of ice cream to each glass. Top each with another 60 ml of soda and serve with spoons.

Notes

Want to serve many floats at once? Save time by lining a baking sheet with parchment paper and scooping the second scoops of ice cream out on to the baking sheet. Place it in the freezer along with the glasses, prepared as above, and freeze until ready to serve. An offset spatula will help you quickly transfer the scoops to the glasses.

This can easily be made vegan by choosing your favourite plant-based ice cream.

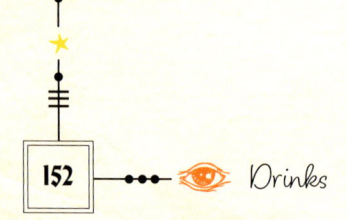

Pink Smoke Drink

When whipping up a bubbling brew,
One never knows what it might do.
Some may turn green, or start to stink.
But this one yields a lovely pink,
Just like the smoke from that foul home
From which three cursed sisters roam.

Its hints of sweetness come in three:
Lemon, cherry and raspberry.
And light meringue with water's fizz
Makes this the finest brew there is.
Pry open thy mouth. Ready? Drink!
There, now. It's perfect! Don't you think?

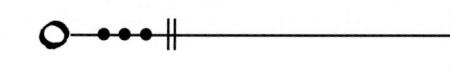

Yield: 1 serving | GF, V

For the Raspberry Lemonade Concentrate

- 120 grams frozen or fresh raspberries
- 3 tablespoons dried butterfly pea flowers
- 100 grams sugar
- 120 ml fresh lemon juice

For the Drink

- 2 maraschino cherries
- 1 tablespoon cherry syrup
- 1 teaspoon egg white powder
- About 240 ml sparkling water

To make the raspberry lemonade concentrate: In a medium saucepan, combine the raspberries, 240 ml water, butterfly pea flowers and sugar. Cook over medium-high heat for about 10 minutes, or until the sugar is completely dissolved and the raspberries are broken down. Allow to cool completely.

Strain with a fine-mesh sieve into an airtight container and discard the solids. Stir in the lemon juice. Refrigerate until needed.

To make the drink: Fill a double old-fashioned glass with ice.

In a cocktail shaker, muddle the cherries and cherry syrup. Add 120 ml of raspberry lemonade concentrate and the egg white powder and stir. Add a few cubes of ice from the glass to the cocktail shaker.

Fill the glass half full with sparkling water.

Shake the cocktail shaker vigorously for at least 1 minute. Pour through the sieve over the sparkling water. Make sure after the liquid has left the cocktail shaker to shake out the foam on to the surface of the drink. Serve immediately.

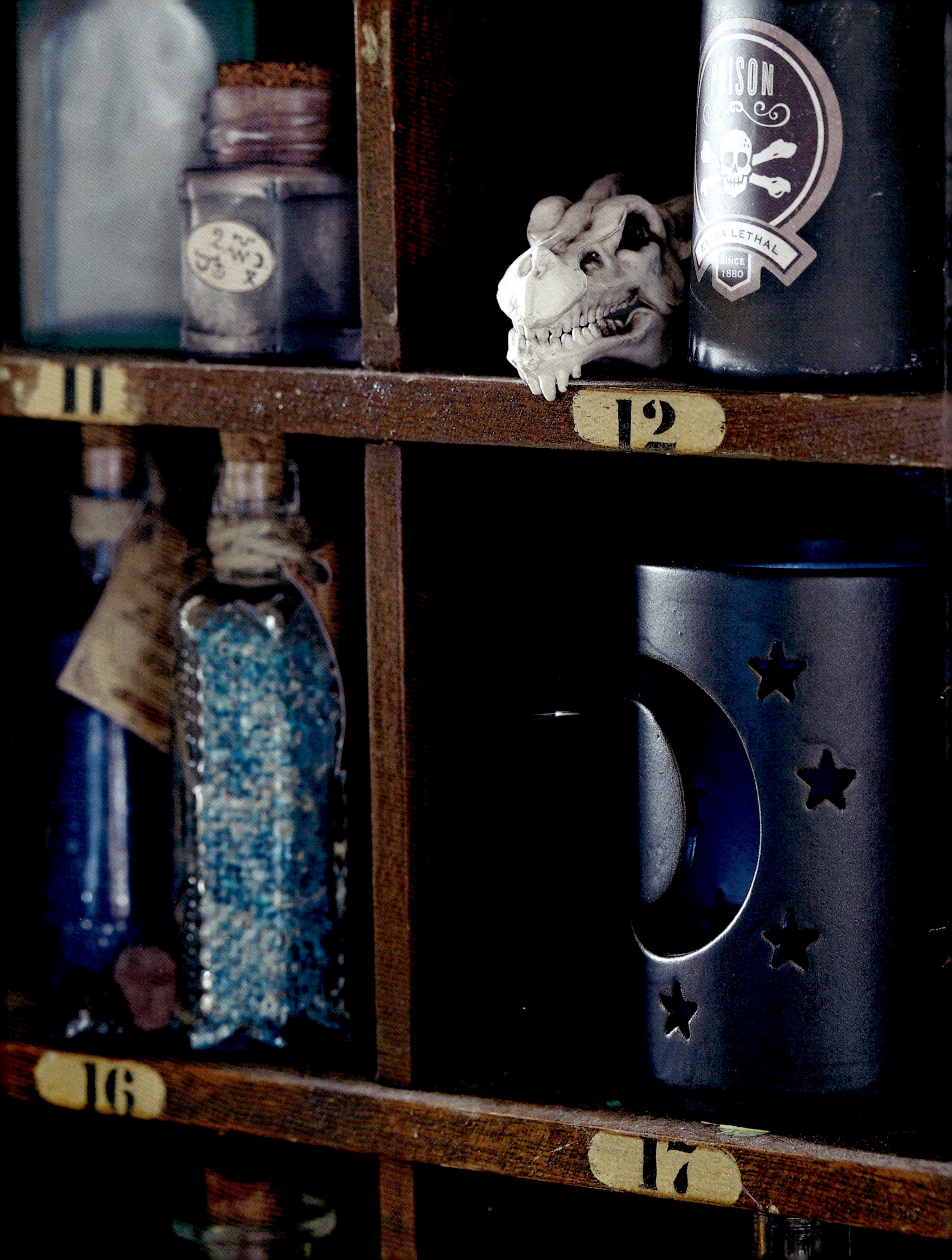
11
12
EXTRA LETHAL
SINCE
1880
16
17

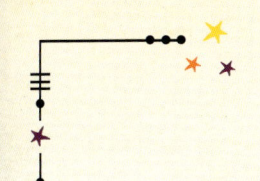

Conclusion

Curses! The dawn nears, and our time together must draw to a close. Hopefully, these alimentary offerings have brought a ghostly glimmer – and perhaps a sprinkle of magic – to your table. After all, tis not every day that one can summon a menu with such a distinguished trio in mind. Whether your tastes run towards the spicy – in which case, we do hope you sampled The Master's Fried Peppers – or the sweet – perhaps the sinfully sinister Gravestone Sugar Cookies were more to your liking – we fervently hope that your appetite has been fully sated. But should you find yourself with an insatiable hunger, by all means light the black flame candle and start your adventure anew. The Sanderson sisters would certainly understand!

We're devilishly delighted that you've joined us on our culinary carousing. After such a fine feast, you're no doubt ready for a good, long rest – just like the ever-mindful Sanderson sister who once loudly declared, "I *am* calm!" It is our deepest desire that you come back to these pages again and again. After all, there is much magic to be found within books – whether that tome is bound in human skin or mere paper. We do hope these recipes have *put a spell on you*. As Winifred says, "Life is sweet – be not shy." Now, on thy feet – so sayeth I!

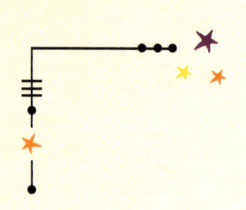

Dietary Considerations

Starters and Sides
Graveyard Cheeseboard: **GF*, V**
Billy Butcherson Zombie Fingers: **GF, V, V+**
All Hallows' Eve Feast Grazing Board: **GF*, V*, V+***
Miss Olin Nutty Brown Bread: **V**
Massachusetts Baked Beans: **GF**
Ten Chocolate Bars, No Liquorice, Candy Toll: **GF*, V**
Pretty Black Meatball Spiders
Circle of Salt Soft Pretzels: **V**
Pan Hag: **GF, V**
"Amok, Amok, Amok" Guacamole and Homemade Chips: **GF*, V*, V+***
"No Witches Here" Pumpkin Butter: **GF, V, V+**
The Master's Fried Peppers: **GF, V, V+**
Dead Man's Toes
"Oh, Cheese and Crust" Homemade Crackers: **V**
Popping Cranberries: **GF, V, V+**
Roach Muffins: **V**
Pastry Boots: **V**

Main Dishes
Mrs Dennison's Roasted Pumpkin Tacos: **GF*, V, V+***
Shiskebaby: **GF, V, V+**
"Another Glorious Morning" Breakfast Sandwiches for Dinner
Winifred's Guts for Garters Squash: **GF**
Knockout Skillet French Toast: **GF*, V**
Full Moon Blue Cheese Onion Tart: **V**
Mummy's Scorpion Pie
"Who's Going for the Jacuzzi" Lobster: **GF***
Spicy Cauliflower Ears: **GF*, V, V+**
Roasted Red Spice Chicken: **GF**
Maggot-Stuffed Pork Chop
Green Mummy Roll-Ups: **GF, V**
Rat Loaf: **GF***
Spicy Nightshade Stir-Fry: **GF*, V, V+***
Pumpkin Risotto: **GF, V, V+***
Waterwheel Pot Pie: **V**
Sanderson Sisters Barbecue Fillet: **GF**
Cheese Puff Chicken Tenders: **GF***

Graveyard Gnocchi Grubs: **GF, V**
Hollywood Barbecue Chicken Pizza: **GF***
Tie-Dye California Smoothie Bowl: **GF*, V, V+***

Desserts
Blood Orange Jack-O'-Lantern Tarts: **GF*, V**
Halloween Candy Ice Cream with Gummy Worm Ganache: **GF*, V***
Thackery Binx Treats: **GF, V**
"Hey, Cupcake" Cupcakes: **V**
Winnie's Spellbook Cake: **V**
Classic Caramel Apple Dip: **GF, V**
Broomstick, and Other Transport, Treats: **V**
Winnie's Magical Popping Candy: **GF, V, V+**
Black River Brownie Bars: **V**
Gravestone Sugar Cookies: **V**
Witch Cookie Lollies: **V**
Dad-cula Fang Strawberries: **GF, V**
Twisted Winifred Spirals: **V**
Puffed Rice Potion Bottles: **GF***
Tart Face Tart: **GF*, V**
Cat Tongue Cookies: **V**
"Bonjour!" Crème Brûlée: **GF, V**
Fly Ice Cream: **GF, V**
Frogspawn Boba Matcha Cheesecake: **GF*, V**
Dust Bombs: **GF**

Drinks
Most Refreshing Drink: **GF, V, V+***
"I Put a Spell on You" Brew: **GF, V**
Life Potion Witches' Drink: **GF, V, V+***
Renaissance Party Cider: **GF, V, V+**
Pumpkin Spiced Golden Milk: **GF, V, V+***
Burning Rain of Death Drink: **GF, V, V+**
Winnie's Popping Potion: **GF, V, V+**
Sarah's Sassy Sipper: **GF, V, V+**
Mary's Magic Elixir: **GF, V**
Sunrise Punch: **GF, V, V+**
"Ice" Cream Float: **GF, V, V+***
Pink Smoke Drink: **GF, V**

Fry Station Safety

If you're making something that requires deep-frying, here are some important tips to keep you safe:

- If you don't have a dedicated deep-fryer, use a casserole dish or a high-walled sauté pan.
- Never have too much oil in the pan! You don't want hot oil spilling out as soon as you put the food in.
- Use only a suitable cooking oil, such as rapeseed, sunflower or vegetable oil.
- Always keep track of the oil temperature with a thermometer; 180° to 190°C should do the trick.
- Never put too much food in the pan at the same time!
- Never put wet food in the pan. It will splatter and can cause burns.
- Always have a lid nearby to cover the pan, in case it starts to spill over or catch fire. A properly rated fire extinguisher is also great to have on hand in case of emergencies.
- Never leave the pan unattended, and never let children near the pan.
- Never, ever put your face, your hand or any other body part in the hot oil.

Glossary

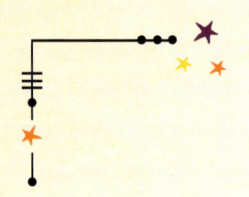

BLIND BAKING: Blind baking means baking pastry or crumb crust without any filling. This method is used when the filling will not be baked at all, such as with a whipped cream or pudding, when the filling needs less time than the crust to bake, or when the filling is quite wet, such as pumpkin pie, and you want to protect the crust from sogginess.

BLUE SPIRULINA: Blue spirulina is extracted from a blue-green algae that grows in ponds, lakes and alkaline waterways. It is rich in vitamins, antioxidants and proteins, providing a deep blue colour when used in recipes. It is available online and in most health food stores.

BUTTERFLY PEA FLOWERS: Butterfly pea flowers are commonly used in herbal tea drinks. When added to a recipe, they provide a beautiful deep blue colour. If combined with acids, like lemon juice, the colour shifts to pink or purple. They are available online and in some health food stores.

SUGAR THERMOMETER: Sugar thermometers, sometimes called fry thermometers, are long thermometers that can be clipped to the side of your pan and withstand very high temperatures of at least 260°C. They are used to measure temperatures of frying oil or sugar during the creation of syrups, candies and certain icings.

CHOCOLATE MELTING POT: A plug-in device with a removable silicone pot that melts chocolate and then keeps it warm and at the correct temperature for dipping and coating things like cake pops or berries.

CUTTING IN BUTTER: To work cold butter into dry ingredients until it is broken down into small pea-size pieces and dispersed evenly throughout the mixture. It is important that the butter is very cold so it does not begin to soften. These little pieces of butter surrounded by the dry ingredient are what create the flakiness in pastry.

DEGLAZE: Deglazing is adding liquid, usually wine or stock, to a hot pan to release all of the caramelised food from the pan. These caramelised bits, called fond, are full of flavour and should not be left behind. Deglazing is often the first step in making a delicious sauce.

CASSEROLE DISH: A casserole dish is a heavy cooking pot often made out of cast iron that is ideal for making stews or deep-frying because it will hold and distribute heat evenly. It works well with high or low temperatures and is a versatile cooking tool that is a handy addition to every kitchen.

EGG WASH: Whisk together an egg and 1 tablespoon of water until light and foamy. Use a pastry brush to apply when the recipe requires.

FOLDING IN: This refers to gently adding an ingredient with a spatula in wide gentle strokes. Do not whisk or stir vigorously. Folding allows any airiness already established to stay intact.

LUSTRE DUST: A food-safe glitter that can be purchased online or in specialist baking departments. It can be mixed with clear alcohol to create a shimmery paint or brushed on dry.

MACERATE: Macerating is similar to marinating but for fruit. Combining the fruit with a little bit of liquid, such as citrus or vinegar, and often a bit of sugar, allows the fruit to soften and release some of its juices, resulting in a delicious syrup.

MILK: The word milk in this book is always referring to dairy milk unless otherwise noted. In most cases, any percentage of milk fat will do unless otherwise noted.

PARSLEY: When parsley is used as an ingredient in this book, please use flat-leaf parsley, as opposed to curly parsley.

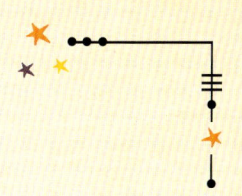

PEELING GINGER: The easiest way to peel fresh ginger is with a teaspoon. Simply use the edge of the spoon to scrape away the peel. This keeps the ginger root intact, with less waste, and allows you to easily navigate all the bumps and lumps.

RENDERING FAT: The term "rendering fat" used in this book refers to cooking off the fat of the piece(s) of meat. The fat should melt into the pan while the meat left behind becomes brown and crispy.

SALT: Feel free to use your salt of choice unless it has been noted in the recipe. Rock salt is the one most commonly used throughout the book.

SHIMMERING OIL: Shimmering oil is hot but not to smoke point. You know it's "shimmering" when it spreads out quickly across the pan, has a rippled look across the surface, and glistens.

SILICONE BAKING MAT: Silicone baking mats can withstand high temperatures in the oven and low temperatures in the freezer. They are very helpful in baking because they are easy to roll dough out on and can then go from prep station to chilling to oven without having to move the dough. They are extremely non-stick and easy to clean.

SPIDER: A spider is a long-handled spoon with a fine-mesh basket in the shape of a shallow bowl. Traditionally, the mesh is hand-tied with wide lattice-like openings, and the long handle keeps your hands away from pesky things, like bubbling hot oil. Its unusual name comes from the spider-web pattern created by the wire.

SUMAC: Made from ground berries of the sumac flower, this sour, acidic spice is most commonly used in Mediterranean and Middle Eastern cooking. It is particularly popular in dry rubs, marinades and dressings. Try sprinkling some over your food just before serving for extra flavour and a punch of colour. If you are unable to find sumac at your local supermarket, you can use lemon zest, but use less than the called-for amount of sumac as lemon zest has a more potent flavour.

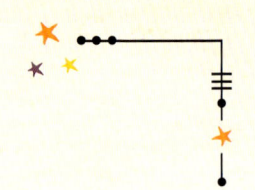

⦿ EXPANSE

First published in the United States 2023 by Insight Editions
First published in Great Britain 2023 by Expanse
An imprint of HarperCollins*Publishers*
1 London Bridge Street, London SE1 9GF
www.farshore.co.uk

HarperCollins*Publishers*
Harper Ireland, Macken House, 39/40 Mayor Street Upper,
Dublin 1 D01 C9W8, Ireland

Copyright © 2023 Disney. All rights reserved.

ISBN 978 0 00 862184 1
Printed in China
001

A CIP catalogue record for this title is available from the British Library.

All rights reserved. No part of this publication may be reproduced, stored in a retrieval system, or transmitted, in any form or by any means, electronic, mechanical, photocopying, recording or otherwise, without the prior permission of the publisher and copyright owner.

Stay safe online. Expanse is not responsible for content hosted by third parties.